Falling Upwards

Falling Upwards

Essays in Defense of the Imagination

Lee Siegel

BASIC
BOOKS

A Member of the Perseus Books Group
New York

Copyright © 2006 by Lee Siegel
Published by Basic Books
A Member of the Perseus Books Group

With the exception of the Introduction, the essays in this book originally
appeared, sometimes in substantially different form, in the following
publications: *The New Republic, Harper's, The Atlantic Monthly, The New Yorker,
The Nation, The Los Angeles Times Book Review, Talk, Slate,* and *Double Take.*
"D. H. Lawrence and the Romantic Option" originally appeared as the
introduction to the Modern Library edition of D. H. Lawrence's *The Lost Girl.*

Books published by Basic Books are available at special discounts for bulk
purchases in the United States by corporations, institutions, and other
organizations. For more information, please contact the Special Markets
Department at the Perseus Books Group, 11 Cambridge Center, Cambridge MA
02142, or call (617) 252-5298 or (800) 255-1514, or e-mail
special.markets@perseusbooks.com.

A CIP data record for this title is available from the Library of Congress
ISBN-13: 978-0-465-07800-4; ISBN-10: 0-465-07800-1

06 07 08 09/ 10 9 8 7 6 5 4 3 2 1

For Christina

To live. To please. To be loved. To love. To write. Not to be duped. To be oneself—and yet, to be *successful*. How to be read? And how to live, despising or hating all sides.

— PAUL VALÉRY, "ON STENDHAL"

CONTENTS

Contents

INTRODUCTION

AT A LITERARY PARTY on a winter night not long ago, someone whose name I didn't recognize—he seemed to be just a few years out of college—introduced himself to me and uttered this declaration: "Someday someone is going to sue you for the stuff you write, pal." Then he turned on his heels, as they used to say, and disappeared into the crowd. It was a strange curse for anyone but an offended author to call down on a critic's head. But it was a significant one. You could trace recent developments in the culture by imagining what my audacious scourge might have said or done at other moments in time.

In the fifties he might have thrown a drink in my face, or passionately engaged me over something I'd written, or he might have engaged me and then thrown a drink in my face. In the sixties and early seventies, he could well have shouted an aesthetic or political declaration, or perhaps waved a pocketknife in the air to prove the weakness of words before stark existential vitality, etc.—and then got down to cases with me on the level of ideas. By the eighties and into the nineties, when most intellectuals and writers seemed to be ensconced at the universities—he probably would have been in graduate school; I most likely would have been teaching somewhere—I might at least have been the object of his attempts at theoretically refuting my existence as a thinking, integrated self. *At the very least, a personal deconstruction.*

But instead here my antagonist was, relishing the prospect of me being litigated against in court. Not challenged, or refuted, or forensically trounced, but dragged out of the unregulated, unsocialized, free and untrammeled realm of intellectual friction and ferment into the hard, constricting halls of justice. Not disagreed with, but forced to make amends. Not exposed as conventional, or banal, or as being complicit with society's official big picture— capital crimes in intellectual life—but officially chastened by society itself. Kafka's comic nightmare of spirit-crushing legalism was this writer's earnest dream of intellectual redress. The incident that winter night was a mildly theatrical example of a new reality: the general reversal of relations between the literary vocation—and the intellectual and artistic vocations, as well—and the status quo. It is my hope that the essays in this book, written over the last ten years, will serve as a counterstatement to that sour inversion.

There has been a lot of talk, and for a long time, about "the triumph of the counterculture." This development has resulted, we are told, in moral relativism, open and permissive sexuality, the decline of civility, and disrespect for authority and the rule of law. That such qualities have been on the rise in American society for the past thirty-five years is hardly disputable—whether they are pernicious developments or benign ones, or maybe even necessary counterbalances to less perceptible but even more constricting conditions, is an ongoing argument. But these qualities are rarely defined. In fact, they are not just antisocial forces released into American life by the dramatic sixties. They are, above all, aesthetic traits that slowly have made their way into mainstream public conduct from the realm of art.

Art and life once had a clear border between them. It was in *King Lear,* not in the sentiments of English judges or politicians, that Keats thought he had discovered the supreme example of what he called "negative capability," which is the displacement of moral judgment by the sympathetic inhabiting of other people's perspectives. Another name for that disposition is moral relativism. You find explicit carnal romping in Boccacio's fourteenth-century tales, not in the papal edicts of his time, or in the pronouncements of the Florentine senate that shaped the society in which Boccacio lived. In ancient Athens, disrespect for authority and the rule of law resulted in exile or death; in ancient Greek tragedy the punishments for such defiance filled the audience with compassion for human frailty, and with who knows what degree of painful regret over destiny's iron byways. When people wring their hands over the integration of "countercultural" values into everyday life, they are really talking about the eruption into public spaces of sentiments once limited to artistic expression.

Now, some traditionalists, from across the political spectrum, believe that the key to social harmony is to insulate an otherwise healthy society from these countercultural, aesthetic excesses that have arisen out of the unsupervised abundance of American freedom. Others, from equally diverse ideological positions, have an ironic response. In their view, the business culture prizes, even creates, seemingly subversive—i.e., aesthetic—values because such values open larger commercial opportunities: what you get as a result of more appetites, fewer moral judgments, and a widespread lack of self-restraint is a greater variety of services, commodities, and markets. For the traditionalists, aesthetic values operating in everyday life are a deviant amorality. For the ironists, they are a deviant respectability.

These circumstances have produced a curious attitude. As society has welcomed into the public realm behavior, sentiments, and psychological revelations once kept secret in art, the work of art itself has come under suspicion. The signs of this art-suspicion are everywhere. There is the wild popularity of "reality" television, for instance. And the relentless inflation-deflation machine applied to celebrities, who are almost always artists—actors, musicians, etc. And the movie-dramas and cable television series that expose the actual lives behind the professional pretense of famous and not-so-famous actors.

Distrust of art is why cinematic techniques are coming to dominate the fine arts, as painting gets outpaced by video, and more and more photographs—especially giant Cibachrome prints—look like movie-stills. Movies are so universally familiar, so much a part of everyday "water-cooler" conversation, that any allusion to film seems reassuringly to ground the imagination in concrete facts. And Hollywood movies themselves are increasingly discussed in literal terms. Though movies have always had profits in mind above all, up until now even commercial films were appraised as crafted fictions. Nowadays the "movie-business" is emphasized more than the fictions that the movie-business creates, as if the people who write about film wish to ensure its segregation from the environs of the imagination completely.

And art-suspicion is why more and more novels and plays are based on real events, or on earlier novels and plays. It is why best-selling novels, like *The Da Vinci Code,* read like actual histories, and why best-selling nonfiction books like *The Tipping Point* use stories to seem to make sense of life the way good novels used to. Art-suspicion is why the novel is blurring into the memoir; why would-be novelists fictionalize from behind the respectable mask of a "memoir"; and why such novels that do get written *as novels* are often timid, self-conscious, precious, and uptight—amazingly, the younger and "hotter" the novelist, the less likely it is that you are going to find in his or her work original evocations of sex, or vibrantly obscene language, or refreshingly illiberal sentiments. Finally, art-suspicion itself has been strengthened by a general distrust of authority, which has been fueled by the Freudian notion that a flawed psyche stands shakily behind every confident assertion. Nowadays, the artist wishes to prove that he is not an arrogant, hypocritically flawed purveyor of self-assured fictions, but a psychologically imperfect, well-meaning self like everyone else. That is another reason why the novel is collapsing into memoir.

Just about everybody who reflects on these matters seems to agree that the arts are losing their capacity to create an original experience, though no one has been able to say why. It seems harder and harder to make a work of art that does not conform to the dictates of the trivializing media, or that does not follow the lead of marketing experts in direct consultation with gallery owners and book and magazine editors—it seems difficult to make a work of art even partially detached from all the myriad diluting and polluting tributaries flowing out from the huge Deadening Sea of buying and selling. In myriad ways and forms, the artistic imagination in America seems to be plunging toward the literal. But of course people still write novels; they continue to make paintings and films. They even do so in greater numbers than ever before, which perhaps is yet more evidence that art is now serving a sharply different function than the aesthetic one it used to perform.

And yet, most strangely, no one appraises works of art themselves in the context of these new circumstances.

Articles in the news sections of newspapers, and in the newsy "front" of opinion magazines, take into account changes wrought by politics, technology, and finance. But for the most part, critics review books in newspapers and magazines pretty much the same way they did fifty years ago. Thumbs up, mostly, sometimes thumbs down in the newspapers; a mind-numbing neutrality in the more "refined" magazines; long, well-mannered expositions of a book's contents, an argument about the nature of the novel here, a spurt of self-consciousness about the tone of arts-reviewing there. A cautious blandness rules in the criticism of other art-forms, too.

But aside from knowing allusions to inflated prices for paintings, or to exorbitant book advances or movie deals, we hear no news about radical changes in the fundamental shape of the arts. We hear nothing about how the individual work of art in our time, *in the particulars of its form and content,* has assimilated not just the values of commercial society, but the vast supple consciousness that a universal spirit of commercialism fosters: get your own, and get it fast, and do it behind a virtuous appearance and with an optimistic air.

Such an omission amounts to a lie about our culture. Because it's often the artists themselves—novelists, painters, filmmakers, television writers—who seem to believe that art is exploitable for nonartistic purposes. They seem to have given up on the idea of art as an autonomous end. Making art now often serves as a means to advancement; the artists—or the people presenting themselves as artists—seem more like ambitious entrepreneurs who have turned the self into a small business.

How could it be otherwise? How could commercial society assimilate once socially transgressive aesthetic values without the artists themselves eventually learning how to assimilate, under the guise of art, the values that drive commercial society? As society has embraced aesthetic ways of being, art has become more, as the people in the Personnel Department like to say, "goal-oriented." And so novelists have felt more comfortable about fitting their stories into a marketing niche, and business-minded people have felt more relaxed about sitting down and writing a novel instead of going to work on Wall Street—for everyone still covets the aura of being an artist.

Still, this is not the way things permanently or entirely are. It's the way some things are—for the moment. The businessification of the arts—and the entrepreneurizing of the artist—hasn't become such an entrenched condition that you can't glimpse through its gaps a different, freer situation.

After all, art and commerce have always mingled; Shakespeare probably created the complex rhetoric of *Troilus and Cressida* for an audience of lawyers. In the right circumstances, money is a blessing on culture. How silly seems the old Marxist idea that oligarchic or plutocratic elites impose their taste on the masses. It was Victorian wealth that made possible middle-class readers, buyers of books who supported attacks on Victorian hypocrisy by writers like Charles Dickens and George Eliot. Merchants and then industrialists, not starving idealists, supported Athenian drama in the fifth century B.C., Florentine painting in the fifteenth century, the French novel during the Second Empire, the efflorescence of artistic genius in post–World War II America— works of culture that could sustain and steel the most alienated starving idealist. Business can shower incalculable advantages on art. It's when art becomes a business, as it has now, that the quality of the imagination is strained.

I SHOULD BE BLUNT AND SPECIFIC about just how art got refashioned into a commercial enterprise, rather than remaining the beneficiary of commerce. A general distrust of art cleared the way for artists to feel more comfortable about employing art as a means to more practical, respectable ends. But material conditions helped this development along: behemoth European conglomerates in book publishing driven by the need to recoup large investments; art galleries struggling to pay rents inflated by the stores at-tracted by the galleries; art museums that have to expand or die; dance companies bereft of public funding; the whole cultural world fretting about being eclipsed by the movies, while the movie executives fret about being overtaken by television. And everyone in terror of being made irrelevant by the next wave of inundating technology.

Yet the people who run the big publishing houses, the ma-jor museums, the prestigious galleries, and the successful film-companies aren't afraid of bankruptcy, unemployment, or some other economic calamity. They don't worry about not making a profit. They worry about not increasing profits. Financial ex-pectations have become so high in this moment of soaring prosperity that money-minded people care more about win-ning than earning—and they care about not losing most of all. This is a radical rub.

The desire to earn a living, even to become rich, is healthy and rational. The wish to beat by large margins last quarter's al-ready profitable figures makes ordinary employees who serve the shareholders feel like they are working for an impersonal hunger and not for flesh-and-blood human beings, who presumably op-erate with some practical, if not moral, restraints. And the profits in certain areas do indeed keep increasing, just as the kinds of work rewarded by ballooning profits keep getting more surpris-ing and diverse. All this crazy accumulation, and all these unex-pected venues for accumulating—*Alan just made $12 million with his idea for motorized slippers!*—generate shivers of irrationality down to the roots of cultural attitudes. The general impression of ubiquitous superremuneration has made wealth the sole mark of success. People take up what has always been modestly rewarding artistic work expecting the same windfall that is bestowed on people who pursue careers in finance.

Because business wants individuals to become big-spending earners at as early an age as possible, young people are made to feel that they have to meet society's criteria for success as quickly as they can. This has a terrible effect on art-making. The general anxiety now is that if you don't have a gallery, or a movie about to be released, or a six-figure advance for a book soon after college, you have bungled opportunities previously unknown to humankind. In such an atmosphere of desperation without a cause, the work of art becomes, as they say in business, "fungible." Learning to make art takes time. But instead of the artist patiently surrendering his ego to the work, he uses his ego to rapidly direct the work along extra-artistic shortcuts, toward the success that seems to be diffused all around him like sunshine. The frenzy to make the kind of killing in art that one would expect to make in business is probably what lies behind the explosion of literary and journalistic frauds. In a commercial society that constantly arouses the libido and makes satisfaction a sacred goal, any shortcut to satisfaction is permissible. Lies become a consumerist tool. Their effectiveness as a tactic earns them the quality of truth.

Out of all this new mire and complexity comes the reversal of relations between cultural values and the entrepreneurial status quo. Twenty-five-year-olds with nothing to tell or say now publish their "memoirs" because marketing shamans have determined that the "youth" demographic must be won over in order for civilization to survive—the precocious reminiscers end up telling or saying what the marketers claim their readers want to hear: tales of drinking, drug-addiction, sex-addiction, violence, etc. (In other words, they end up portraying a vision of life that middle-aged publishing and entertainment executives lasciviously project onto the appetites of young audiences.) Media honchos publish cynical, dreadful novels on the basis of the "demographic" they bring with them. Book publishers drop an author if his first book didn't make a profit, rather than sticking with him as publishers used to do, and supporting and nourishing him over the long haul. Writing-or-painting-or-filmmaking-by-identity becomes as formulaic as painting-by-numbers. And everybody seems to be bidding for the reader's attention and sympathy by writing bouncily about criticism-proof subjects like terminal illness and the Holocaust. Almost unreal prosperity—the sunshine of self-interest everywhere—has created a weird, American style of writing profitably about tragedy in a sunny, upbeat sort of way. All that sunshine, incidentally, makes it hard to criticize for a living. It can make a critic want to seek out and celebrate art that honestly exposes the cruelty and sorrow in life.

But as I said, this is how only some things are. Truthful, authentic art keeps being made outside, far outside, the increasingly closed circles of the great cultural centers where the inversion of art and business turns art's head. The critic's passion should be to expose the shams, the false consciousness, the cleverly accommodating patter that are turning expedience into culture, and making an essentially social transaction into a novel or a play. The true critic's function should be to hearten the true artist.

Yes, of course, critics *shouldn't* have to do anything, and there are as many different ways to write criticism as there are people practicing it. There are still brilliant, replenishing intellects around, making sense of things in all the arts. But criticism that hopes to affect artists' creative prospects, and the quality of a reader's intellectual choices, is the most intimate, and effective, and exciting kind of criticism.

The critic who aspires to such a meaningfully consequential criticism is not a glorified reviewer. He does not merely evaluate a work of art, or peremptorily argue this or that aspect of a genre, or mechanically bemoan the falling-off from some golden age.

Rather, he uses each critical occasion to show, *in the particulars of its form and content,* how an object of discrimination reflects the life around it in the broadest sense possible, either as an example of manufactured sentiments thwarting life itself, or as an instance of joy and freedom—he interprets the work under scrutiny almost as if it were a lesson in freedom, or in some of the ways of being, or not being, free. This critic serves the ambitions of the true artist struggling to break through all the travesties, inversions, and deformations of his calling to a rich, unfettered imaginative place.

To accomplish that the critic has to operate as a writer. He should not produce essays consisting of two paragraphs of opinion at the beginning, then twenty-eight paragraphs of synopsis with an unobjectionable *aperçu* obligingly woven in here and there, followed by two resoundingly final paragraphs of opinion at the end. He should be witty, and coarse, and antic, and subtle; his essays might well be the products of a mime, an ironist, a buffoon, a provocateur. *Do unto art what you would have art do unto you.* It is the difference between a job and a vocation. As for negative, even vehemently negative, criticism, it has to be as much a form of understanding a specific work as a mode of attack. For the rest, the proof is in the pudding.

Before the extinction of grand intellectual frameworks, critics used to be not just finicky appraisers but intellectually and stylistically avid writers. They plied their trade at now-defunct journals that collected around them writers united by grand political or aesthetical frameworks—figures who used to argue with similar writers gathered around rival journals. But that was before the hyperscrutinizing media grew more important, more transgressive even, than any artistic or critical movement; and before the media reduced everything, whether an isolated murder or a piece of exceptional music, to a *trend.*

Now critics work in the media's giant gleaming maw, mostly as reviewers, necessarily shorn of passion and obsession and beautiful axes to grind. For not only is the media, like art, subject to the inversion of intellectual and business values. Obviously, the media itself is a big business, a very big, profitable, perennially anxious business that doesn't so much sneakily abet the status quo as openly seek to become it. The ambitious critic who wishes, like any serious person, to fulfill his destiny in his work—who wants to be consequential—sooner or later has to take perilous aim at his peers.

But of obstacles along life's way there is no end, and anyway, nothing speeds a critic's progress along like plentiful obstacles. Hating or despising all sides is nice work if you can get it, too. And loving, and being loved. Dear reader, accompany me, if you will. I was lonely and asthmatic as a boy.

PART ONE

The Imagination and Its Obstacles

Harry Potter and the
Fear of Not Flying

ONCE UPON A TIME, a boy on a broomstick flew into a nation that was significantly free from tradition and prescribed custom. So great was the country's freedom in this regard that it turned every social incident and every cultural expression into a symbolic occasion that might supply a sorely needed orientation to national life. If two teenagers went on a rampage of killing in a high school, the slaughter had partly to embody the nation's surrender to television or computers. If a series of books came out about the adventures of a nearly adolescent boy swooping around on a broomstick, the rapturous reception of these books had partly to embody the craving for an antidote to the national submission to television or computers. Yet the popularity of the Harry Potter books actually has everything to do with our symbolizing tendency itself.

That is because all this fancy pop-critical theory quickly hardens into leaden, clinical fact, testified to by an array of experts who are glad to make themselves available to all the technologies of punditry. Why the killing? Not just because of television and the Internet, but because of early trauma, poor self-esteem, a broken home, inept guidance counselors and school psychologists, and so on. Clunk, clunk, clunk: it is like dully making change for events of tremendous denomination, though none of the routine inquiries ended up applying to the Columbine killers. Swamped by these so-called facts of mental life, the specificity of what happens in the world outside the mind gets lost; the world seems to turn on what takes place in the mind, and what takes place in the mind is whatever the electronic sages tell us does.

What's more, if you protest against the clinical facts that supposedly define you—they also include the fact of where you come from, and of what group you belong to—you are deemed outside the pale of a century of improvements in scientific plain-seeing. You are "in denial," which is like saying that you are allied with the powers of darkness and irrationality. Our cultural productions reflect this state of affairs. Memoirs stress the standard, formative facts; works of art hallow the standard, formative facts. Now, this relentlessly rational organization of inner and outer reality, of cultural documents and works of art, makes for a fantastic situation. For underneath it all, life flows incalculably on, and we know and feel this.

For this reason, the rapturous reception of the Harry Potter books is heartening, because J. K. Rowling is a literary artist, and her books possess more imaginative life than the majority of novels that are published in this country in any given year. They are full of marvelous invention and humor and fun, but they have more than that. They are not fantasy-escapes from mundane existence, as they are being hailed; they are escapes from a general condition of hyperrationality that, because it ignores the element of incalculability in life, has become unreasonable to the point of seeming receptive to fantasy and the occult as escapes from life. With Harry Potter, Rowling has brought reality back into the literature of escape, and back into our fantasy-culture. What a rarity, a literary imagination that is not self-conscious, and studied, and uptight.

The Harry Potter novels spin the tale of an orphan who is eleven when the series begins, and grows older by a year in each successive volume. One night, the infant Harry appears on the doorstep of the Dursleys, his aunt and uncle and their gluttonous bully of a young son, Dudley. Harry spends ten years with them, during which time they treat him cruelly—they make the sadistic Aunt Spiker and Aunt Sponge of Roald Dahl's *James and the Giant Peach* look like hospice-workers—making him sleep in a cupboard and barely giving him enough food to survive.

Uncle Vernon and Aunt Petunia have told Harry that his parents died in a car accident. But Harry's parents had a secret, which Harry discovers on his eleventh birthday: they were powerful and respected members of England's wizard community. And they never died in a car crash. They were killed by the evil wizard Voldemort, who lost much of his power when he tried to finish off the infant Harry but, for some inexplicable reason, failed to do so, leaving Harry alive and with a scar in the shape of a lightning bolt. Indeed, Harry with his green eyes, and Voldemort with his green light, mysteriously share a granule of the same nature, though Harry is unambiguously good and Voldemort is unambiguously evil.

Harry is saved from his wicked stepparents by his parents' wizard friends and sent to Hogwarts, a famous private school for wizard children, though he has to return to his aunt and uncle over the summer holidays. The books tell the story of Harry's adventures at Hogwarts, where, among other things, he discovers that nonwizard people are called Muggles; and learns how to play the game Quidditch, which is conducted while flying through the air on broomsticks; and finds his best friends in the bookish daughter of two dentist–Muggles and the son of an impoverished wizard family; and does battle with a mountain troll in the girls' bathroom; and learns how to make friends with a hippogriff (you stare unblinking into its fierce orange eye, bow, and wait for it to bow).

WHAT IS IT WITH THE BRITISH, why are they so good at creating stories in which there is this world and an alternative world? J. M. Barrie, Frances Hodgson Burnett, E. Nesbit, Lewis Carroll, J. R. R. Tolkien, C. S. Lewis—they all come from somewhere in Great Britain. (Rowling herself is Scottish.) Of course, there is the creative stimulus of living on cozy little islands shrouded by fog. And there is the nice constant scare of the surrounding sea making your neighbors seem more alien and more likely to arrive unexpectedly; and the venerable class system, which enacts alternative worlds side by side; and, for a time, there was the strange, distant galaxy of empire. Or maybe it is just that the battlements and the turrets of British common sense are so solidly established that British writers can imagine its opposite with luxurious sanguinity.

But why are we so entranced by the creation of alternative worlds in the first place? The answer might have something to do with the conventional premise of so many children's stories, which is that they revolve around children whose parents are dead or absent or diminished. (Nesbit, the Fabian socialist, liked to make her fathers bankrupt or falsely accused of selling secrets to the Russians.) This is partly the reflection of a child's tyrannical wish to have total sovereignty over a parent-free world, and it is also a reflection of the adult author's childlike impulse to have total sovereignty over his or her created world. But surely there is also an attenuated Christian influence: Jesus in Jerusalem refusing to acknowledge his parents, Jesus exhorting his followers to leave their parents and their homes and to follow him. The unaffiliated, deracinated state is a state of pure spiritual receptivity, and this is the condition of much children's literature, which introduces the child to the idea of change. And since the gradual withdrawal of parents is an inevitable thing, the classic children's stories are often semiparables of the terrors and the pleasures of separation.

The appeal of alternative worlds goes much further, deep into the vicissitudes of our maturity. As our parents recede, we rely on our imaginations to construct another authority—which is to say, another world. The pressure that our ego exerts on the objects of its hunger and its need amounts to a desire to enchant the people around us. Yet beyond our magical circle of bonds and affection lies the other world, the world outside the reach of our enchantments. We have to negotiate between these two regions on a daily basis, and to keep our balance as the boundaries move, and to maintain our poise throughout the times when our world takes on the aspect of the mundane, and the world beyond acquires the allure of enchantment (it notices us, it seizes us and holds us in its power, victory is ours).

So the children's story of a solitary imagination, operating avidly and resourcefully in the shifting world, is also the naked, subterranean story of our adult days. The point is not that a good children's story is, as people like to say, written also for adults. The point is that a good children's story is the story of the making of an adulthood. That is why the best children's stories have a wit and an urbanity that make their most extravagant inventions all the more believable.

From J. M. Barrie's *Peter Pan and Wendy:*

"What is your name?"

"Peter Pan."

She was already sure that he must be Peter, but it did seem a comparatively short name.

"Is that all?"

"Yes," he said rather sharply. He felt for the first time that it was a shortish name. . . .

She asked where he lived.

"Second to the right," said Peter, "and then straight on till morning."

"What a funny address!"

Peter had a sinking feeling. For the first time he felt that perhaps it was a funny address . . .

"Don't have a mother," he said. Not only had he no mother, but he had not the slightest desire to have one. He thought them very over-rated persons.

From C. S. Lewis's *The Lion, the Witch and the Wardrobe:*

In one corner there was a door which Lucy thought must lead to Mr Tumnus's [a faun] bedroom, and on one wall was a shelf full of books. Lucy looked at these while he was setting out the tea things. They had titles like . . . *Nymphs and Their Ways* or *Men, Monks, and Game Keepers: A Study in Popular Legend* or *Is Man a Myth?*

From Ian Fleming's *Chitty Chitty Bang Bang:*

Now, Joe the Monster was in fact head of an international gang of robbers and ruffians and he was known in France as Joe le Monstre.

Rowling herself, with her narcissistic wizard-professor Gilderoy Lockhart, to take just one example from her books, masterfully does this dry trace of a satirical tone, though with a touch of farce. The renowned author of *Magical Me,* among other volumes, Lockhart praises his student, Hermione Granger, Harry's bookish friend, for supplying the right answer to an exam question that Lockhart poses about himself:

> . . . but Miss Hermione Granger knew my secret ambition is to rid the world of evil and market my own range of hair-care potions—good girl!

I'm sorry, but I find this sort of thing hilarious. I also find it replenishing, since I cannot think of any "adult" fiction that attempts genuinely to satirize the celebrity-fraud. Most wondrous of all is that Rowling does not use the archness, and the worldliness, and the knowingness to protect herself or to promote herself, to remind us that she is too sophisticated to be taken in by her own fictions. On the contraire, as Joe le Monstre would say. As in Barrie and Lewis and Fleming, Rowling wants to prove the strength of her fiction by testing its capacity to assimilate the worldliness. This is because Rowling, like her predecessors, has total confidence in her imagined world, and is unafraid of delivering herself up to her fancy. Or, as Peter Pan puts it, when the human children ask him to tell them how to fly, "You just think lovely wonderful thoughts . . . and they lift you up into the air."

THE ABILITY TO FLY is the most pressing issue of our time. And it is not just the trend-diviners and the glossy social-scientistic savants who make it hard to know how to fly. There are also the fantasists themselves, for instance the so-called magical realists, who pretend that fantastic occurrences are continuous with reality. Magical realism snubs the intractable evidence of reality, and thus never allows readers to exercise their capacity to believe the unbelievable against all the evidence of reality. In snubbing reality, magical realism slights the power of imagination.

But Rowling writes her tales in a manner that may be called realistic magicalism—which preserves the discontinuity between fantasy and reality. She takes it for granted that, against all the stubborn evidence that she has preserved to the contrary, her readers will nevertheless leave the ground with Harry Potter. In maintaining the gravitational pull of reality, she pays homage to the magical leap of imagination.

And there are still other obstacles to the genuine levitation of the spirit. For one thing, you have to leave your consciousness of self behind, and that is a foolish thing to do nowadays, like leaving your car unlocked on a city street. For another, developing the confidence that you may ascend above the sum of your gritty givens might stick you with the appearance of being an egotist—like puffed-up Peter Pan, or the conceited Phoenix in Nesbit's *The Phoenix and the Carpet,* or like all flying creatures. That would be disadvantageous in a society whose citizens feel more comfortable around narcissists with fragile egos like Lockhart than around egotists with selfless natures like Harry.

But Rowling knows the value of flying, and so do her readers. This is why she makes the game Quidditch, a combination of soccer and rugby, an event of central importance. The worst effect of a crisis at Hogwarts—a rogue troll wandering about the halls, Voldemort's minions on the loose, the dangerous Dementors going around making everyone feel sad and hopeless—is that a Quidditch match is canceled. And the happy resolution of every book involves Harry's house, Gryffindor, winning a crucial game of Quidditch. Indeed, Harry is never so happy as when he is playing the game; it keeps his mind off his troubles.

Harry would make a very bad contemporary memoirist, because when he is zooming around on his broomstick and thinks of his parents' violent deaths, sometimes remembering their screams, the experience of flying seems unreal to him and he nearly falls off his broom to his own death. The formative trauma, for Rowling, is the true unreality. Only the airborne imagination fosters self-forgetfulness, which makes work possible, work that sustains a life. Thus Quidditch, with its echo of "quiddity," meaning the essential quality of a thing. Quidditch, a vital, self-forgetful busyness, is the essential activity of Harry Potter's world.

ROWLING HERSELF seems to have the habit of pure artistic confidence, of egotistical self-abandoning. She appears to be totally immersed in her imagined world, and you can see this in her books' layers of literary allusion. At the beginning of Antoine de Saint-Exupéry's *The Little Prince,* the strangely disconsolate narrator tells us that as a boy, he once drew a picture of a boa constrictor. He showed it to several adults, who failed to recognize it for what it was. They thought the drawing showed a hat. This, says the narrator, was the beginning and the end of his career as a painter, for "grown-ups never understand anything by themselves." The capacity to read properly a child's drawing of a boa constrictor becomes a test of the litheness of adult imagination.

Now, it happens that in *Harry Potter and the Sorcerer's Stone* the Dursleys allow Harry to accompany them to the zoo, where he meets a boa constrictor. To Harry's astonishment, he and the reptile have a conversation, which comes down to the boa constrictor's desire to see Brazil, where he has never been, despite the information conveyed by the card on his cage: it reads, "Boa Constrictor, Brazil." Though Harry is not aware at this point of his magical powers, he somehow has the effect of making the glass front of the reptile's cage disappear, which allows the boa constrictor to slither out to freedom, hissing to Harry as he departs, "Brazil, here I come. . . . Thanksss, amigo." Of course, Harry's nonwizard relatives could not hear Harry talking with the snake. In this way, the capacity to hear a boa constrictor speak becomes a test of the litheness of adult imagination.

There is also a willow that, rather than serving as benign backdrop to the adventures of *The Wind in the Willows'* Mole and Toad, "whomps" anyone who comes near it with its giant branches; and a wardrobe that the children use, not as a portal to a magical world, but as a hiding-place in which they can eavesdrop on adult conversations (in other words, as a more realistic portal to a more available magical world); and a phoenix named Fawkes, referring to the moment in Nesbit's tale when the children discover the phoenix on Guy Fawkes' Day (a good day for a socialist). My favorite allusion is a flying car with its own mind. It does its work and then trundles away from its owners into the Forbidden Forest, where it goes native, tooling around and covering itself in leaves and branches and mud.

There is no reason for these references, it seems to me, beyond the writer's wholehearted absorption in her universe. That, too, is perhaps why these books are so appealing: in our practical and utilitarian artistic atmosphere, they are ends in themselves. But I don't mean to make Rowling out to be another Joyce. Though she has produced works of literature, they are still primarily books for children and young adults. Their reported popularity among adults says more about the dearth of good fiction than about the books themselves.

In fact, parents expecting a respite from the violence in popular culture will be surprised by the amount of violence that Rowling introduces into her tales. I cannot think of any classic children's story that has as much of it. Rowling is a clever writer, and she has assimilated just about every basic bit of business you might encounter in an action movie. At one point, she even has Harry and his friends pointing their wands and kicking in a door. Legs get broken, the children get thrown against walls, blood drips, bones crunch. Sometimes the characters even cry out, "Aaaargh!" that trusty old comic-book exclamation.

If Rowling has absorbed Fleming's *Chitty Chitty Bang Bang,* she has also mastered the conventions of the James Bond movies. So far, every book ends with the standard Bond wrap-up, in which the captured British agent—in this case, Harry Potter—waits patiently to be killed while the villain helpfully explains the fine points of the plot, reviews the highlights of his villainy, and discusses his plans for the future. Then comes the violent reversal and the happy outcome.

But this patina of rough action is all to the good. Most little boys spend much of their time thinking about ways to decapitate other little boys—and of course never do. Most little girls spend much of their time thinking of ways to please little boys, mainly by laughing at their most embarrassing qualities or crying as hard as they can whenever they are around. Rowling's violence is a blessed acknowledgment of the nature of children.

Harry and his friends Hermione and Ron Weasley are good kids, but they are not angelic, Wordsworthian kids. They usually do the right thing, and they always feel bad when they do the wrong thing. But they pass through a spectrum of hurtful impulses along the way, some of which they act on. This means that their goodness is not only a passive gentleness, easily wounded by the world. It is also the goodness of being able to act in the world. Since they are built with the potential to do harm, Harry and his friends are also built to endure harm. The inexorable violation of their childhood innocence will not lodge its leaden factuality in their minds like burrs; it will not spell their doom as persons. Harry's scar is not only evidence of a deep emotional injury but, more consequentially, it is also the sign by which everyone in the wizard world recognizes him as the famous Harry Potter, the boy who defeated the villain Voldemort.

The many-sided nature of children is also, perhaps, what Rowling is getting at when she hints that Harry partakes of Voldemort's nature. As the French name implies, Harry has stolen from death its terrible power, but only as a way to fly from death: what Harry has gotten from Voldemort is the instinct of self-preservation, which is a mercurial, double-sided thing. Such a portrait of children's complexity, at least to the degree that you find it in Rowling's tales, is something new in children's literature. She has hit our contemporary moment right on the head.

Rowling's complicated violence has a functional purpose, too. It draws in children who might otherwise be won away by empty fantasies of violence. Once distracted by Rowling's highly enjoyable scrim of action, they will find a fusion of entertainment with an autonomous artistic will. Each book follows the hero's archetypal journey—in the form of a detective story—from increasingly turbulent surface, to life-endangering depths, and back up to sunlit surface. (Uncle Vernon, whose absence of imagination perfects his cruelty, manufactures drills for a living.) And in every book, Harry confronts his parents' deaths at the same time as he fights to preserve his life, an ordeal that seems to have to do with Harry finding a way to stop dwelling on his parents' deaths.

Inside that pattern, Rowling structures her books with a different theme that she develops through reiterated words, images, and motifs. Her tales are remarkably unified for children's stories. In the first volume, Harry first learns about his wizard nature, and discovers that he is not the worthless boy that his aunt and uncle have told him he is. The theme is the nature of identity, which is hidden, elusive, and immovable. And so when he goes shopping for a wand right before school begins—it is required—Harry finds that the wand chooses him. The nicest conceit is the Mirror of Erised, with its strange inscription: "Erised stra eh ru oyt ube ca, fru oyt on wohsi." Read in the opposite direction, it says, "I

show not your face but your heart's desire." It teaches, both literally and figuratively, the idea that you are what you want and not
what you appear to be, and that what you want follows from
who you mysteriously are, and that your desires can also change.
The book's conclusion has Harry fighting for his life with "The
Man with Two Faces."

The second book, *Harry Potter and the Chamber of Secrets,* deals
with origins and class. It portrays fame as a reward for character
and as a path up through society, and it depicts celebrity—in the
figure of Lockhart—as a scourge on character, and as an irritant
to social harmony. Rowling, for all her uncanny inventiveness,
means business. In this volume, the moral is that your choices,
not your origins, define you. Seemingly good people disclose
their villainy; apparent transgressors reveal their innocence; trans-
figuration becomes an issue; and the phoenix, whose origins are
ashes, saves the day.

The third volume, *Harry Potter and the Prisoner of Azkaban,*
pushes the artfulness further. It is about depression, black moods,
days when a kid just can't go on, because everyone tells him—or
her—that he is nothing, and that things will never change. Sirius
Black is the villain, who turns out to be the good guy, because
things do change, after all. And the Divination teacher, Professor
Trelawney, ends up getting everything wrong, because nobody
can tell you what the score is; you have to find out for yourself.

People such as Professor Trelawney set themselves up as reality-
instructors, but they are projecting their own inadequacies. They
hope that by convincing you to bow to your supposed limitations, they will make up for their inability to overcome their own
limitations. But you have to travel along the axial lines of your
own unique existence—wait a minute, that's Saul Bellow's *The
Adventures of Augie March*! Americans may love the Harry Potter
books because they tell a British school-story, but the British

must love them because the real lessons learned at Hogwarts remind them of America.

Rowling's world is very artfully patterned. Consider, finally, her conceit of having owls deliver the mail in the wizard world. Harry has his very own courier, an affectionate though high-strung snowy owl named Hedwig. Hedwig happens to be the name of the little girl in Henrik Ibsen's play involving another bird, *The Wild Duck*. Roald Dahl certainly had Ibsen's play in mind when, in *The Witches,* he has the Norwegian grandmother tell the story of a little girl with a pet duck who is abducted by means of nefarious magic. I have no idea if Rowling is making kindred literary mischief. But it doesn't matter. Ibsen's play is about the "life-lie" that we tell ourselves in order to bear as much reality as we can. It is about life-lies that deform and destroy, but also about those that become a part of truth because they make life possible. And J. K. Rowling has similarly qualified our spiteful and ungenerous adult notion of denial, and drawn out of it a beautiful human affirmation. She is spinning an honest and necessary deceit about the world.

A Book of Virtues for the Right-thinking Left

THE BEST RESPONSE TO A STORY being another story, I can't resist the temptation to begin talking about this anthology, *A Call to Character,* by telling a few tales of my own.

One day, my father, a less than modestly successful businessman, came home from work. That's it. That's the end of the first story. He lost his job and did not go back to work for a long time, no matter how hard he tried to find another job. What sometimes happens happened next: he declared bankruptcy, and eventually he and my mother divorced. There's no moral at the end of that story either—only my life, which continued unpredictably and incalculably (as did my parents' lives).

I'd always been a reader, but at around the time my father became unemployed when I was sixteen, I turned more purposefully to books—especially fiction, poetry, and drama. That good, bad, glad, sad, mad Hamlet; helpless, murderous Raskolnikov; Cordelia, so absolutely right and so absolutely wrong; haughty, vulnerable Darcy; monstrous, pathetic Ahab; poor, weak, stupid, heartbreaking Hurstwood! Unlike my father's bankruptcy and my parents' divorce, the incidents in those characters' lives never stood humiliatingly alone, trapped behind the bars of monotone facts. I read about situations and personalities, words and gestures, that rose up into the imagination on layers of meaning—so many layers that all these overlapping meanings could cushion a guy when he bounced off the hard rock of social reality and started falling. Art imprismed me in its extenuating colors, and the multiplicity of truth—of morals to be drawn—set me free.

I went off to college after that, and the first semester there I found myself in a course on nineteenth-century European philosophy, taught by a Professor Bridges. There were mostly kids from humble circumstances at this school, kids who, like me, wore their best clothes self-consciously and glowingly to class. Bridges himself strode into the room on the first day in a flannel shirt, jeans, and work boots, and delivered the news that he stood for radical change, in the tradition of Marx and Engels, Lenin and Trotsky. That was fine with me. So long as the revolution had room for people in nice shirts and pants, I would be there. I excitedly prepared to listen to Professor Bridges blow a hole in the hard social facts, the way my favorite authors did.

But that's not what happened. Professor Bridges just kept bouncing our heads off the hard social facts. Bourgeois art—and he considered all "high" art bourgeois art—lied, deceived, oppressed, and betrayed. It offered a way out as a way of keeping us in the system. It did not accurately reflect the forces that crush, as art must always do; rather, its multiple meanings smothered the impulse toward concrete collective action. Bridges was cruder (and more casually dressed) than other supposedly radical professors I encountered when, years later, I attended graduate school in a tonier academic setting. But his crudeness was just the thing to overrun my defenses. I began to hate my bookish ambitions, and to hate the telltale formality of my clothes. He stripped me bare inside and out, and I sat there shaking with the shame and anger I'd felt when my father lost his job.

Since then, as American politics has moved to the right, I've dug in my heels left of center. And as the culture has moved to the left, I've—well, let's just say that I've stuck to "high" art and to its saving complexities, those complexities that are neither liberal nor conservative. Two years ago I reviewed William Bennett's *The Book of Virtues* for *The Nation* and tried to give Bennett a good taste of his own scourge. My father's experience led me to respond caustically to all that cruel blather about lack of character being a more fundamental social reality than social arrangements themselves. And yet no one had screwed things up like my father. Thus, entangled like Laocoön in those layers of meaning, I read through this new moral anthology, edited by the progressive educators Colin Greer and Herbert Kohl—a volume described by its publisher as the "liberal alternative to the bestseller *The Book of Virtues*"—and began to recall Professor Bridges.

In purpose the two anthologies are decidedly similar. Both contain stories, poems, and essays meant to be read aloud by parents, so as to facilitate the moral education of children during their preadolescent years—though Bennett thoughtfully adds that he has included some difficult material for children to read as they grow older. Bennett's goal is "to help children achieve . . . moral literacy." Greer and Kohl aim to "encourage young people to read, talk and think about moral issues." In both books editorial commentary highlights the various moral messages that the authors intend their selections to illuminate.

Open these two big books to their tables of contents, however, and they begin to split apart like the primal elements. Bennett divides his anthology into ten sections that cover the moral "field," as he puts it, from self-discipline to faith. Greer and Kohl weigh in with sixteen sections, from courage to love, the sections themselves sorted under four main headings: "Values That Relate to One's Self," "Values That Relate to People One Knows," "Values That Relate to People One Doesn't Know and Nature," and "Values That Relate to Love." The two anthologies share six values: self-discipline, compassion, responsibility, courage, loyalty, and honesty. Bennett has four that didn't make it into Greer and Kohl's volume: friendship, work, perseverance, and faith. Greer and Kohl have a whopping ten that Bennett never thought of: integrity, creativity, playfulness, generosity, empathy, adaptability, idealism, balance, fairness, and love.

You know that when you have "work" in a volume without "playfulness," and "playfulness" in a volume without "work," you're looking at a genuine difference of opinion. But the gulf between *The Book of Virtues* and *A Call to Character* is at its widest when it comes to the values they share. Take the booming introduction to "responsibility" in Bennett: "Responsible persons are mature people who have taken charge of themselves and their conduct, who own their actions and own up to them—who answer for them." Here are the multiculturally sensitive Greer and Kohl on responsibility—after having specified that they compiled this anthology for children aged eight to thirteen:

> Responsibility is . . . a readiness to step forward as needed, a capacity to make sound preparations for certain and uncertain prospects. . . . This means paying attention, because it is inattention to the hurt, which can be caused by thoughtless habit and ill-considered convention, that produces so much ill will and conflict between people.

In the former you hear the deadly yin of defunct entitlements, in the latter the pedantic yang of the condescending group leader. Both visions of character are essentially public visions with public aims—character as a vehicle for social change.

One person's concept of responsibility has often been another person's burden, and fine sentiments won't pay your health insurance. God loves the poor and helps the rich, as my paternal grandmother told me when I once asked her why she didn't lend my father money. But I marvel at how there can be such a chasm in this country over the idea of character, with liberals on one side and conservatives on the other. It speaks of an intellectual hatred between the two sides, and as William Butler Yeats wrote in "A Prayer for My Daughter," "An intellectual hatred is the worst."

I don't think of character as a public issue. The public issues that rend America are, for the most part, insoluble conflicts, beyond the art of compromise. You can't have capital punishment and not have capital punishment, have gun control and not have gun control; a fetus cannot be a little bit aborted. In public conflicts one side or the other always gains the upper hand. But civil society depends on people who, once outside the political realm, know how to abstain from demanding victory, how to embrace contradictions with Whitmanesque ardor. Unlike the capacity to choose sides in a conflict, the ability to live amid contradictions requires character. And the first step toward character is the capacity to build solitude out of loneliness, to learn how to be alone with yourself.

Greer and Kohl stand for what used to be proudly called the liberal agenda. If I were a parent—and my wife and I hope to be parents someday—I would want my children to learn the importance of taking and acting on a public stand, and on most issues I'd want them to stand beside Greer and Kohl. But when the rally was over, the chanting done, the sun setting, and my children all alone, I would want them to have good old-fashioned inner resources—for their sake, and for the sake of their society. I would want them to know and accept life's crepuscularity. I would not give them treats or favors or hugs or kisses unless they repeated after me, every morning and every night: Life is not this thing or that thing, or one thing or another thing! Life, to put it not so simply, is life.

So I would want my children to be able to pull themselves up by their own bootstraps, but never to assume that everyone else is able to do the same. I would want them to see truth sometimes as social handiwork but sometimes as an absolute. I would want them seldom to spare themselves the rod, but to go ahead and spoil the poor and the vulnerable. I would want them to care deeply, creatively, playfully, generously, empathetically, idealistically, about the people and the wider world around them, but I would want them to survive. And I would want them to flourish. But above all, I would want them to know that the future offers more than two opposing courses of possible public conduct; I would want them to live intensely through life's paradoxes and ambiguities.

Among other things, art and literature humanize us into enduring life's paradoxes and ambiguities, its setbacks, calamities, and disappointments. They teach us to be alone with ourselves, so that we might grasp our "own inborn strength," as Joseph Conrad called it, which enables us to endure what we have to endure without sacrificing identity to survival. That is character. Yet— irony of ironies—here are Bennett, Greer, and Kohl screwing a utilitarian handle onto the imagination, abusing the very faculty that most makes character possible.

No child is going to nourish character out of life's twilit nooks and crannies from reading either the conservative anthology of virtue or this recent liberal one. If these two books were all they had, kids would have to choose between Chaucer on the one hand and Langston Hughes on the other. They would find John Donne and Alfred, Lord Tennyson facing off with Derek Walcott and Seamus Heaney; Plato, Aristotle, and Ralph Waldo Emerson versus Albert Einstein, Bertrand Russell, and Gandhi;

the Grimm Brothers' tales versus E. Nesbit's enchanting dragon stories; Goethe and Tolstoy versus Denise Levertov and Luisa Valenzuela; the Book of Exodus versus Lewis Carroll. It's as if in the deepest, most luscious and mysterious folds of the imagination, children were to find an administrative aide insisting that they sign up for either Mr. Bennett's homeroom ("Wow, what's his problem?") or Mr. Greerkohl's ("Yuck, he's always smiling").

Greer and Kohl are paragons of character; they know the pitfalls of their enterprise, yet they press on. One of the many worthwhile books that Kohl has written, *Thirty-Six Children,* is a marvelous, impassioned account of his experience teaching in a Harlem public school in the sixties, and I suspect that much of the passion and the commitment in this anthology come from him. *A Call to Character* cautions wisely and sincerely about respecting children's "complex inner lives," carefully emphasizes how "wonderful and complicated" children are, and talks about the importance of avoiding "preaching or didactic teaching" when raising "issues of concern" with children.

But the authors do protest too much. Once you start using stories to discuss "issues of concern," you begin taking the edge off that wonderfully complex inwardness—especially when you know exactly where you're headed: "A grounded understanding of social character values such as loyalty, honesty, and empathy can evolve through the conversations that reading stories makes possible." But what if a kid doesn't want to have a moral talk about what she's read? What if she reads a story chosen to illustrate empathy but remains stubbornly convinced that it's about the complicated inner life of a hedgehog named Georgina? Does she get a dunce cap? A show-and-tell trial?

Because Kohl and Greer are sensitive to the potential for impertinent readings, they've taken no chances. And because they take no chances, a better title for their anthology would have been *Thirty-Six Robots.* Like Bennett, they introduce their selections with little prefaces meant to isolate the moral meaning under consideration. And like Bennett's, these prefaces rarely have anything to do with the literary works they precede. Typical is the preface introducing an excerpt from Arthur Miller's *Death of a Salesman,* which warns, "If, like those of Willy Loman's sons, our unexamined prejudices get in the way, we can end up disconnected from others." Yet Arthur Miller's heart-wrenching play is not about unexamined prejudices. And Willy Loman's epitaph is not "Here Lies a Man Who Was Disconnected." But all that is moot, since Greer and Kohl's excerpt is from the scene where Willy begs his former boss's son to keep him on the job—a scene that doesn't even have Willy's sons in it. Throughout the anthology the contrast between the authors' prefaces and the selections themselves is nerve-wracking: it's the difference between a more perfectly ordered world as shiny as a new pair of shoes, and that precious, dirty, fraying old pair of sneakers (one of which lies hidden in shadows under the bed) that poets call the human heart.

Bad as this is, what is most surprising is *A Call to Character*'s deep disrespect for the act of storytelling itself. Greer and Kohl speak impressively about "the power of stories to bind adults and children and teach in depth and with love." But they are so zealously open to their vision of stories as vessels of social change that they are closed to their stories' and poems' openness. Gouging brief selections out of longer works, they succeed in destroying any magic or charm that might shield their choices from their intentions. Excerpts begin bewilderingly, without any adaptation or background explanation, and stop the reader dead in his tracks.

What is anyone, let alone a child, to make of a single page from *Northanger Abbey*? Eight paragraphs from the complicated finale of *Invisible Man*? Three paragraphs from *The Hunchback of Notre Dame* (moral: "Deep pleasure can come in prized pursuits")? The answer is that readers are not supposed to make any sense of these selections. They are there because Jane Austen was a woman, Ralph Ellison an African American, and Victor Hugo a chronicler of social injustice. For Greer and Kohl, female, African American, and poor children don't have imaginations, only wounds. Thus stories can "heal," but whether or not they give pleasure is irrelevant.

Some don't even aspire to healing. Instead they teach children how ruthless life can be. Barry Lopez's pointless tale "Coyote and the Skunk Kill Game" has a dishonest skunk who blinds, and a rapacious coyote who clubs to death, some good-natured and very poignant prairie dogs and rabbits. The two murderers dig a mass grave for their victims and cook them; the skunk then eats the corpses after getting rid of the coyote on a ruse. Moral: "Calculated dishonesty can also be a form of group or clique identity, making people fear to be left out." If you're going to choose this as a bedtime story for your kids, you might as well read them the Contract with America.

Or better yet, simply listen to Henry James. He's just right for liberals (cosmopolitan, ambivalent), and perfect for conservatives, too (a classic, good manners). "We work in the dark," James wrote. "We do what we can—we give what we have." And after we have given our children all the love, protection, and guidance we are able to, the best thing we can do for them is to leave them alone in a lamplit room with Henry James—or Langston Hughes or Chaucer or Plato or Denise Levertov or the Book of Exodus or Lewis Carroll—and close the door gently behind us.

Seize the Day Job:
Sacrificing Saul Bellow on the
Altar of One's Own Career

THE NOVELIST SAUL BELLOW is many things to many people. To some, he is the self-made literary Bourbon who restored the soul to American letters; to others, the Jewish Jackie Robinson who smashed his own idiom through WASP exclusions. To still others, he is the wisecracking custodian of the best that has been thought and said; or the patient stylist in Flaubert's line, laboring to make language a prehensile attachment to the eye. To my mind, this is all either piffle or partial truth. Bellow's genius consists in his being one of the greatest meshuganas who ever lived.

"Meshuga" means harmlessly crazy in Yiddish, but I am going to take liberties and use it in the sense of being gripped by divine laughter. Bellow himself characterizes this state of being in "Him with His Foot in His Mouth," a story about a man, Shawmut, whose truth-compulsion guarantees his social isolation: "In various ways I have been trying to say this to you, using words like seizure, rapture, demonic possession, frenzy, Fatum, divine madness, or even solar storm—on a microcosmic scale." Shawmut's irresistible urge to tell it straight manifests itself in witticisms that arouse the wildest life-giving laughter. It is the opposite of the spasms of blind self-regard that destroyed many of Bellow's friends and contemporaries: John Berryman, Randall Jarrell, Robert Lowell, Jean Stafford, Delmore Schwartz. Meshuga is the other side of destruction, a reconstitution in the form of a momentary flying-apart. The Meshuga Principle ventilates what self-destructive outbursts of deep forces actually work to repress.

Bellow once wrote a wise and affecting essay called "Mozart: An Overture" about his lifelong love for the composer. Mozartean laughter is, in fact, the very quality that fuels his meshuga energy. "That's the *animal ridens* in me, the laughing creature, forever rising up," thinks Augie March to himself at the conclusion of *The Adventures of Augie March,* a novel that begins almost farcically with an old woman at the mercy of an animal— a dog—and ends with several dogs bounding into the air and kissing the face of their master, an image of happy parity between humans and their physical nature. This communion between the individual and his or her animal power is one of Bellow's great themes. Here is most of the final paragraph of *Herzog:*

Coming back from the woods, he picked some flowers for the table. He wondered whether there was a corkscrew in the drawer. Had Madeleine taken it to Chicago? Well, maybe Ramona had a corkscrew in her Mercedes. An unreasonable thought. A nail could be used, if it came to that. Or you could break the neck of the bottle as they did in old movies. Meanwhile, he filled his hat from the rambler vine, the one that clutched the rainpipe. The spines were still too green to hurt much. By the cistern there were yellow day lilies. He took some of these, too, but they wilted instantly. And, back in the darker garden, he looked for peonies; perhaps some had survived. . . . He turned his dark face toward the house again. . . . He set down his hat, with the roses and day lilies, on the half-painted piano, and went into his study, carrying the wine bottles in one hand like a pair of Indian clubs. Walking over notes and papers, he lay down on his Recamier couch. As he stretched out, he took a long breath, and then he lay, looking at the mesh of the screen, pulled loose by vines, and listening to the steady scratching of Mrs. Tuttle's broom. He wanted to tell her to sprinkle the floor. She was raising too much dust. In a few minutes he would call down to her, "Damp it down, Mrs. Tuttle. There's water in the sink." But not just yet.

At the close of a novel in which an intellectual has tried to reconcile his experience with his ideas about experience, Bellow creates a brief existential harmony. The passage undulates between nature and culture—from the natural woods to the civilized corkscrew; from the physical act of breaking the bottle to the movies, that civilized simulacrum of uncivilized behavior. There is the hat and the roses; the *half*-painted piano; the wine bottles and the Indian clubs; the civilized notes and papers that get savagely trodden on; the protective screen, which gets pulled loose by the wild vine. And the novel ends at a perfect Mozartean pitch, with dust, the primal element of death, about to be joined with water, the primal element of life. Herzog is set to issue instructions for the improvement of his condition; he is about to commence the operation of civilization once again. But he pauses. He wants his thoughts to stop. He wants the serenity, if not the actuality, of death for just a few seconds longer, which is all that he will be able to bear.

REARRANGING LIFE'S GIVENS in such a way is a refusal to accept the tyranny of life's givens, and that is the essence of laughter and the function of art. It is also the promise of democracy. Bellow fittingly ends *Humboldt's Gift,* his epic story of a genius-poet of humble origins who achieves fame before ruining himself, with an old joke from Jewish immigrant culture: "They used to tell one about a kid asking his grumpy old man when they were walking in the park, 'What's the name of this flower, Papa?' and the old guy is peevish and he yells, 'How should I know? Am I in the millinery business?'"

Such a guerrilla-like eruption of the Meshuga Principle can have a terrible effect on people who lack the imagination to question the circumstances life has presented to them. They get very nervous. They reach for their credentials; they brandish the signs of conventional success; they withdraw into cliques and coteries. Their defensiveness is the response of a sham meritocracy to a true democratic spirit. Sadly, James Atlas's biography of Bellow is animated by these very anxieties.

Now, IF JAMES ATLAS is out of his mind (to borrow a line from Moses Herzog), it's all right with me. The unfolding of his condition, however, reveals a lot about American literary life. The brute fact of the matter, as it seems to me, is that Atlas, the author of *Bellow: A Biography,* which required over ten years to research and to write, appears to have been driven insane by his subject's cosmic laughter.

Bellow, raised in Chicago, was the child of poor Russian Jewish immigrants. Atlas, too, is an American Jewish writer, of the next generation, and brought up in more comfortable circumstances (in nearby Evanston, as he tells us in his introduction). There is something novelistic about the meeting of these two men in the pages of Atlas's startlingly deficient biography. It is an almost Jamesian encounter between a man who made mistakes and took wrong turns and failed and created out of his life great art that transforms experience into truth; and his chronicler, who never took a false step and whose right moves finally caught up with him. It is an encounter between two opposing versions of American experience; and it is an encounter between two very different versions—there are, of course, many—of American Jewish experience.

What exactly happened to James Atlas, a solid and reliable literary journalist, who for the past twenty years or so has been on the staff of such distinguished publications as *The New Yorker* and *The New York Times Magazine?* His writing for those and other magazines offers clues. First there appeared articles in which Atlas blithely declared the death of the independent intellectual in America ("The intellectual vocation . . . is largely obsolete, an archaic profession; the intellectual has gone the way of the cobbler and smithy"). Then there emerged, in piece after piece, Atlas's strange—and, alas, representative—obsession with social and economic status ("If you don't have a six-figure book deal by the time you're thirty-five, you've failed"). Next Atlas turned up and proclaimed in print that the great modernist novels of Proust and Joyce and Mann were not worth reading ("I am bored to tears and long for nothing more than the latest issue of *Vanity Fair*"). Worst of all, the poor man was slipping in a reference, every chance he got, to the fact that he had attended Harvard ("As we walked toward the Harvard Yard, where a quarter of a century earlier I had dodged tear gas with a wet handkerchief over my mouth . . . "; "I called him up from a phone booth at the Harvard Club. He'd heard about my project, and was full of enthusiasm"; "A month later, in Harvard Square, I went to the Harvard Coop, where I'd shopped as a student"; "Meanwhile, the pledge envelope from Harvard—I finally promised a hundred just to get them off my back—lies in the drawer"). One can almost imagine, at the end of Atlas's relationship with Bellow, the biographer keeping his Harvard diploma in his inside jacket pocket and desperately fingering it whenever Bellow said something wise or witty or wild.

It's especially Atlas's fateful rendezvous with this wildness of Bellow, with Bellow's demonic vitality, that seems at the root of his curdled spirit. Atlas himself, after all, has had little time for meshuga side trips. Not long after college, he published a first-rate and widely admired biography of Delmore Schwartz, and since then has advanced from one prestigious magazine position to another. Recalling his decision to write a biography of Bellow, he confides in the introduction that it "came at a difficult moment in my life." And what exactly was this difficult moment? A crisis induced by despair, grief, heartbreak? "I was," Atlas confides, "between projects." He was between projects.

The confrontation between such emotional constriction and Bellow's *animal ridens* is perhaps one reason for Atlas's ludicrously hostile and resentful approach to Bellow's life. It might help to explain why Atlas suppresses material that puts Bellow in a flattering light, material that an honest biographer would never consider excluding. He tiresomely refers, again and again, to what he at one point calls Bellow's "ill-concealed racism," his evidence being Bellow's honest if disturbing fictional expression of his fear of poor blacks' rage and violence in the seventies. Yet Atlas never mentions, while briefly touching on an early Bellow story, "Looking for Mr. Green," that Bellow sets the story in Chicago's black ghetto with the greatest empathy and that he identifies the elusive Mr. Green, who is black, with life itself. Atlas doesn't even tell us that the story has any black characters in it.

An even worse omission, given Atlas's recurrent charge that Bellow is insensitive to women, has to do with Anne Sexton. The poet cherished Bellow's writing, especially his novel *Henderson the Rain King,* the themes of which she drew on in several poems. The two pursued a lively and revealing correspondence, according to her biographer Diane Wood Middlebrook, in which Bellow seems touchingly to encourage the suicidal Sexton to cling to life. Atlas never mentions this material; indeed, he never mentions Sexton at all.

ATLAS AT ONE TIME WROTE A NOVEL, a thinly disguised memoir in the first person, entitled *The Great Pretender.* "For as all of Russian literature was said to have come out of Gogol's overcoat," Sven Birkerts wrote prophetically in a review of the book, "so all of *The Great Pretender* has come out of Bellow's hat. . . . Atlas would like to swallow [Bellow] whole and be him—parricide by anthropophagy."

Enjoy this sample:

> "You're destroying me," I complained. "I'm going to end up at Northern Illinois University."
>
> "So what's wrong with Northern Illinois University? People do go there, you know."
>
> Yeah, but not people whose fathers gave them a complete set of Gibbon's *Decline and Fall of the Roman Empire* for their twelfth birthday. Make good, Sonny. Make good or else.

Not surprisingly, the novel flopped. A bilious biographer was born. The Bellow we meet in the pages of Atlas's book must have been given the Nobel Prize by a Jewish charitable organization.

> In truth, [Bellow] hadn't fared well in menial jobs; his stints in his family's coal companies had ended disastrously.

> [Bellow] was unaware that in Parisian literary circles to discuss one's work was considered gauche.

[Bellow] lacked the reserves of self-esteem needed to engage in rigorous self-criticism.

As the biography proceeds, as Bellow becomes more and more accomplished, and more and more famous, Atlas cuts him down to size. We get Bellow's philandering, his vengefulness, his temper, his philandering, his vanity, his five marriages and four divorces, his selfishness, his philandering, his philandering, his philandering. Atlas seems so flustered by Bellow's countless affairs with women that at one point he sputters out an insinuation that Bellow is actually gay, a speculation tossed off like a schoolboy taunt and never returned to.

Maybe Bellow really is the biggest shit in the world. Maybe he really is the selfish, sexist, thin-skinned, retaliatory monster of egotism Atlas wants us to see him as. Once you've established his flawed character, what do you do with it? The occasion for writing about Bellow's life is his work, and the work is the only justification for scrutinizing Bellow's life. Otherwise all this not-very-shocking personal material is just what it is: unverifiable gossip. And it's not even gossip deepened and selected by time into history. Bellow is still alive—still writing, for that matter.

In a nearly seven-hundred-page biography, Atlas doesn't offer a single sustained reading of Bellow's fiction. Of the stunning scene that concludes *Seize the Day,* in which Tommy Wilhelm, the novel's protagonist, breaks down at a stranger's funeral and sinks "deeper than sorrow, through torn sobs and cries toward the consummation of his heart's ultimate need," all Atlas has to tell us is that Wilhelm is really Bellow and that this climactic moment is "an elegy to Bellow's father, dead only a year before." Never mind that Bellow portrays Wilhelm's father as a stingy, brutal monster, a wholly unsympathetic character who drives his son into despair. Some elegy. Atlas does not even

examine the interview Bellow gave to *The Paris Review*'s "Writers at Work" series, an extraordinary window onto his life and
art. Instead, he reduces the fiction to the bare actual facts that
provoked the artist into transforming them, depending for his
literal interpretations of the fiction on the integrity of people
who once knew Bellow: "Schwartz appears as Sandor Himmelstein in *Herzog,* a reliable guide to this episode in Bellow's life,
according to Ralph Ross."

I have never read a biography in which the author seemed to
take his subject so personally. Atlas incessantly reminds the reader
that the novelist long depended on his wealthy businessman-
brothers for money. Bellow was a poor kid from a poor family,
and Atlas lingers nastily over the young writer's penury, and over
his setbacks and rejections. The biographer is obsessed with Bellow's professional failures and ordeals: his short-lived literary
magazines; his unsuccessful plays, which Atlas spends an inordi-
nate number of pages discussing; and, above all and always, Bellow's struggle to make a living from his writing. Bellow's first
novel, *Dangling Man,* got mostly rave reviews, including one from
Edmund Wilson in *The New Yorker,* and placed the young author
at the heart of American literary life. That's unusual for a first
novel. Atlas is unimpressed:

> He was thirty years old, and his one book had gotten some
> good reviews. . . . Yet he was still a Hyde Park intellectual
> with a closetful of ill-fitting suits, a wife and child to help
> support, and a postmark that read Stock Yards Station—in
> effect, nowhere.

Later, after Bellow has published his second novel, gone to Europe on a Guggenheim, and been celebrated by the cream of literary society in New York and London, Atlas reminds him that he

was still the threadbare artist, ill dressed and perpetually short of cash. He had a reputation among the *Partisan Review* crowd but was virtually unknown to the general public.

And, four years after the Yiddish inflections of *The Adventures of Augie March* had resurrected American literature and established Bellow as the most important novelist of his generation, Atlas contemptuously describes Bellow as "a novelist with no job and no fixed income." Why a man who does not consider writing novels a real job would want to write the biography of a novelist is a mystery.

Atlas, in fact, writes like Bellow's father (though of course without that father's stormy affection), an immigrant who naturally disapproved of his writer-son's limited financial prospects. His biography bursts with numbers and sums quoted from Bellow's advances, sales figures, royalties, and tax returns: "The $600,000 advance made back about $160,000 on the trade edition, and subsidiary rights added another $200,000, leaving 'at risk' some $240,000." Augie March, meet Charles Schwab. Commenting on the young Bellow's yearning for a more meaningful life than the one his lower-middle-class origins offered him, Atlas again sneers, "Going into Dad's business: What could be more contemptible than that?" The biographer's philistine attitudes are almost self-satirizing:

> The two older brothers whose bed [Saul] shared, Moishe and Schmule . . . were healthy, vigorous, dynamic; no one in the family was surprised when they went on to become big deal makers in Chicago real estate. . . . Their worldly success was a persistent rebuke to the impecuniousness of their intermittently broke and never wealthy

brother. Together with [Bellow's father], who at last became a prosperous businessman in his forties, they formed a triumvirate from whose judgmental gaze the novelist struggled to free himself—without much success—throughout his days.

If only he could return his Pulitzer Prize and his three National Book Awards and his Nobel Prize and do it all over again! He might have become the dynamic Laundromat king of the South Side.

The most damaging effect of Atlas's single-minded prosecution of Bellow's life is that it hampers Atlas's professional competence. His biography is filled with contradictions and errors, with poor judgments and outright distortions. We read that Bellow was "disdainful of any effort to get ahead in the literary world—a form of defensiveness," and then about twenty pages later learn that Bellow was "ever expedient in matters of literary politics." At another point, Atlas writes that *The Adventures of Augie March* was "a modest triumph," explaining that it "never made the bestseller list." Yet one page later, he tells us that *Augie* "had made Bellow famous." A triumph not so modest. And fifty pages after Atlas has conceded that Bellow had become famous, he tells us that Bellow, several years after *Augie March* appeared, was still "well on his way to fame." The biographer has fame-block!

Atlas describes Bellow as "a novelist who was to make the process of becoming American one of his major themes." But the process of becoming American is not a theme in a single one of Bellow's novels and short stories. Bellow's characters, Jewish or not, are Americans who are in the process of becoming persons. For Atlas, Willis Mosby, the main character in Bellow's short story "Mosby's Memoirs," is an "older, more reflective version of [his] creator." Yet Bellow portrays Mosby as a casually vicious anti-

Semite who admires Hitler's managerial skills. And Atlas thinks that in *Herzog* the phrase "potato love" reverently refers to a "powerful devotion to the family." In fact, Herzog isn't referring to family feeling at all. He uses the term to refer to his envious friend Sandor Himmelstein's pretense of affection for him, to Himmelstein's "amorphous, swelling, hungry, indiscriminate, cowardly potato love." Of course, this is also the kind of stifling inauthenticity a generation of sensitive Jewish sons and daughters—generations of everyone's sensitive sons and daughters, for that matter—struggled to free themselves from.

ATLAS'S IDENTIFICATION with a particular kind of immigrant father—there were also the fathers who supported and encouraged their wayward artistic children—represents a sea change in American Jewish writing. Leave aside the fine points of exactly what it means to be an American Jewish writer, not to mention the danger of committing a coarse anachronism in using the designation. It is safe to say that the American Jewish sensibility once was characterized by a skepticism about current conditions, which was in fact a way of affirming life. It had laughter and was devoid of the cold calculation that wears sentimentality like a fig leaf. It seemed to come from nowhere. American Jewish literary expression had a special kind of ethical beauty; an inconsolable joy; a pregnant mirth drawn out of life's sadness. That sensibility is just about extinct. There are beautiful exceptions, to be sure. Leon Wieseltier's *Kaddish,* a masterpiece of filial piety, is the history of a soul in the form of a meditation on a ritual, which barely refers—imagine!—to the author's self or to his father. It is a pointed sublimation that stands on their head two generations of American Jewish autobiographical outpourings. And all the world-historical polemics of the much sentimentalized New York Jewish intellectuals don't rise to the moral courage of Philip

Gourevitch's book on the Western complicity with genocide in Rwanda. But these are, again, beautiful exceptions. For the most part, rather than the heirs to Bellow and Roth and Mailer (and the New York intellectuals at their best), today one sees younger American Jewish writers who are more like characters straight out of the satirical fiction of Bellow and Roth and Mailer.

One writer smoothly inserts a proprietary reference every chance he gets to the Holocaust (he got married on the anniversary of Kristallnacht as a gesture of defiance, and then he writes about getting married on the anniversary of Kristallnacht as a gesture of defiance); another pursues a power-fantasy of New York Jewish intellectual authority in a culture column for an online magazine, displaying a comical blend of insecure assertiveness and obsequious careerism that even Roth could not invent; another writes cute little affirmations of suburban life, as if she were making small talk while examining teeth; and still others continue to write about being Jewish, male, and horny, as though they were organizing briefs for distant, historic cases as a law-school exercise. Where have all the fine independent American Jewish minds gone? Such cautious calculation is a form of rebellion against their artistic and intellectual parents. But it is also the windfall of a lazy inheritance, thanks to the hard-earned affluence of their actual parents.

When is the last time you read a piece of writing by a Jewish writer in his or her twenties or thirties, or even forties, that approached life with the fresh, vital Archimedean angle on life that has been the hallmark of American Jewish writing? (God knows, I'm not holding myself up as an exception.) It is not at all that Jewish writers have become, en masse, anhedonists incapable of deep mischief. It is that many American Jewish writers, who have been the custodians of the meshuga spirit in modern America, who gave American writing and American culture a new life after the Second World War, now (like Atlas) seem smugly to associate the chance-taking and the inspired condition of their cultural forebears ("But you will be wondering what happened to 'the inspired condition.'"—*Herzog*) with a life of self-destruction and failure. Make good, boys and girls. Make good or else.

Of course, today's American Jewish carefulness and complacency are part of the general atmosphere. Literary, artistic, and intellectual worlds used to set up their own hierarchies against the outside world's conventional hierarchies. The creative world's ranks were ordered according to personal gifts and idiosyncrasy, audacity and the capacity for self-reinvention. Now, in New York, you go to a literary, artistic, or intellectual party and you encounter the same pecking order that exists in the conventional world. Everyone is from Yale, Harvard, Princeton, or such like; they are standing around in the same formation, with the same nervous, contracted ambition, as they did in college, and everyone comes from money. In Bellow's day, the city's creative precincts were full of the peers of privilege, but they also brimmed with people from everywhere and from every level of society; yes, blacks, women, and gays, too. Not that outsiders don't break in now and again. One might have reservations about the young writer Dave Eggers's work, but at least he's not a calculating creature of old school ties. (He is a raw, original, calculating creature.) But Eggers is just one more semi-inspiring exception. Let's not kid ourselves. We are living now in the age of Atlas, the anti–Augie March.

THE ADVENTURES OF AUGIE MARCH is the great novel of the young person who not only almost ended up at Northern Illinois University but who experimented with life in the search for a calling rather than just a career. Like *The Adventures of*

Huckleberry Finn and Ellison's *Invisible Man,* Bellow's teeming picaresque tale sprang, in part, from the author's experience of traveling upward through society. If American democracy is ever put on trial, the American picaresque novel will be Exhibit A in its defense. Augie comes from, as Atlas likes to say, "nowhere." He is the kind of literary hero a money snob and an Ivy League snob like Atlas doesn't want to know from.

Augie is, among other things, a spiritual record of how a kid born into poverty uses culture. The novel rolls in culture references as if in clover. One of the fiercest critical arguments about Bellow is whether his dense cultural allusions mar his fiction. True to form, Atlas chalks these cultural allusions up to Bellow's "childish intoxication with 'the big ideas'"; "the products of a provincial Chicago boy's efforts to show that he wasn't provincial." (An ambitious poor boy or poor girl should never meet a teacher like James Atlas.) Augie, however, is proof of the artistic potency of Bellow's cerebral flights. As poor kids do, the young Bellow used culture to raise himself above his origins; Bellow the triumphant adult uses culture in his novels to, as it were, raise himself above culture, to drop back into experience. In Bellow, culture and an irreverence toward culture become, like laughter, a universal principle of upward human motion.

Here is a pertinent moment from *Augie March,* in which William Einhorn writes an obituary for his wealthy businessman-father—the "Commissioner"—for a local newspaper. Einhorn is Augie's first great teacher. Einhorn himself is self-taught and erudite, and also a cripple confined to a wheelchair. In other words, he is the very image of the man uplifted by the power of culture; ideas propel him where his legs have failed. Augie loves him. The older, completed Augie, looking back on his life, tells us that "William Einhorn was the first superior man I knew." Einhorn is no clumsy autodidact. He even talks like Augie, mixing racy street idioms with high-flown culture references in spontaneous bursts of eloquence and poetry:

> "Augie, you know another man in my position might be out of life for good. There's a view of man anyhow that he's only a sack of craving guts; you find it in Hamlet, as much as you want of it."

Bellow has Einhorn using culture in his obituary the way Bellow treats culture in his novels. He plays games with it:

> The return of the hearse from the newly covered grave leaves a man to pass through the last changes of nature who found Chicago a swamp and left it a great city. He came after the Great Fire, said to be caused by Mrs. O'Leary's cow, in flight from the conscription of the Hapsburg tyrant, and in his life as a builder proved that great places do not have to be founded on the bones of slaves, like the pyramids of Pharaohs or the capital of Peter the Great on the banks of the Neva, where thousands were trampled in the Russian marshes. The lesson of an American life like my father's, in contrast to that of the murderer of the Strelitzes and of his own son, is that achievements are compatible with decency. My father was not familiar with the observation of Plato that philosophy is the study of death, but he died nevertheless like a philosopher, saying to the ancient man who watched by his bedside in the last moments . . .

Now, Einhorn doesn't talk in such a pompous, awkward way. Why does Bellow have him write like that? Einhorn is shrewdly using culture as a lever for his own purposes, just as his creator does. This is the very next paragraph:

We then went to his father's room. . . . [Einhorn] handed me things with instructions. "Tear this. This is for the fire, I don't want anyone to see it. Be sure you remember where you put this note—I'll ask for it tomorrow. . . . So this was the deal he had with Fineberg? What a shrewd old bastard, my dad, a real phenomenon."

Far from proving in his life that "great places do not have to be founded on the bones of slaves," Einhorn's father was a "shrewd old bastard" who knew how to climb to the top of the heap in iron Chicago. With the obituary's overblown, almost baronial cadences, Einhorn fabricates the image of a noble Commissioner—whose business Einhorn has inherited and needs to keep respectable. At the end of the chapter, Einhorn sums things up for Augie:

We never learn anything, never in the world, and in spite of all the history books written. . . . There's a regular warehouse of fine suggestions, and if we're not better it isn't because there aren't plenty of marvelous and true ideas to draw on, but because our vanity weighs more than all of them put together.

In one stroke, Einhorn acknowledges the pretense of his obituary, which is a kind of history, and an insightful one at that; places it in relation to his ego; and teaches Augie a lesson about social reality and the virtues and limitations of culture. Yet it is Einhorn's reading that has led him to be skeptical of a purely literary education. The power of books helps him affirm the primacy of experience, which leads him back to books, which he once more tests against experience. It is like the undulating dialectic between nature and culture at the end of *Herzog*.

Einhorn is Bellow's image of the ordinary man who labors to bring out his innate nobility—the nobility of the individual. Such regalness of the spirit is not conferred; it is extracted through hard work and alert living. Bellow's heroes are usually introspective because they are engaged in the process of paying unsparing attention to themselves. They wish to, in Augie's phrase, find the "axial lines" of their own specific existence and to follow them into their mortal allotment of dignity. Not surprisingly, Atlas mistakes this introspection, which requires a substantial sense of self, for the narcissist's self-obsession, which is the product of a reduced sense of self.

"Narcissism" happens to be the clinical condition that Atlas attempts to pin on Bellow. He mentions the "narcissistic traits that a succession of psychiatrists diagnosed in him." Not narcissism in the colloquial sense, in other words, but clinical narcissism. The problem is, Atlas never quotes a single psychiatrist or therapist making such a diagnosis. In one of this biography's lowest moments, Atlas finally stumbles upon Heinz Kohut, a famous psychoanalyst who was the grand theoretician of the narcissistic personality. In the late sixties, Bellow saw Kohut for a short time in Chicago's Hyde Park, where both men lived. Although Kohut, who died in 1981, never disclosed the identities of his patients in his notes, Atlas thinks he knows which patient Bellow is, and he thinks he has figured out that Kohut, too, diagnosed Bellow as a clinical narcissist. Yet Atlas doesn't even cite the source that he is relying on when he quotes Kohut's diagnosis of an anonymous "forty-year-old university professor."

Aside from the obvious ethical and professional questions Atlas's irresponsibility raises, his malicious encounters with Bellow's life are at the heart of his inability to grasp the nature of Bellow's art. Atlas uses Kohut's theories to support his fantasy about Bellow's psyche. He quotes Kohut: "The artist stands in proxy for his generation. He anticipates the dominant psychological problem of his era." But Atlas drops the art from Kohut's accurate, though trite, observation about artistic genius, and he keeps the psychological problem. So radical is Atlas's denial of the fact that he is chronicling the life of one of the twentieth century's greatest novelists that he writes about Bellow as if Bellow had never written any fiction at all.

It's hard to square clinical narcissism with what is Bellow's attachment to friends from seventy years ago, or with Atlas's own evocation of Bellow's powerful, if evidently tormented, family feeling. And it's hard to square the clinical narcissist's solipsism and inner emptiness with Bellow the novelist's curiosity and sympathy, with his extraordinary openness to other people's lives, with his uncanny, sensuous grasp of the sights, smells, sounds, and textures of physical reality. Clinical narcissists do not have a capacity for surrender to the world's sweetness and strangeness. Still, maybe Bellow is a clinical narcissist. Who knows? Again, it is a question of what to do with that bit of information. Meanwhile, the art is waiting.

THE WORLD'S SIREN SONG, its sweetness and strangeness, is the ordeal of Bellow's heroes. Life fills them with such a sense of promise and beauty that, in the end, they turn inward as a way to escape the inevitable disappointments that plague passionately receptive natures.

"Men of most powerful appetite have always been the ones to doubt reality the most," says the African king Dahfu to Henderson in *Henderson the Rain King.* These life-famished figures are contemporary; they cannot, Dahfu continues, "bear that hopes should turn to misery, and loves to hatreds and deaths and silences, and so on." They are contemporary in precisely this sense: the more their desires expand, the further reality recedes.

So Bellow's heroes leap away from disappointing reality into ideas, and then away from insufficient ideas into sex, and away from sex into fantasy, and back to culture, and then back to experience—and on and on, in an infinite regression of distancing from the episodes in life that fall short of life's promise. They must protect their psyches from the insult of inadequate conditions. This psychoacrobatic motion is anarchic, like laughter; and it reproduces the odyssey of Mozart's music, which modulates from earth to sky to the far end of heaven and back to earth.

Bellow's heroes are in flight from reality to the heart of existence. They flee from life for love of life. Henderson is both strengthened and harried by a small persistent voice deep inside him that repeats, "I want I want I want." There is something terrible about these protagonists who are so consumed with desire. They burn life away with the intensity of their wanting, feeling, thinking, and almost always find themselves alone, barely alive, far away from other people. It is as if their defeat by desire were also the fulfillment of their desire. A wish for deprivation lurks in the depths of their voracity. Joseph reflects in *Dangling Man:*

> Of course, we suffer from bottomless avidity. . . . And then there are our plans, idealizations. These are dangerous, too. They can consume us like parasites, eat us, drink us, and leave us lifelessly prostrate. And yet we are always inviting the parasite, as if we were eager to be drained and eaten.

With the exception of the Rabelaisian *Humboldt's Gift,* all of Bellow's novels end with the heroes in isolation: plunged into darkness in a movie theater *(The Victim);* walking along the edge of an icy North Sea *(Augie);* submerged in tears at a stranger's funeral *(Seize the Day);* running along the Arctic tundra *(Henderson the Rain King);* gazing toward cold infinite spaces from an astronomical observatory *(The Dean's December);* stationed at a laboratory near the North Pole *(More Die of Heartbreak);* diffused into a disembodied, oracular voice that seems to come from somewhere beyond life *(Dangling Man, Mr. Sammler's Planet, Ravelstein).* These figures seem to will themselves into simulated oblivion. Such an end seems foreordained: a thin pane of glass exists between the Bellovian fictional persona and the other characters in the novels. *Herzog* concludes with a subtle melting of the third person into an atmosphere that speaks; as if the self, in the absence of God, were consoling itself by impersonating the neutrality of a divine voice:

> In a few minutes he would call down to her, "Damp it down, Mrs. Tuttle. There's water in the sink." But not just yet. At this time he had no messages for anyone. Nothing. Not a single word.

Thus does the Bellovian hero give himself up utterly to the world that he has rendered with such self-forgetful vividness and accuracy. And thus does he end up sacrificing the world, and the world of other people, to his sanity. World and self vanish into the absolute freedom of a fresh beginning. It is a kind of fecund nowhere, both chilling and charged with inspiring possibility.

I spent the day with Bellow once and told him a joke. It was an old joke from Odessa. One day Cohen tells Goldberg, his business partner for fifty years, that he wants out. The distraught Goldberg asks several times why Cohen wants to end such a long association, and finally Cohen tells him, in exasperation, that the reason is because Goldberg is pretentious. Goldberg is shocked; he is speechless for a moment, and finally he replies, "Who? *Moi?*" Bellow laughed richly, his eyes glittering, and then he said, "But that is not just a joke." He would say that. The self-deluding mystery of the "*moi*" is Bellow's turf, just as it has been the turf of every great writer since Sophocles. (If you wanted to sum up *Oedipus Rex* and *King Lear* with two words, they would be "Who? *Moi?*") But only those who have a *moi* know what it means to want to solve the riddle of it, or to escape from it, or to endure it with laughter.

Persecution and the
Art of Painting

THE STAGE VILLAIN in Clement Greenberg's most famous essay, "Avant-Garde and Kitsch," is the nineteenth-century Russian painter Ilya Repin. Greenberg picked up his aversion from Dwight Macdonald, who had referred to Repin in an article on Soviet cinema as the "leading exponent of Russian academic kitsch in painting." Declaring Soviet socialist realism the supreme example of kitsch, Greenberg found it precociously embodied in Repin's work.

Take a Repin painting of a battlefield, Greenberg proposed. You will see why peasants cannot get enough of this artist's easy satisfactions, as opposed to, say, Picasso's formal abstrusities. Repin's painting simply mirrors what the peasant finds in the physical world around him. "There is no discontinuity between art and life"; and also Repin trickily and banally "heightens reality and makes it dramatic: sunset, exploding shells, running and falling men." In such a way, "Repin predigests art for the spectator and spares him effort, provides him with a short cut to the pleasure of art that detours what is necessarily difficult in genuine art. Repin, or kitsch, is synthetic art."

Whatever the lasting merits of Greenberg's essay, about one thing he was indisputably wrong. Repin never painted a battle scene in his life. And Greenberg had never seen a Repin. (He confessed to his ignorance in a footnote that he added to "Avant-Garde and Kitsch" when he reprinted it twenty-two years later in *Art and Culture,* but in his *Collected Essays,* which appeared in 1986, the footnote was dropped.) Greenberg's aesthetic was still muffled in the chrysalis of his politics. In fact, Repin is one of the greatest painters who ever lived. His best work, his *unheimlich* portraits and dynamically psychologized crowd scenes, easily surpasses this country's Ashcan School, as well as John Singer Sargent and Winslow Homer. His portraits are the equal of Thomas Eakins's late masterpieces. But then, socialist realism, Repin's supposed legacy, numbers among its mediocrities some of the finest realist paintings produced in this century, and a bounty of masterpieces.

It is not a coincidence that Greenberg had a battle in mind when he fabricated a painting for Repin. The vast bloodbath of the communist genocide in Russia threw giant obscuring shadows over the life that kept unfolding even in the midst of the suffering. This is history's *trompe l'oeil*: with the passage of time, terrible events eclipse what they do not destroy. In the case of Russian art, socialist realism has disappeared into the darkness of its heyday. To a large extent, it earned its oblivion; but the qualities that it shared with nineteenth-century Russian realism have whisked the earlier period into oblivion with it.

There cannot be more than a handful of nineteenth-century Russian realist works owned by public collections in this country, if there are any at all. You almost certainly didn't read about them in high school or college; and certainly not in Linda Nochlin's *Realism,* one of the most illuminating commentaries on the style in nineteenth-century European painting, which doesn't mention a single Russian realist painter. Neither do the textbooks: Marilyn Stokstad's *Art History* gives just one tiny paragraph to the history of Russian realist painting and one tiny paragraph to Repin, the only Russian realist referred to at all.

Stokstad does not spend much time looking, either. Repin's portrait of Moussorgsky, she writes, shows the latter "with tousled hair and a rugged demeanor, a man of the people rather than a slick sophisticate in the Western mold." Repin was indeed, like Moussorgsky, a part of the nationalist trend sweeping Russian culture at the time; but Repin's portrait of his friend is not about anything so trite and typical as Moussorgsky's ties to the collective Russian soul. Painted rapidly in a ward for alcoholics a day before the composer's death, the work catches the once-prosperous Moussorgsky at the end of a long binge, impoverished, at the brink of madness, his eyes red and shadowed and swollen, his final energy seeming to consist of its dissipation. This, rugged?

Stokstad's description ironically resembles the politically correct introduction to a catalogue raisonné of Repin's work that appeared in the Soviet Union before communism's collapse: "Repin . . . put his genius at the service of the people." Stokstad misunderstands Repin for the same reason that other scholars remain indifferent to him: they all lump him in with the socialist realists. As a result, few people know that in Russia, under the knout of terrible events and beneath the crippling lashes of official culture, artists ate, went for walks, and became new Old Masters.

STILL, THE INSTINCT to make Russian nineteenth-century realism complicit with twentieth-century socialist realism is far from inaccurate. For socialist realism was not just a phenomenon of socialism. It arose as much out of the traditions of Russian culture as out of communist impositions. It was virtually inevitable that a realism with moral import became the dominant artistic style in Russian painting in the twentieth century.

Art in Russia had always been led by its officially subordinate nose: by the church, or the tsar, or the state-sponsored academy. For this reason, painters working in the icon tradition retained a medieval style well into the days of Leonardo and Michelangelo. Russian painters did not even begin to paint in oils until the eighteenth century. Just as communist commissars inveighed against abstraction, censors in the Russian church at the time of the Renaissance in the West railed against any hint of realistic depiction. Russian avant-garde absolutism (think of Kandinsky's manifesto *Concerning the Spiritual in Art*) may eventually have been anathematized by Soviet cultural custodians; but it grew out of a deeply embedded authoritarian strain in Russian life, which in fact had nourished and protected great icon painters such as Feofan Grek and Andrei Rublev just as much as it stifled many of their successors.

And even more consequential than the direction of art from above was the absence of direction from below. The Enlightenment that evolved in the West was imported and distributed by Catherine in Russia. Russian art lacked a Kant, a Diderot, a Shaftesbury; and it also lacked a solidly established bourgeois culture that might absorb such ideas. When Kant argued for art as an autonomous realm outside society and politics, he provided the philosophical foundation for two centuries of romantic and avant-garde art. (He also established the foundation for modern conservative taste, as the bourgeoisie metamorphosed from the revolutionary class to the ruling class to the beleaguered class.) In Russia, the reverse situation prevailed. Beginning in the nineteenth century, Russian artists and writers located art's autonomy precisely in its engagement with society and politics, in opposition to the censor's huge and clumsy hand.

So an intriguing situation came about in European art. In western Europe, the socially (and obliquely) critical realism of Courbet and Millet was giving way by the late 1860s to impressionism's formal experiments. At the same time, art in Russia was defining its modernity by the intensity of its social criticism. The artists working in this style were known as the Peredezhniki, or the Itinerants, for their practice of organizing exhibitions that traveled around Russia. They were their country's first home-grown art movement; and they were the first Russian artists to break with state-sanctioned styles. Rebelling against the lifeless Frenchified academy, these St. Petersburg painters took their inspiration from the literary critic Vissarion Belinsky and the social critic and novelist Nikolai Chernyshevsky. Both men believed that art should be, in Chernyshevsky's words, a "textbook of life," though Chernyshevsky was the more radical materialist, lamenting that "until now our art has been unable to create anything equivalent even to an orange or an apple."

Socialist realism, as Matthew Cullerne Bown observes in his poised and groundbreaking study, starts here, with Belinsky's and Chernyshevsky's insistence on art's social and political obligations. For the most part, these ideas ruled Russian art until the collapse of the Soviet system, though they were gradually twisted by the law of unintended consequences. A socially critical art hostile to the official culture became assimilated as an official style hostile to genuine social criticism. The fates are never kind with the avant-garde.

And the Itinerants were indeed the advanced artists of their day. They proved highly receptive to Belinsky and Chernyshevsky—as did Dostoevsky and Tolstoy—and even to the extreme notions of Dmitri Pisarev, who rejected wholesale the concepts of beauty and taste, and thought that the random shape of jelly was on a par with the greatest architecture. (This was fifty years before Marcel Duchamp's fanatical quotidianism.) Thus Ivan Kramskoi, the driving force behind the Itinerant movement, wrote to Repin from Paris in 1873—where he almost certainly would have seen work by Courbet, Manet, Degas, and possibly Monet—to express his anxiety that Russian painters were succumbing to mere formal principles. "We must move without fail towards light, color and air, but . . . how should we proceed, if we are not to lose on the way an artist's most treasured quality—his heart?" Content should always be exalted above form, he warned. "For better or worse, we are not Frenchmen. This should never be forgotten."

Like the French realists and protoimpressionists, Russian realists were shunning academic art's classical, mythological, and biblical themes for contemporary and everyday subjects. But they were also rejecting the Western way in which the revolution in content was yielding to a revolution in form. And, surprising though it may sound, their emphasis on subject matter put them one step ahead of the French.

We like to think of innovation, especially in the visual arts, in formal terms, with the history of Western art told as a tale of progressive abstraction, of inexorable reduction to the artistic medium itself. In this sense, Kramskoi's reference to the heart hints at a significant counterstatement. Interestingly, the words "heart" and "soul" appear over and over again in the discourse of socialist realism, most notoriously in Stalin's infamous comment that writers should be the "engineers of human souls." It is an odd vocabulary to appear in a culture and a society based on a draconian materialist ethic; but it has the effect of exposing the radical subjectivity at the core of communist thinking, and it explains how the regime's fears of formalism's self-enclosure enabled it to objectify and to anathematize its own nature. In Russian history, invocations of "heart" and "soul" have often justified a tragic deformation of rational thinking.

But there is another tradition in Russia, exemplified especially by the late Tolstoy, in which the heart has its reasons that reason cannot know. By reminding his peers to retain the incurably human element in artistic creation, Kramskoi was not celebrating irrationality. He was honoring wisdom. A wisdom of the image—the indispensable tool of the iconist's trade—is Russian realism's most daring innovation. That quality is what Bown is getting at when he writes about how socialist realist artists kept smuggling into the tinny, dishonest official "humanism" genuine humanistic elements from the bottomless stores of Russian culture.

Such a tendency began with the Itinerants, who sifted a real newness of content out of Chernyshevsky's mistrust of art and out of Pisarev's crudeness. You can see this if you compare Kramskoi's *Christ in the Wilderness,* painted in 1872, with Manet's *The Dead Christ with Angels,* painted in 1864. Both paintings rattled their respective cultures for the manner in which they stripped Jesus of transcendence, the way they set divinity down in the context of the mundane. But Manet's wonderful painting achieves its power principally by means of formal effects: the harsh frontal lighting, and the way Manet clips the angels' wings by abruptly cropping the canvas, and the modernist manner in which he drives the composition up to the picture plane, so that you never really lose the sense of looking at a painting. What a difference a few thousand miles make! Kramskoi's picture is the "window" onto reality that traditional painting had been since the Renaissance. The foregrounded stonescape upon which Jesus is seated looks as if it could have come out of Taddeo Gaddi.

Compositionally, Kramskoi is several centuries behind Manet. Kramskoi's innovation lies, rather, in his depiction of the face and the hands of Jesus. Here is how Pisarev advised artists to represent the face, which is the spiritual vanishing point of figurative (and much semiabstract) Russian art:

> When we see from a person's face that he is healthy, intelligent and has lived through a lot in his time, then his face pleases us, not as a pretty picture, but as the program of our future relations with this person. Judging by his face, we are inclined to get closer to this person, because his face tells us what the most impeccable Greek profile could not.

This philistinism later shaped a good part of socialist realist doctrine. (Bown overzealously calls this depressing passage "a powerful call to life and for an art to reflect it.") Yet Kramskoi modulated Pisarev in the same way that some socialist realist painters inflected the commissars' strictures.

He may be sitting in a boundless rocky wilderness, but Kramskoi's Jesus has the demeanor of a modern, urban man. Anomie enshrouds him. No supernatural phenomena appear around this Christ; his temptations come from within, and they take the form of familiar anguish and doubt. He is clasping his hands tightly between his knees, like a humble petitioner in a bureaucratic waiting room. He is looking down into this world, not through or beyond it. Appearing in shadow just under the hem of his robe, his bare feet make him the helpless object of compassion—or perhaps of a passerby's briefly engaged glance—rather than its source. He could be sitting crisis-ridden in a St. Petersburg park.

This is hardly the kind of programmatic reassurance that Pisarev had in mind for art. Yet neither does a viewer need to know about superseded aesthetic forms fully to comprehend the painting, which is what Manet's *Dead Christ with Angels* demands.

What Kramskoi requires is an intuitive leap into what his painting knows of forms of thinking, feeling, and living. The painting leads you along an invisible line of experience clarified by the imagination, as a Renaissance painting leads your eye along receding lines of motion organized by perspective. Like the best Russian realist paintings, *Christ in the Wilderness* is as "necessarily difficult" as Greenberg's formalism. It is wisdom painting.

II.

Kramskoi is at the magnificent core of Russian realism. You have to experience that style in order to grasp the value of much socialist realist painting. That is why Bown begins his study with a survey of the earlier period. You must see the work of Isaac Levitan, a Jew whose landscapes gave nationalist Russia its self-image, and whose caressing brushstrokes make the world look like eternity's flushed or shivering skin; or the paintings of Vasily Vereshchagin, who painted some of the most remarkable scenes of war in the history of art. (His *Fatally Wounded* approaches *The Dying Gaul* in its unsettling mystery.) And there are many more extraordinary Russian realist painters: Aleksander Ivanov, Nicholas Ge, Boris Shishkin, Vasily Surikov, Nikolai Yaroshenko, Aleksei Savrasov, to name a few. Repin is nonpareil. His *Religious Procession in the Kursk Province* and *Ivan the Terrible and His Son Ivan* (depicting the former's impulsive murder of the latter) make Courbet look meek.

There is nothing in other nineteenth-century realist traditions that comes close to the ontological complexity of Russian realist paintings. They enfold you in sheer inarticulable being. If the best of them share a common quality, it is the way they use the vexed heaviness of flesh, and the separate life of things, to demonstrate the vexed career of the spirit. They fling the soul like meat to the heart. In our cultural moment, when so much art lies supine on the cushions of irony and banality, an exhibition here of Russian realist painting might have the same invigorating effect on an enfeebled American postmodernism that the Armory Show once had on a nascent American modernism.

SOCIALIST REALISM tried to turn the Itinerants' realism on its head, but that project never entirely succeeded. The doctrine behind socialist realism was so muddled and fluid that in 1987 one prominent Soviet art historian admitted that the term itself should be abandoned since "we do not know what socialist realism is." That was over fifty years after socialist realism had been declared the official style. In fact, as Bown fascinatingly shows, from the time of the revolution until the disintegration of the Soviet system, the question of what a Soviet-style art should be frequently gave rise to the kind of polemic that we associate with aesthetic debate in the West. And such contention appeared in official publications.

To be sure, the arguments took place within definite parameters, especially at the height of Stalinist repression in the 1930s. Bown reprints a discussion of a portrait of Voroshilov, the Red Army commander, conducted between Sergei Gerasimov, one of the most powerful art-world commissars under Stalin, and three of his colleagues:

GERASIMOV: Out of the intelligent, remarkable face of Voroshilov the author has made some kind of an idiot. This is a counter-revolutionary work.

E. Lvov: I consider that the portrait needs to be corrected, it has not been done on purpose. However, it is necessary to take into account that when the jury was shown this work they all burst out laughing. Consequently, the work is counter-revolutionary.

Yu. Slavinski: So reject it with harsh criticism.

E. Katsman: It is necessary to suggest that this thing is destroyed, not only not accepted.

Such "evaluations" must have paralyzed countless imaginations, and not only under Stalin. More chilling was the case of a painter named Nikolai Mikhailov. In 1935, the entire fifty-member board of the all-powerful Union of Soviet Artists (MOSSKh) met to accuse Mikhailov of using a painting to incite the assassinations of Voroshilov and Stalin. The work in question was *Farewell to Comrade Kirov,* done by Mikhailov just after the murder in December 1934 of the Leningrad party-boss, Sergei Kirov. The artist depicted Stalin and Voroshilov standing over Kirov's coffin, paying their respects. MOSSKh officials liked the painting so much that they hung it in their headquarters. But when a photographer snapped a picture of Mikhailov's canvas that appeared in a Soviet newspaper, the photograph seemed to the commissars to show a skeleton—a kind of skull and crossbones, from their description—grabbing Stalin by the arm and Voroshilov by the neck. Hastily accused by the terrified union leaders of both counterrevolutionary activity and sketchy, impressionistic technique, Mikhailov got ten years and was probably executed. If proof were still needed that Kirov was killed on Stalin's orders, the commissars' fevers of Raskolnikovian paranoia would be enough.

Stalin persecuted artists, but not nearly on the scale that he hunted down writers. In fact, he appointed the artists themselves, among others, as the custodians of aesthetic policy. A different situation prevailed in fascist Italy, where Mussolini never drew up an official line for artists to follow, and in Nazi Germany, where the state simply imposed one. One reason for Stalin's relative leniency might have been that he was a failed poet, not a failed artist. (Exhibitions of "degenerate" art did not hold the interest for him that they did for Hitler, the unremarkable watercolorist.) And with his withered arm, below-average height, and pock-marked face, he might have felt beholden to those responsible for his public makeover.

Perhaps because his own appearance terrified him, Stalin had a visceral respect for appearance in general, and for those who created it. And though he reduced with one swipe of the pen the number of art organizations in his kingdom, he probably enjoyed allowing room for the polarizing squabbles that had character-ized the Russian art world from before the revolution. As people involved in the state's massive propaganda activities, artists per-formed a manipulative function that served the state's purposes. Regarding artists as, in some degree, public servants, Stalin might have felt that mutual suspicion, rather than outright terror, was the best way to enforce their obedience. (It was for this reason that he encouraged competition among the various factions of the secret police.)

The result was the institutionalization of an art world of self-advancing maneuvers and professional turf wars that continued to foster at least some of the stylistic variety that had existed in Soviet art since October 1917. For pluralism is not too bold a term to describe much of the configuration of official art be-tween the revolution and Stalin's consolidation of power. From the storming of the Winter Palace, and through the limited free-market period of the New Economic Policy (NEP) in the 1920s, the artistic styles vying for absolute authority made Paris during the same period look like a quiet academic salon.

Though still active at the time of the revolution, the Itinerants had conceded their advanced position to coteries that made highly stylized yet mostly figurative art: the World of Art, Jack of Diamonds, Union of Youth, and the Moscow "Cezannists." The latter were themselves superseded by more formally radical—and more abstract—cliques such as rayonnists, symbolists, cubists, cubofuturists, constructivists, and primitivists. It was the constructivists who emerged ascendant. They are the group to whom people refer when they talk about the Russian avant-garde, also known as the futurists.

The constructivists composed the extreme left wing of the art world, and they were opposed mainly by Kasimir Malevich's suprematists. The latter had embraced the revolution, but they bridled at its subjugation of the artist to the state. The suprematists were also unmoved by the constructivists' theories about marrying the artist and the industrial designer. In 1918, Malevich painted *White on White* as a spiritual challenge to the constructivists' scorn for easel-painting and their exaltation of the machine. In a parodic blow for materialism, Aleksander Rodchenko, an archconstructivist, retorted with a painting entitled *Black on Black*. There is a metaphor here for revolutionary situations.

But the suprematists were no match for the way the constructivists bullied and elbowed their way into the revolution's highest political echelons. After the Bolshevik coup, the constructivists briefly ruled the roost by means of political-cultural organs, especially through the establishment across the country of countless "proletarian culture organizations," known as "proletkults." "The Streets are our Brushes," they announced, "the Squares are our Palettes." They looked forward to painting all the buildings in Moscow gray, and the windows black. They insisted, in the words of a sympathetic critic, that "communism, as a theory of culture, cannot exist without futurism."

As they saw it, their politics did not lie in their artistic style, which was, for the most part, abstract. Instead they defined their revolutionary commitment in terms of a totalizing method of production: collaboration with workers; collective creation; the decoration of streets and public buildings; an art that would aim at creating a New Person and a New Society, after which art itself would disappear into industry, engineering, and communications and wither away like the state. And this utopian aesthetic outraged Lenin's utopian politics.

Lenin did not exactly pore over aesthetic problems. His criterion for art was a simple one. As he told a group of art students during a surprise midnight visit to their hostel, art should be "comprehensible to a worker and to everyone else." Lenin rejected the constructivists' avant-garde vision of the artist-worker. In doing so, he was asserting the bourgeois notion of a distinction between the artist and the nonartist. Such a notion sorted better with the way in which Lenin conceived of the gulf between the political avant-garde and the mass of citizens.

Anyway, Lenin had a deeper reason for his aesthetic caution. As he told Gorky, after confessing to a fondness for Beethoven's "Appassionata" Sonata:

> I can't listen to music often, it acts on my nerves, I want to say sweet nothings and caress the heads of people who, living in a dirty hell, can create such beauty. But today it's not possible to caress anyone's head—they'll bite your hand off, and it's necessary to crack skulls, crack them mercilessly, although ideally we are against any kind of violence on people.

Did the professional revolutionary have a primal fear of the vicissitudes of the heart? That would explain a lot about the trajectory of revolutions. Or was Lenin dead to Beethoven and to art in general, and just bullying an artistically superior hero of the revolution with his moral superiority while showing that he was as aesthetically sensitive as Gorky himself?

By 1919, Lenin had halted the constructivists' snapping advance and put brakes on the "proletkults." (Though they had the last word: the most famous constructivist public structure left in Russia is Lenin's tomb.) This was partly owed to the increasing influence of the "proletkults," which were being sponsored by Lunacharsky, Lenin's Commissar of Enlightenment and a possible rival. But the explanation goes deeper. A utopian politics gazing at a utopian art sees the lethal skull and crossbones of its own ego. And there was a practical consideration, too. An abstract politics needs the ballast, in the cultural realm, of recognizable images.

BY THE MID-TWENTIES, the "proletkults" were just about defunct. The resilient Lunacharsky began promulgating easel-painting and realist style. Thus the Soviet art world became broadly and momentarily divided between two figurative groups: the more formally experimental OSt (Society of Easel Painters) and the more traditional AKhRR (Association of Artists of Revolutionary Russia). The AKhRR had appropriated the Itinerants' style, while mostly rejecting its socially critical content, after the latter disbanded. Eventually the AKhRR won out.

Yet the notorious Soviet campaign against formalism persisted. The reason is that Russian artists, like Kramskoi, would have felt uncomfortable with a modernist absence of subject matter even without the ukases of socialist realism. The fury of antiformalism was also due to the fact that formalism never left Soviet art. As Bown meticulously shows, complaints about bourgeois subjectivist experimentation with form led to a "documentary" approach in reaction, which led to dissatisfaction with mere naturalistic "copying," which produced more formalist forays, which provoked a crude conservative response, and so on. The futurists left the scene by 1930, but their restless utopian energy kept animating the debate over what kind of art would replace their utopian vision.

Here are some of the official art organizations and semiofficial groups that strove to establish their aesthetic between October 1917 and Stalin's radical streamlining in 1932 (the abbreviations themselves are futurist verbal designs, a new language of revolution): AKhRR; AKhR; NarKomPros; OSt; FOSKh; Oktyabr; VOPrA; the Four Arts; OMKh; RAPKh; OSSO; IzoBrigada; Bytie; Rost; OKhO; OKhS; LORKh; TRaM; OMAKhR. Much of this ferment reflected the economic pluralism of Lenin's New Economic Policy. And much of it was due to the period of "class struggle," during which the regime massacred a recalcitrant peasantry.

With that accomplished, a single decree in April 1932 abolished all art world sects and factions. In June 1932, Stalin created the Union of Soviet Artists (MOSSKh) to replace them. And in 1934, Gorky, Nikolai Bukharin, and Andrei Zhdanov, Stalin's Minister of Culture, set down the three chief criteria of socialist realism, though these principles had been knocking around for years: "ideinost" (ideological consistency); "partinost" (party spirit); and "narodnost" (commitment to representing the life of the Soviet people).

Like Lenin, Stalin showed little interest in aesthetics. He liked Repin's *Zaporozhe Cossacks Writing a Letter to the Turkish Sultan,* and probably had a copy of it hanging in his bedroom. (Maybe Greenberg and Macdonald got wind of that and thus felt no twinge of conscience in dismissing Repin without having seen his work.) Isaac Brodsky, Stalin's court painter, and a fairly gifted artist, said that Stalin's highest praise for a painting was that it contained "living people." Lackey critics and union officials from the worlds of art and literature repeated that phrase throughout the period of the purges. Stalin's flair for obliterating

irony—a little like the sculptures depicting mythological punishments that Louis XIV placed in the gardens of Versailles to
deflate his courtiers—makes you wonder how he meant "living
people" to be taken. He himself refused to pose for any of his
myriad portraits. The famous sculptor Vera Mukhina wriggled
out of pressure to depict Stalin by insisting that she could work
only "from life."

Stalin loved movies, especially action movies, and it is not
clear if he, or his commissars, had any more of an "eye" for painting than your average television critic. The official response to
Samuil Adlivankin's *A Visit to the Tank Drivers* provides a wonderful illustration of their ocular lassitude. The painting depicted a
crowd of soldiers holding aloft a baby with an oversized tank driver's hat on its head. According to an eyewitness, Stalin went up
to it at the Red Army show in 1933, with Voroshilov, Vyacheslav
Mikhaylovich Molotov, and Sergei Ordzhonikidze, the head of
heavy industry. They laughed, and Ordzhonikidze said to Stalin,
"This is our kind of picture." Though it exists now only in reproduction, the painting is in fact skillful and even enigmatic. The
child's mother and the soldiers are smiling, but the child itself is
not. Its eyes are hidden completely in shadow. The picture pos-
sesses an intriguing trace of self-reflection.

"Can the victorious results of the heroic struggle to build socialism, the joy of our happy flourishing life, really be expressed
by the familiar standard smiles, by purely external effects of color
and light?" This is an excerpt from an art review that appeared in
a Soviet newspaper in 1938, the peak of both the Stalinist terror
and the campaign against formalism in the arts. Note the language. The sentence begins with an homage to the triumphant
system, asserts the satisfaction of the people living under it, and
finishes with a *de rigueur* dig at the formalist bane of technique
for its own sake. And there, buried in the middle of the sentence

is criticism of the "familiar standard smiles." Yet smiles were the hallmark of socialist realism's enforced optimism. Anyone who disparaged them as "familiar" and "standard" might also take a negative view of the familiar and standard rhetoric about "victorious results," "heroic struggle," "happy flourishing life," and so on. The writer could venture such a dangerous remark only because, even under Stalin, the definition of socialist realism remained in flux.

III.

Appearing for the first time in 1932, the term "socialist realism" embodied a heritage of ideological, aesthetic, and philosophical perplexity to which not even Stalin could bring order. The commissars' inability to come up with an art that conformed to their purposes was symbolic of the regime's inability entirely to master the human substance under its control. It is as if art contained its own antibodies against the antihuman element. The failure of socialist realist doctrine in the Soviet Union is, ultimately, entangled with the essential incalculableness of human reality. A science (and a politics) for representing that reality could not be found.

Since the end of the nineteenth century, Russian Marxists had tried to hatch a realist art that would be serviceable to the new society. From that time until 1932, various formulations had been proposed: heroic realism, realistic idealism, naive realism, synthetic realism, dialectical realism, constructive realism, proletarian realism, dynamic realism, compositional realism, industrial-technical realism, political realism. And all these notions foundered on the imperative of Georgi Plekhanov, the first Russian Marxist and an admirer of Belinsky and Chernyshevsky: "Without an idea, art is impossible."

The idea, of course, was the perfectibility of society. And that was the rub. A realism guided self-consciously by an ideal was, essentially, a paradox. One result of this predicament was a search for an art that had futurist content but no futurist form. The other was a paranoid hatred of abstract art's "idealism." Both outcomes must have made the art of the futurists themselves appear repulsively redundant.

Various figures took a shot at defining revolutionary art. Lunacharsky, who liked to dabble in aesthetics, devised the notion of biomechanics. Taking up the baton from Plekhanov's materialism, he applied it to the human figure through the medium of human biology. Influenced by Ernst Mach's mechanistic philosophy, the Commissar of Enlightenment expatiated on what the New Person in the New Society would look like: healthy and happy and physically gorgeous. The greater the concord among the body's various elements, the greater the harmony of the individual's mental state, and the closer to perfection the society. Art should induce this total balance through the way it operates on the faculties. Thus Lunacharsky promoted, as Bown puts it, "a maximum of visual excitement": visual rhythm, rousingly warm colors, and an aversion to broken or irregular forms.

One of Bown's many virtues is that, in his discussion of Lunacharsky, he debunks the Russian philosopher Boris Groys, who has had a lot of influence on the art scene in Russia today. Groys argued that Stalin took over from the futurists the concept of the state as a total work of manipulative art. Like some far less interesting pundits and commentators in this country, Groys reduced politics and history to an exotic strain of aesthetics. But Bown shows that it was not the futurists' aestheticized politics that influenced Stalin. It was Lunacharsky's politicized aesthetic that influenced the futurists, some of whom threw themselves at the commissar's feet. Behind the "society of the spectacle"—in our day, beyond even the evil geniuses of the big and the small screen—are the more significant facts of social and political relations. That was certainly Lenin's feeling.

The antagonism between Lunacharsky and Lenin set the stage for the perpetual struggle between formalism and naturalism. For there were really no "realistic" criteria to guide the portrayal of a life that people could recognize and the projection of a communist future that people could believe in. For one prominent critic, Soviet art was realistic "but only in the sense which Comrade Trotsky gives to that term." For another, "identical attitudes are not at all identical at different historical periods and they create in different epochs their 'realistic style' differently." The commissars must have found it unnerving—or did some find it liberating?—that the element of contingency that they had suppressed in social and political life was slipping in through the back door of official art.

Socialist realist doctrine faced another problem: history itself. As the regime's fortunes changed, its art had to change with it. So the proliferation of styles during the NEP period of "class struggle" during the 1920s gave way to the lugubriously merry canvases of the 1930s. In the thirties, art had to portray the dialectical forces gestating a utopian future. But the war came, and it enabled artists to depict life's dark side, the representation of which Stalin had earlier proscribed.

And then postwar art reinstituted the official optimism through the Theory of Conflictlessness, which held that since the classless society had been achieved, art should dispense with illustrating dialectical strife. Collectively produced "brigade paintings" were meant to add to the illusion of utopian harmony. With Khrushchev's rise to power, the Severe Style came to the fore: formally innovative, monumental, socially engaged, harsh, disillusioned. And as the system declined into the Brezhnev era's

corpulence and corruption, the attempt to impose a socialist realism from above gave way to a voluntary—and immensely creative—appropriation of it by artists from below.

Such flux reflected socialist realism's underpinning principle:
"socialist in content, realist in form." And since, contrary to fashionable present-day opinion, images are more indeterminate than
words will ever be, such a principle could really mean, in shrewd
and gifted hands, an invitation to defiance and distortion.

This is not to say that Soviet artists didn't knock out a steady
line of deceitful, mind-bruising abortions of the imagination.
And it is not to say that plenty of artists, some talented, some not,
willingly went along with the cultural commissars and made life
miserable for more conscientious figures. Also, Bown is too dismissive of the so-called nonconformist artists, active from 1956
until communism's collapse, who painted outside the official
boundaries. They created some striking and powerful art (though
their status as dissidents has sometimes blinded critics to the large
amount of second-rate work they also produced). And you feel
uncomfortable when Bown brandishes Soviet artists' incomparable technical training as an argument for socialist realism's artistic
merit. He has to do this to spare himself ethical contortions over
all the depictions of bountiful harvests fabricated at a time of
state-organized famine, and the zillion portraits of a deified Stalin
done amidst the purges, and the representations of happy and ro-
bust workers produced at the zenith of forced labor.

Still, Bown is correcting seventy years of Western ignorance
and neglect, so a bit of zeal is pardonable. And he is not overstat-
ing his case when he asserts that "the painting of socialist realism,
broadly defined, comprises our century's outstanding movement
in realist painting." By "broadly defined," I think he means a general cultural style out of whose criteria an individual can hew his
or her own personal style. Van der Weyden and Van Eyck painted

in the same prevailing style, but in radically idiosyncratic ways, as did Vermeer and Rembrandt, or Courbet and Manet. (It is only after impressionism that different individual styles really begin to take on the appearance of different cultures.) In socialist realism, to be sure, a particular artist's style often is unstable—a sign that the artist is either a genius or a hack; but the best socialist realist artists painted in a consistently distinctive way. And this despite the fact that, to get a commission from the union, an artist had to choose an approved title for the painting before embarking on it.

WHAT WITH THE VAGUE and perpetually evolving official criteria, the conflicts between critics and artists, the official tastemakers' careerist position-taking, and the changing times, Soviet artists found a way to express themselves. After all, patrons had been handing out commissions based on exacting or unattractive subject matter since the Middle Ages. And the realist tradition was the birthright of the Soviet artists. Steeped in the older style, they found it possible to bend aesthetic instructions to their own uses. You might call their response "painting between the lines."

What they could do with crowd scenes! There is no art that ponders the modern crowd with anything like the attention of Soviet art. Consider the Ashcan School's crowds as a contrast. The American faces are generic blurs, represented mainly for the sake of atmosphere. But socialist realism uses its crowd scenes to portray the distinctness of individuals. The main influence here was the icons' emphasis on the face, but also Konstantin Stanislavsky, who advised actors to plumb their own experience to find the emotions animating their characters. Impelled by socialist realism's calls for cinematic, participatory qualities in painting, artists used Stanislavskian technique to imagine the psychologies of the figures they were portraying.

The official imperative was to show the personal benefits of collective harmony. Superficially heeding this, painters could present visual evidence for personal autonomy. This is in the line of Repin's extraordinary *A Religious Procession in Kursk Province,* a vastly peopled picture that delineates general social suffering in each of its minutely differentiated faces. In socialist realist crowd scenes, the centuries-long attention to the face in Russian art, brought to a peak of perfection by the nineteenth-century realists, came to the artists' aid.

Thus Arkadi Plastov's *A Collective Farm Festival,* painted in 1938, portrays an outdoor banquet in a yard behind a stone building with a wooden roof. The painting hums with color and movement, and it includes the requisite smiling faces. Indeed, fluttering above the happy goings-on is a red banner sporting Stalin's grotesque motto: "Living Has Got Better, Comrades, Living Has Got Merrier." Stalin's portrait, propped up by two sticks, appears behind and above the banner, at the painting's compositional acme. The whole thing conforms to official standards. At first glance—and this was 1938, the final year of the Great Purge—it is morally repugnant. But the viewer has to look more closely, which even Bown doesn't venture doing.

For a start, the work is stunningly executed. It is also devoid of the surreal element that plagues many socialist realist works, the result of the artist's self-conscious adherence to external criteria bobbing unnervingly away from the eye along the painting's own subconscious undertow. Plastov's painting begins organically to work against itself. Faces are partially or completely hidden behind the heads of other people. A woman stands off to the side, isolated, almost scowling. Two bearded peasants speak discreetly to each other, a private island in the midst of the public celebration. What's more, these men appear directly under Stalin's picture, along an almost straight line that ends in the foreground with a woman who has her back turned to the viewer. The very top of the line is Stalin's face; and the eye follows the line down to the woman's behind. And not only does one of the bearded peasants have his arm flung around the other's shoulder; a wolflike hound stares rapaciously at a basket of apples as a young girl reaches toward them. A Soviet viewer would have known that the mass murder of the peasantry was concluded only six years earlier.

Like Kramskoi's *Christ in the Wilderness,* Plastov's painting has knowledge; and it calls for a leap into what it knows. Its demand upon the viewer's response is as strenuous as the demand posed by any Western avant-garde work, and you find this again and again in socialist realist art. Plastov himself was criticized for showing labor as exhausting: "toil" should be the joyous hero of socialist realism, Gorky had said. Critics also reprimanded him for concealing his faces. But he remained in favor, and officials of the prestigious Surikov Institute in Moscow wrote to him, extending an invitation to teach. He demurred, explaining that staying in his village was better for his art.

THE CROWD could be a kind of bourgeois sanctuary for the socialist realist artist. Within its unlimited psychological space, the disclosure of meaning on a face could hide an inwardly migrating imagination. The depiction of the relationship between the individual and the crowd was politically sanctioned, after all. And in the 1920s, the deadening-sounding official call for painters to illustrate history's dialectic provoked the same creative response. The master of that decade was Alexander Deineka, who also created the ceiling mosaics for the Moscow subway's remarkable Mayakovsky Station. Showing history's dialectical mechanism required simultaneous scenes of past, present, and future; and Deineka, a modernist, used that pretext to employ temporally distinct, cubistic planes in dismayingly titled masterpieces such as *The Defense of Petrograd* (1926) and *Building New Factories* (1927).

More traditional painters used the dialectical theme in their own way. In Boris Ioganson's *In an Old Factory in the Urals,* painted in 1937, a worker stares with defiance at his opulently clad boss. Behind them toil workers plunged in darkness. As Bown observes, Ioganson has captured present, past, and future in the figures of debased proletariat, wicked overseer, and proud worker. Yet Bown tells us that the boss was modeled on Alexander Gerasimov, who, with Sergei Gerasimov (no relation), was the all-powerful overseer of the art world. And his sneering assistant has the face of a prominent critic! How did this painting make it past the censor?

A visual gesture in socialist realism could be worth a thousand images. Bown doesn't say so, but you could write the history of Russian art from the nineteenth century through the entire Soviet period by looking at the constructivists' favorite compositional device: the diagonal. One of socialist realism's cardinal criteria was that a painting had to convey the idea of forward and forward-looking motion. Thus the organization of a painting by dynamic diagonals, a trick borrowed from baroque art, appears in much socialist realist work. Probably the most famous example is Alexander Gerasimov's *Lenin on the Tribune,* from 1929. Lenin's gaze toward an unseen future beyond the picture frame on the viewer's right is underlined by a flag pointing in the same direction along an upward diagonal line. But since diagonals were also the constructivists' trademark, socialist realist artists could manipulate a proscribed formalist icon by quoting them.

In Nikolai Baskakov's *A Windy Day,* from 1961, the foregrounded figure leans almost out of the canvas, along a diagonal that indicates the prescribed positive outlook. Yet the horizon behind him is just above his ankles, tethering the forward motion to earth. Horizons during that period of revelation and liberalization generally appear lower in paintings. Twelve years earlier Dmitri Mochalski painted *After the Demonstration (They Saw Stalin),* in which he has a young man carrying the identical flag that appeared in *Lenin on the Tribune.* This time, however, it points along a diagonal in the reverse direction. These paintings could be hinting at nothing at all. But who can say for sure? Their ambiguity is a sign of their freedom.

The erudite Bown does not venture such interpretations. Considering how diabolically wily centuries of official culture have made Russian artists and writers, he should have let himself go a little, especially in the case of Pavel Globa's *Galya of the Birds* (1950). Even in reproduction, I find this picture strangely alluring. Bown refers to its "obligatory optimism." The country girl walking in the foreground at the head of a flock of geese is indeed smiling; in accord with convention, she is looking out past the frame on the viewer's right toward an invisible future. The wind is playing around her apron and the hem of her skirt, lifting the bottom of the kerchief that she has tied around her head. But the line of geese runs along a diagonal toward the back of the painting, not the front. The geese bend forward, reaching for the girl's skirt, but they can't get to it. And you cannot tell whether the sun is setting behind a sere brown hill or rising. There is a puzzling sadness rippling through the obligatory optimism, a sense of loss irradiating a moment of hope.

The uncanny thing is that the painting's diagonals duplicate those in that ur-artistic moment of social criticism, Repin's *A Religious Procession in Kursk Province.* Formally the paintings are exactly alike, right down to the two geese in the foreground stretching out their necks the way the two lame beggars in the foreground in Repin are stretching forward. So what does the reference mean? Laying a pastoral scene over Repin's could refer,

I suppose, to communism's triumph over regressive social conditions. Yet the girl is gazing into an unseen future, not into a triumphant present. The future that Repin's work looked forward to was an oppressive political system's upheaval.

I do not want to make it seem like the worth of the best socialist realist paintings lies in their subterfuge. I am trying to demonstrate the subterfuge to prove that a creative breadth did exist. There are paintings reproduced in Bown's book, and many more in private and public collections in Russia, that strike the viewer for purely aesthetic reasons, for the sometimes astounding way in which they reveal the struggle to turn a socially burdened eye inward while staying true to a shared social and physical reality. That is not just a Soviet aesthetic problem.

Of the many public services Bown so intelligently performs, one is the revelation of Soviet art before and after Stalin. The still lifes painted by Ilya Mashkov during the twenties, to take one example among dozens, have been pushed to the side entirely by futurist art; but they are the earthy counterparts, laden with being, to Willem Kalf's elegantly ethereal seventeenth-century masterpieces. The paintings reproduced by Bown of scenes from the Second World War are alone worth the price of the book. They find their consummation in the work of Geli Korzhev, one of the founders of the Severe Style, and one of the greatest artists of the twentieth century. For my money, no American realist can touch him. Korzhev's portraits are the end of the line for the face in Russian art: his weathered, bruised, scarred, wreaked-upon figures strip history naked and expose it on the peak of a human pathos.

Manet once wrote, "The artist does not say today, 'Come and see faultless works,' but 'Come and see sincere works.'" His place in the modernist line of descent eventually pulled Manet's sincerity out from under him. But many socialist realist paintings are at their most sincere when they are at their most ironic. That deeply human note is alien to us because our irony is as utilitarian as the idea of "partinost": it is a tool for the earnest upending of earnestness. It has the form of humor without the substance of wit. So we are blind to beautiful, spiritual irony; to irony that outrages convention by discovering meaning, rather than affirming convention by merely rearranging meaning.

This is the sort of artistic truth that is buried in these paintings. And many of these works are just plain sincere about the root elements of existence. The regime's hateful and hypocritical calls for artists to show hope, endurance, and joy sometimes resulted in officially approved images of hope, endurance, and joy that served as antidotes to all the outrageous official hypocrisy. The complexity of some of these paintings is almost unfathomable, and profoundly moving. If nothing else, they prove beyond the shadow of a doubt that the regime's own artists could beat the censor and traduce the state. In an unbearably sad position in an unbearably sad place, they made some of the most accomplished and affecting art of our time.

PART TWO

Faking It

Prophets of Profit:
How Artists Slyly Critique
Their Wealthy Patrons

No one, to my knowledge, has yet written a comprehensive world history of artists and the people who commission and pay for their art. But when such a study does get put together one day, the relationship between the Nabis and their wealthy Parisian benefactors—usually rich Jews of German or Russian descent—will make an especially vivid chapter.

The Nabis, the subject of the Metropolitan Museum of Art's wonderful exhibition "Beyond the Easel: Decorative Painting by Bonnard, Vuillard, Denis, and Roussel," were a group of painters active in Paris from about 1890 to 1930. They included two world-class painters—Pierre Bonnard and Édouard Vuillard—and two minor ones—Maurice Denis and Ker Xavier Roussel. On the surface, their work was, well, all surface. Denis summed up their aesthetic in one renowned sentence: "A picture—before being a war horse, a female nude, or some anecdote—is essentially a flat surface covered with colors in a particular order." The Nabis aimed primarily to make art that would neither provoke the intellect nor vex the emotions. At least these were their publicly stated intentions. On closer examination, they seemed to be up to something more.

For one thing, the Nabis may have concerned themselves with surface, but their work wasn't superficial. Though they abandoned the easel in favor of painting on Japanese screens and on ceramics, and though they often applied themselves directly to living-room walls, they animated their work with dreamy, sometimes haunting layers of symbolism. They also worked in opposition to the impressionists, banning the portrayal of natural light from their work and exaggerating the insignificance of the impressionists' human figures to the point where, in the Nabis' pictures, the figures sometimes blend into the wallpaper. "Nabi" means "prophet" in Hebrew, and besides using the allusion to appeal to their Jewish patrons, the four painters thought of themselves as being in the vanguard of their time.

Not everybody agreed. Degas couldn't stand them. The label "decorative" brought out fear and contempt among hard-core modernists: since simplicity can be misconstrued as superficiality, to call modernist art decorative is like flinging its worst fear into its face. In the eyes of their critics, what the Nabis considered painterly refinements were acts of aesthetic grossness. The fact that their works adorned the apartments, mansions, and villas of Paris's haute-bourgeoisie didn't add to the Nabis' popularity among the modernists, either.

A preoccupation with the Nabis' patrons' wealth also shapes the Met's presentation of the show, as well as some prominent critical reactions to it. *The New York Times*'s Holland Cotter wrote: "Concocted for well-heeled homes," the Nabis' creations were "promotional statements about social stability, collective prosperity, collective prosperity, . . . inert, closed-in, exhausted." It was decorative art that was merely "soothing," not "shocking." The Met's wall texts also stressed the art's decorativeness to the exclusion of its deeper qualities, though in a spirit of admiration, not hostility, going on at length about the lavish existence of the Nabis' patrons. Perhaps Cotter was crankily responding less to the show than to some of the more complacent aspects of prosperity. Perhaps the Met's commentary was, in its good-natured way, reflecting one of those complacent aspects, describing the opulence of the Nabis' work in lush shelter-magazine terms.

But the Nabis' art could be read, to a great extent, as a sly commentary on their patrons' taste. If you look closely at some of these paintings, you'll notice a wry, ingenious playfulness. One of the first paintings that greet you as you enter the exhibition is Bonnard's *Woman in a Garden: Woman in a Checked Dress.* Painted on a narrow, vertical panel, the picture represents a woman against a background of leaves and general greenery, with two other female figures in the near distance. But this is not any kind of recognizable garden. Several of the leaves, unattached to branches, appear superimposed over the dress's checkered pattern. The lower part of the dress seems to grow out of a fork in the tree at the bottom of the painting; leaves and tree are in the process of becoming fabric. To top it all off, the white hat, partly laid over with leaves—one of them heart-shaped—is so abstract that it looks more like a jagged patch of sky shaped into a hat. And the two women in the distance are rendered against a green expanse so oddly speckled with yellow that it seems embroidered rather than painted. Indeed, the entire garden is one-dimensional, stuck onto the background the way the dress is stuck onto the woman's figure. The painting transforms nature into a thing. This is a garden you might find on a rack in Saks.

As you walk through the show you notice how the Nabis have frozen nature into a commodity. In Denis's *The Muses,* which portrays a group of women in a forest, some sitting and some standing, the ground is literally rendered as an oriental rug. Vuillard's *Under the Trees* is even more defiantly playful. The painting is divided horizontally by a mass of foliage, whose bisecting border Vuillard represents as the fringe of a dress. Artificial, acquirable things, Vuillard seems to be saying, have replaced the romantics' and the impressionists' trees and valleys, rivers and seas.

Vuillard's *Vanity Table* is a portrait of a woman at her vanity table, but in this, as in several other works, he has titled his painting not after her but after her physical possession. The solitary figure on the right side of the painting is barely distinguishable from the dense subdued brilliance of the wallpaper, the flowers, the tablecloth underneath the flowers, the vanity table itself. The feeling such works evoke is, first, one of serenity, even comfort; and then a sensation of emptiness, loss, and nostalgia. It is as if you are watching a room become a memory of the people who once inhabited it at the same time as the people themselves slowly disappear from the room.

By the end of the show, by the time you have seen Bonnard depicting his human figures in hues of purple and green and pink, just like his bottles and vases, you get the feeling that the Nabis had a high time at the end of the day, sitting in a café and laughing over their guileful last word. It is as if they were saying to their benefactors: Do you want to escape the outside world to your haute-bourgeois apartment-castles? We will give you a world in which nothing exists but your interiors. Do you want to accumulate things, and more things? We will show you a world of only things. Do you want an art that might offer you a portal back to all that is natural in life, which you have lost? We will give you an art that is entirely artificial, so that you may long for what you have lost. The biblical prophets, after all, were great chastisers of convention and of material excess.

You could say that the Nabis not only pulled the rug out from underneath the rival artistic styles of late romanticism and impressionism. They also, for all their gratitude to their patrons, pulled their benefactors' pretensions out from underneath their rugs. In this way, the Nabis snatched artistic triumph from the jaws of their material success.

From Stalin to SoHo

In Moscow last year, I had lunch at a hotel café with a Russian art critic. I'll call her Regina. A few minutes into our meeting she excitedly handed me a book of photographs by Oleg Kulik, a youngish performance artist. In these pictures, Kulik seemed to be having sex with a goat, a dog, and a bear. Regina spoke about the authenticity of Kulik's gesture, the purity of his conception, the honesty of his position. (His aesthetic position.) After she had enthused for a while, a group of Russian businessmen swaggered in, accompanied by an extravagantly dressed prostitute, and sat down at a nearby table. Regina glared at them as she carefully returned the photographs to her bag. "That's disgusting," she said.

Kulik is wildly popular in Russian artistic circles these days. In Moscow, in St. Petersburg, one encounters younger writers, artists, intellectuals who call for the exaltation of unreason, of antihumanism, of "stench," "filth," "evil." It is a sentimental nihilism laced with Russian histrionics, a nostalgie de la boo-hoo-hoo. But it is not unserious. And if you point out the obvious—that those were precisely the qualities of the former regime—your interlocutor will say, Yes, precisely! and explain to you that what the communists called "reason," "humanism," and "morality" was the very opposite. These Russian artists and writers, you see, are performing an ideological unmasking.

If this sounds familiar, it should. Such ideas appear at first to be warmed-over Western postmodernism, though directed at a different set of adversaries. The almost fanatical references that Russian intellectuals make to Barthes, Lyotard, Foucault, Baudrillard, and the others only add to the feeling that you have seen the future and it is the past. And yet the difference between Russian postmodernism and Western postmodernism is chasmic. In the placid and prosperous West, one was sometimes hard-pressed to adduce living examples to convince the devout postmodernist that morality was not just an ideology of power. Under the Soviet regime, however, Russians had before them stirring counterevidence of the unstable meanings, the plentiful simulacra, the harvest of unreason reaped by the regime. In the dramas enacted around Sakharov, Sharansky, and other dissidents, Russians could witness a moral certainty that could not be reduced to ideology or power. But the pomos of Russia critique and deconstruct and interrogate Sakharov's morality right alongside communism's immorality! Communism's burlesque of a stable moral stance seems to have destroyed the possibility of a stable moral stance. In this way, Russian postmodernists are obliterating their intellectual birthright as a way of avenging themselves upon those who tried to obliterate it.

Western postmodernists often transgress only logic and taste. But the transgressiveness of their Russian counterparts is a much sadder spectacle. These are people who have actually experienced the deconstruction of meaning and value, the reinterpretation of truth and falsehood by coercive political and social structures. But they celebrate the mentality anyway. They seem to prefer a hip, paralyzing reality to even the slightest whiff of moral assurance, whether its sponsor is Lenin or Herzen or Tolstoy. The everyday maneuvers and compromises of democratic politics fill them with scorn. They have become professional cynics and professional survivalists—as were the erstwhile commissars they profess to disdain. This is the worst irony of post-Soviet culture. Many members of the Russian intelligentsia travel along the lines of illogic laid down by the regime that they outlasted. Enter Komar and Melamid.

THE COLLABORATIVE ARTISTIC TEAM of Vitaly Komar and Alexander Melamid left the Soviet Union in 1977, when Komar was thirty-four and Melamid was thirty-two. After spending almost a year in Israel, they arrived in New York in 1978, where for the most part they have had their studio ever since. Along with Ilya Kabakov, the New York– and Paris–based conceptualist who emigrated from the Soviet Union in 1987, Komar and Melamid are the world's best-known living Russian artists.

References to twentieth-century Russian history and twentieth-century Russian art abound in Komar and Melamid's work. Their allusiveness is almost a kind of code, and so it is helpful to know how that history has dealt with that art. In 1922, with the approval of Trotsky and Bukharin, Lenin set up the AKhRR, or the Association of Artists of Revolutionary Russia, and instigated the suppression of the Russian avant-garde, who had enthusiastically supported and helped stage the revolution. It was around this time that Lenin and Anatoly Lunacharsky, his "Commissar for Enlightenment," began to lay the groundwork for what eventually became socialist realism.

Socialist realism ran parallel to the illogical logic that infused the official rhetoric: it was a kind of visual doublespeak. The state was not so much lying as it was deliberately displaying its power to make its own truth. Forced labor on one side, and posters depicting smiling construction workers on the other; state-orchestrated starvation, and public images of bountiful harvests; the open secret of Stalinist repression, and portraits of

Stalin as Christ. The *official* program of Socialist realism was a permanently latent irony—the lowest point in the history of irony, you might say—and it disheartened articulate opposition into a permanently ironic self-suppression. Its standards were set forth in 1934 by Bukharin, Gorky, and Zhdanov at the First Congress of Soviet Writers. A socialist realist work of art had to meet three main criteria: *narodnost* (sometimes called *massonost*), or accurate depiction of the life of "the people"; *ideinost*, or an adherence to official ideology; and *partinost*, or party spirit. Art falling outside these boundaries immediately became "unofficial" or "nonconformist."

From around 1934 until Stalin's death in 1953, art burrowed underground. In 1956, Khrushchev's famous speech denouncing Stalin and the cult of personality ushered in a second phase of unofficial art. But that exhilarating spell of freedom came to a halt in 1962, when Khrushchev attended a show of both official and unofficial art, and blasted the latter as anti-Soviet ("Gentlemen, we are declaring war on you!"). Still, Khrushchev had let the paint out of the tube, and the momentum behind unofficial art continued to pick up steam. More and more, unofficial artists began consciously and explicitly, if cautiously, to criticize the system in which they were living. Liberated by the revelation of Western artistic developments and the relaxation of official parameters, emboldened by the interest of a new generation of private collectors inside Russia, Russian artists worked in a dizzying melange of styles throughout the 1960s and into the 1970s.

By the late 1970s, an artist's ability to move from style to style, sometimes incorporating several styles in the same work, had become an established approach. Works representing historical events in Russia were especially suited to this kind of fragmentation. The new aesthetic boasted a major intellectual influence, the literary theorist Mikhail Bakhtin's idea of the "carnivalesque" or masquerade of styles. It also had a basis in social experience: the necessity of using a *personazhnyi avtor*, or an assumed persona, to manipulate one's way through the paradoxical nets of everyday Soviet life. Interestingly, such a disorientation of memory and identity was welcomed by the regime, which allowed officially approved artists also to work in this combinatory style.

Two important artistic trends, sometimes indistinct from one another, emerged from these twisted circumstances: Moscow conceptualism and Sots art. ("Sots" is a compression of the Russian words for "socialist realism" and "pop.") Both styles seemed to comment on the physical and mental depredations practiced by the regime. The former was more cerebral, making use of objects in space set alongside words, or taking up the *personazhnyi avtor* to tell stories that revealed the melancholy or the poignant durability of inner life in the Soviet Union. But Sots art directly incorporated references to official ideology in its work. It applied the style of American pop art to the iconography of the regime's propaganda.

Komar and Melamid were the principal founders of Sots art, and in September 1974 they and Sots burst onto the world scene. The occasion was the so-called Bulldozer Show, an open-air exhibition outside Moscow that the authorities broke up with fire hoses and bulldozers. The exhibiting artists had made sure to invite Western journalists, and reports of the assault circled the globe. From then on, while serious episodes of harassment still occurred, Russian nonconformist artists found it easier to exhibit their work, helped along by the atmosphere of detente.

American readers at that time learned a great deal about Komar and Melamid. Articles appeared in *The New York Times* and then in *Newsweek,* whose art critic became such a fan that in 1977 he accepted an invitation from the artists to collaborate with them on a project. Stunned by their expulsion, the result of a personal grudge, they told *The New Yorker* in 1986, from the youth section of the all-powerful Moscow Union of Artists some months before the Bulldozer event, Komar and Melamid, both Jewish, were understandably intent on emigrating to the West. The sudden acquisition of the dissident's halo had made them sympathetic figures to Western journalists. (The art critic Carter Ratcliff, in a monograph about the duo, had them heroically banished from the Union of Artists after the Bulldozer Show.)

The works that Komar and Melamid exhibited at the Bulldozer Show caught the eye of the expected Western reporters. One of their offerings was an oil painting called *Double Self-Portrait* (1973), a representative example of their Sots work at the time. According to Komar and Melamid, thugs destroyed it at the scene; but the artists re-created it. An oil on canvas, it portrays the artists' heads in the style of official portraits of Lenin and Stalin done before the latter's death. Westerners admired their audacity. *Double Self-Portrait* is an uncannily clever work of art. It has the style of Byzantine mosaics, a gesture that is as much a self-mockery as a careful iconoclasm; and its replacement of Stalin with an image of one of themselves could have been construed as an ironic act of suppression that served as a reminder of the Brezhnev regime's own attempts to cover up the reality of Stalinism in the wake of Khrushchev's revelations.

Unlike some other participants in the Bulldozer Show, who continued to be arrested, committed to mental institutions, or called up for military service, Komar and Melamid escaped similar harassment. Even though they had been ejected from the union, they were allowed to join the Graphic Artists' Organization, a dispensation that gave them precious access to freelance design work. Of course, their position in Soviet society couldn't have hurt them: Komar's parents were both attorneys (his father was a military lawyer), and Melamid's father served as a high-ranking government official. But the larger reason for their good fortune was that they possessed a calculated detachment from their subjects that was the equal of that of any official artist working directly for the regime.

Early on, Komar and Melamid mixed loaded content with a neutral attitude toward it. They did this so expertly that it is almost impossible to define their place in the nonconformist art scene during those years. An even more typically ingenious work than *Double Self-Portrait* is *Meeting Between Solzhenitsyn and Boll at Rostropovich's Country House,* which was done in 1972. It was painted in a combination of Western modernist styles and old Russian icons, the writer's head being depicted in the manner of the latter. Since references to religion were still taboo as artistic subjects, the painting seems to make an equivalence between Western cultural trends and reactionary cultural-political conditions.

What serious dissident in the orbit of communism would satirize the liberal West in 1972? In Paris, fledgling pomos were just beginning to herald the death of the artist as individual; but Komar and Melamid, aided by the atmosphere of *personazhnyi avtor,* had jumped right over theory into praxis. In their work, they were nowhere to be found. They grew more and more popular with Western journalists and critics, who had a natural predisposition toward the plight of unofficial artists. And so, by the time a well-connected relative arranged a show for them at the prestigious Ronald Feldman Fine Arts gallery in New York in 1976, Komar and Melamid had acquired a reputation among commentators outside the art world as the supreme satirists of communist totalitarianism.

A critical and financial success, the New York show encouraged Komar and Melamid to apply for exit visas the following year. The regime refused the request, but the government's obduracy played into the duo's hands. They founded "TransState," a federation of "I-States," announcing that each of them was a nation unto himself. They had already developed what would become their trademark genre: performance art as a public relations *coup-de-théâtre*. At the time of the New York show, they had transposed the regulations from the Soviet internal passport into musical notation and arranged for a cellist in New York and pianists in cities throughout the West to play the Dada-ish composition simultaneously. The charged political background turned first the passport performance, and then the "I-States," into gestures of defiance, and the regime buckled under the bad press, finally allowing the artists to leave.

Arriving months apart in Israel in 1977, Komar and Melamid immediately set about trying to cause another stir. They built an aluminum "temple," carried it to the top of a hill overlooking the Valley of Hinnom, and burned Komar's suitcase. Then they read aloud what they had composed as an "addition" to the Torah—it was an account of their departure from Russia—and smashed the temple into pieces. Nobody in Israel took much notice. (Ratcliff dimly wrote that "because they do battle with the imagery of superpowers, Komar and Melamid could find little in Israeli life to engage their attention.") Shortly afterward, they left for America.

In America, Komar and Melamid found much to do. Establishing themselves as artists critical of the Soviet regime had gotten them out of the Soviet Union. But the vanguard elements in the New York art world were keenly critical of capitalism and bourgeois morality. They were also highly adversarial toward official American policy with regard to the "evil empire." In neither respect, of course, had Komar and Melamid compromised themselves by their work in Russia. (Moscow knew about SoHo.) Indeed, their second show at Feldman, called "Catalogue of Superobjects—Supercomfort for Superpeople," a kind of preparation for their arrival in the States, had mocked Western consumerism.

So the pair consolidated their Western art-world credentials with another collaborative piece. Called *Komar and Melamid, Inc., We Buy and Sell Souls,* it was a satire on the soulless American capitalism that had publicized their situation, enriched them, and helped them to leave the Soviet Union. The people whose souls Komar and Melamid solicited were some of the most powerful and influential figures in the art world. The duo "bought" their souls, and then advertised them for sale in a catalog of souls that they wrote themselves: it included Andy Warhol ("Who does not know the soul of this great artist?") and Norton Dodge, the preeminent collector of contemporary Russian art ("A soul containing a rare concentration of the most varied qualities").

In Manhattan in the 1980s, it was a golden age of artistic self-consciousness: art-historical appropriation; a multiplicity of styles; self-serving proclamations about the end of art; ideological unmasking; society as spectacle; society as "simulacrum"—all floating around in a great gazpacho of irony. Komar and Melamid couldn't have landed in New York at a more auspicious moment. After all, they were experts in infinitely regressive self-distancing. As such, they could meet different prescribed criteria, all at the same time. And so they proceeded with the Americanization of *personazhnyi avtor.* "We're basically non-social persons, derelicts," Melamid explained to a reporter. "We work together as a unit and express no personal cause of our own, but a social tendency," said Komar on another occasion. "Whatever changes in the world balance affects us. As the earth turns, we turn with it."

Downtown artists, critics, and curators could talk about the deconstruction of socially fabricated meaning and value. They could dabble in the representation of depersonalizing and dehumanizing extremes. But Komar and Melamid had come from the *omphalos* of deconstructing, depersonalizing, and dehumanizing extremes—and they worked diligently to keep people from forgetting it. As Melamid told Ratcliff: "The real Stalin time was about life, death. Blood. It was a terrible time but a deep one, the real time. The cultural life of Russia under Stalin. The radio played Brahms, Beethoven. The time of the thaw was about nothing. . . . What was Yevtushenko? . . . What was it about? What was this bullshit? . . . What's the problem? What are you solving with this idiotic poetry?" Never mind that they were ten and eight years old, respectively, when Stalin died, and grew up during the thaw, the only happy period in twentieth-century Russian history since 1917. In New York they didn't want anyone to associate them with the unheroic thaw. Arriving in a culture that reduces catastrophic events to the melodramas of identity, these foot-fast, world-weary émigrés, heavy with the knowledge of life, death, and blood, grasped intuitively how to present themselves.

Thus Komar and Melamid's "Nostalgic Socialist Realism" series. It went way beyond radical chic. It was totalitarian chic. The most committed downtown insurgent couldn't beat it. The style got them into the Palladium, one of New York's hottest night-clubs in the eighties, where they staged a May Day extravaganza called "Lenin Lived, Lenin Lives, Lenin Will Live!" It won them a stream of critical praise, and it earned them purchases by the Metropolitan Museum of Art, New York City's Museum of Modern Art, and the Guggenheim Museum in New York City.

"Nostalgic Socialist Realism" consisted of large oil paintings, heavily varnished into a glamorous sheen and skillfully executed in true socialist realist style. The subject was life under totalitarianism, especially under Stalin: Stalin glimpsed in the back of a car, peeking out from behind a curtain; Stalin admiring himself before a mirror; Stalin getting the gift of inspiration from the Muses (in *The Origin of Socialist Realism*). The paintings were voluptuously rendered, though their content was morally abhorrent. This was the standard-issue irony of the Moscow conceptualists' arrangement of "impossible things," and it was about fifteen years old in the Russian context. But Komar and Melamid brought it up to date by postmodernizing it: "We don't believe in anything. We are not against communism, or against capitalism, or for either. Irony is above everything because nothing is taken seriously." Satirizing official culture, they ended up making use of official irony. The whole thing was—ironic.

And yet. Taking a large red banner in Brezhnev's Moscow and painting on it "Onward to the Victory of Communism," as Komar and Melamid had once done: that is irony. Portraying Stalin in socialist realist style in the United States in the mid-1980s: that is strategy. But Komar and Melamid's admirers, still awed by Russian experience and Russian suffering, continued to extol their work. So the pair gave their paintings another twist. They took the irony out of their "Onward" banner and brought it to America, where they made another large red banner, putting Stalin's image alongside the words "Thank you, Comrade Stalin, for our happy childhood." They made the irony sincere. (In the postmodern weather, of course, the sincerity could still appear ironic.) "Through Stalin art," Komar has said, "we could re-create our childhood." Since their childhood is so bound up with images of the dictator, they extended that tenderness toward Stalin himself. As they explained to *Flash Art* in 1985: "We try to understand Stalin, to love him as we did when we were kids. . . . The gulag and so on was something we learned about later. It was horrible—really horrible—but no one changes from childhood. It is like learning for example that your lovely girl is a prostitute.

You are betrayed. You might hate her. But you still know she gave you the best feeling of your whole life."

In their flattering full-length portrait of Hitler, they were also being ironic and sincere. Visually, the painting absorbs the cultural atmosphere of irony automatically—this, despite the fact that there is no reason why a portrait of Hitler as a distinguished historical figure should be ironic in a society that is not divided on the question of Hitler's moral worth. So, to add a ballast of stable meaning to an irony in danger of faltering, Komar and Melamid explained the picture to *Flash Art*. It turns out that they were shattering taboos. "Hitler was a good thing for us Jews, a kind of Messiah. He threw Jews out of Jewish history into world history. Because of him, Jews are world-personalities. Every nation needs its own Holocaust to understand what is going on in this world. The person without suffering is not a real person. It says in the scriptures that every evil is a messenger from God. Hitler was a disaster for Germans. People forget that the Germans lost and the Jews won."

Komar and Melamid had so many facile and conflicting meanings going that critics and viewers became afraid of choosing the wrong one. In their interviews, the pair found a way to say what they meant without appearing to mean what they said. Only ethical sophisticates could dare to seem so morally stupid. Or was it that only stupid people could impute sophistication to such deliberately empty ideas? Who, in the minatory shadow of SoHo, had the confidence to decide? Komar and Melamid's paintings embodied a permanently latent irony that disheartened articulate opposition into a permanently ironic self-suppression. They were not so much lying as deliberately displaying their power to make their own truth. Why the Soviet regime let two such precious assets get away remains a mystery.

As Komar and Melamid's career began to wane after the "Nostalgic Socialist Realism" series, they maneuvered to stay in the art world's, and the public's, eye. They were not used to being ignored. (In *Painting by Numbers,* Komar remarks: "Maybe it's our mission—Alex and mine—to give world some lesson.") Declaring themselves fed up with the shallowness and the hypocrisy of the New York art world, they moved across the river to Bayonne, New Jersey, a dying industrial town. There they painted socialist realist portraits of old factories and the few remaining foundry workers. They also conducted bus tours of the area that embarked from SoHo. ("Smells terrible here. Terrible smell." "You see this building? It isn't what you think it is. It's a toilet.") They conveyed the fruit of their Bayonne adventure back to shallow and hypocritical New York, where it went on display at their SoHo gallery. Then they left Bayonne and returned to their studio in downtown Manhattan.

WITH STALIN ABSENT from *l'oeuvre de Bayonne,* however, critics felt safe to criticize. They called the show irritating and condescending. So Komar and Melamid turned the other chic. For their "Monumental Propaganda" show in 1993, they devised another collaborative performance/public relations/networking extravaganza, inviting artists and art-world figures to send in suggestions for the preservation of communist monuments. In the catalog essay that they wrote for the occasion, they did their best to capture evolving art-world taste by suggesting that Lenin and Stalin were transvestites. The show attracted some attention, but nothing like the noise of the "Nostalgic Socialist Realism" series. Their rising star was dropping out of sight. Which brings us to their new book, and their "Most Wanted" poll.

In 1993, Komar and Melamid hooked up with the Nation Institute, a nonprofit offshoot of *The Nation* magazine, and commissioned a public-opinion research firm to conduct a poll asking Americans what kind of painting they preferred. Based on the poll, Komar and Melamid made two paintings, *America's Most Wanted* and *America's Most Unwanted,* and exhibited them in SoHo in the spring of 1994. The results of the poll, alongside an interview with the artists, appeared in *The Nation* around the same time. The poll results and the interview have now been published in a book, which includes an essay by JoAnn Wypijewski, who edited the volume, and an admiring commentary by Arthur Danto.

A FEW WEEKS BEFORE *Painting by Numbers* hit the bookstores, *The Commissar Vanishes: The Falsification of Photographs and Art in Stalin's Russia* was released. The reception of the latter explains something about the nature of the former. *The Commissar Vanishes* is a riveting and depressing collection of photographs doctored by Stalin and his henchmen to reflect the changes in the communist hierarchy. As Stalin purged or cast out of favor one person after another—some with blood on their hands, some innocent of any crime—he had various artists and technicians touch up official photographs and make the non-grata image disappear.

As with Komar and Melamid's paintings, a regnant irony welcomed this ghoulish book. Some critics, while pointing out the horror the book revealed, mentioned what they found to be its comic effect. Partly, their reaction resulted from the book's presentation: *The Commissar Vanishes* sounds like a satiric operetta by Kurt Weill, and its editor, David King, introduced each set of manipulated photographs with headings like "Four, Three, Two, One . . . ," "Crowd Control," and "Long-Term Friendships." (Hardy-har-har.) There was another reason why at least some reviewers had no trouble maintaining their lightheartedness. Which one of us, after all, has not wished that he could alter his past? Reviewing the book for *Slate,* for example, Luc Sante cheerfully concluded that "everyone has a little Stalin lurking somewhere within." And if it is widely accepted that everyone has a little Stalin lurking within, then we can forgive Stalin a little; or at least we can lighten up. (And here is Sante, in a review of Komar and Melamid's new book for *The New York Times Book Review,* describing them as "social critics who never fail to locate the comic aspect of a given subject. Trained in dialectical thinking, they are at ease with contradictions. They would probably be dissidents in any country, under any regime." Probably? Certainly! These are people for whom dissidence is a career move.) The notion that Stalinism is a quality of human nature prepares the ground for the notion that a totalitarian system has little to do with the actual ideology and the actual history that set it in motion. Thus, in his preface to *The Commissar Vanishes,* Stephen Cohen—who believes that moderate Bolsheviks such as Bukharin would have spared Russia if Stalin hadn't destroyed them—can instruct that "under Stalin's regime, which ruled the Soviet Union from 1929 to 1953, photographs lied." Never mind that photographs (and newspapers) lied under Lenin's regime, too. And thus David King can describe Bukharin as the "immensely popular, liberal, and most humane member of the Bolsheviks." Never mind that Bukharin was planning with Trotsky to smash the independent trade unions, even as he was carefully and humanely, like a good liberal, imposing an ideological line on independent artists.

Komar and Melamid, too, have an aptitude for the imperative of mainstream adversarial culture in America, which is to keep things nice and equivalent. Melamid to Ratcliff:

Of course, everyone knew all along that to a degree Russia was a slave-labor camp in Stalin's time. But it wasn't until we came here that we learned that in the American army during World War II there were special battalions for

black people. That the U.S. Army was segregated. This
would have been impossible in Russia. . . . Soviet Russia is
ruled by fear, just like the United States. Russians are
afraid of the KGB, food shortages. Here, people fear losing
their jobs, AIDS. . . . KGB, AIDS—these are only symbols.

Can anyone blame Komar and Melamid for their tenderness toward Stalin, who provided equal opportunity for black people
even as he was crushing the life out of everyone else, in a terrible
time, but a deep one, a real time?

PAINTING BY NUMBERS puts Komar and Melamid's trademark
nostalgia on the offensive. As Melamid once bragged to Ratcliff,
"I don't consider myself a naive person who takes a long time to
realize what's the situation. Just the opposite." And so this enterprise is an ideal occasion for the pair to construct a superior attitude ("dissidents in any country") to a country that they grew up
believing was superior to them no matter what they did. They attempt this by drawing connections by numbers between the Soviet Union and the United States every chance they get. This is
partly because they will stretch reality to any proportions to keep
themselves relevant, and partly because they cannot shake a
deeply embedded habit of mind.

  Their book should have been called *The Commissar Reappears.*
When they talk about America, they sound like the old hacks of
Pravda sneering at the socially primitive West. Here are some of
Komar and Melamid's gloating revelations (having lived in the
United States for almost two decades, they have artfully retained
and refined their grammatical mistakes in English):

We made surprising discovery: in society famous for freedom of expression, freedom of individual, our poll revealed

sameness of majority. Having destroyed communism's utopian illusion, we collided with democracy's virtual reality.

This whole system, American system, runs on fear.

I have never seen artists so desperate as they are now, in this society.

[The American] art world is not democratic society but totalitarian one.

In a way, pop art in America was like socialist realism in Russia, because the real pop art of America is not Andy Warhol but Sears. . . . And in that case, in Searstyle, I think behind the banal colors—almond, avocado, java—there is tragedy and the deepest fears of America, the fear of un-employment, the fear of death.

Experts at mocking prescribed aesthetic criteria, Komar and Melamid have mastered the art of meeting them. Here are excerpts from the interview with Wypijewski:

Q: But how do you think people who aren't part of this [American] system express their aesthetic judgment?

AM: . . . People in ghettos, these young people, they spend an enormous amount of money for their dress. They care about the beauty of the thing, much more than people with a bigger income. . . .

Q: And what did you think of the responses you got from people in the focus groups and at the town meetings?

AM: . . . You know, the upper classes treat the lower classes like children. . . .

Q: What's the role of the collector?

AM: . . . I met many big collectors. Ninety-nine percent of them were either really stupid, illiterate people or just vicious people. . . . All of the museums in the United States exist only to serve these people. . . . These people, the rich people, the people in power, they build their castles, which are called museums. . . . Then these great people come in and they have their bar mitzvahs or wedding parties. It's just like the aristocrats and their castles. . . .

Q: Do you think that [in terms of art] America is not that dissimilar from the Soviet Union, only here the commissars are the collectors and curators?

VK: Yes, sure. . . .

Q: In the same way that when you were in the Soviet Union you were painting pictures that countered the official art, do you think that the poll and the pictures that came out of it are a kind of parallel to that in the United States?

AM: Definitely. This is a totally dissident art. . . .

And what about the poll itself, and the paintings based on it? The paintings might not be "dissident"; but the poll is certainly "total." Indeed, everything about Komar and Melamid is total: the irony, the accommodation, the bullying. They once had the employees of a gallery humiliatingly repeat the Russian words for "fuck your mother" over and over again without telling them what the words meant, in order to prove that artists are tyrants and vice versa. "When I paint," Melamid once remarked, "I see I have Hitler in me."

Komar and Melamid found, amazingly enough, that the majority of Americans preferred the same painting. Americans overwhelmingly preferred the color blue. They wanted a landscape with mountains, a river, a bit of forest, and a single tree in the foreground. They desired to see George Washington in the painting, as well as three anonymous figures and two deer. What the majority of people did not want was a painting that was abstract. Even more incredible is that, when Komar and Melamid conducted the poll in countries throughout the world, everyone else wanted the exact same kind of painting, with local variations. And a global majority of respondents also shared Americans' aversion to abstract art, along with their liking for the color blue.

I don't mean to seem like such a square, but it does seem necessary to point out that no pollster could divine the artistic image that people had in their minds as they hurriedly answered 102 abstractly particular and discontinuous questions within twenty-four minutes. The questions themselves include queries about income and "ideology." They are either unquantifiable ("I only like to look at art that makes me happy—agree or disagree?"); or meaningless ("Art should be relaxing to look at—agree or disagree?"); or snide, intimidating, and irrelevant ("When you have a choice between two products of equal quality, how often are you willing to pay a little extra for a design or style you prefer?"; "How important would the appearance or design of the following be in your decision to buy that product: a pair of underwear?"; "How important to you is the way you dress?").

Komar and Melamid get a lot of mileage out of the supposed universal preference for blue: "I believe it reflects people's nostalgia about freedom. It's a very simple metaphor, and very deep at the same time," and so on, and so on. In fact, six years before they did the poll, long before they made their astounding discovery of the universality of the preference for blue, Komar and Melamid had a very precise association for that color. Explaining to Ratcliff, in an interview in 1987, what they thought of the way Gorbachev was transfiguring the Soviet Union, they said:

> This is cheap culture. Easy culture. Like Abstract Expressionism in America. It's nothing. It's empty. It's not good, it's not bad, it's just light blue culture. A culture of false optimism, which says, We're immortal, we're great, we will change the situation. Freedom. We will overcome. Overcome what? What? Your death?

Observe the scornful reference to abstract expressionism. The hostility to modernist abstraction is obsessive among nearly all contemporary Russian artists, critics, and curators, who—understandably—resent being cast by the revolution outside the modernist line of descent. They feel embittered by Western art historians' glorification of the Russian avant-garde, and by the Western canon's omission of Russian art after the avant-garde period. So—lo and behold!—the world's Most Unwanted paintings are modernist and abstract.

With their poll, these opportunistic shtickheads, who never made a self-forgetful brushstroke in their lives, have devised the perfect wish-fulfillment. It allows them to trash the art world that has started to tire of them, and to strike a pose of solidarity with ordinary people, and to sneer at ordinary taste, and to advertise their superiority, and to make new friends who, as usual, will be too uncertain to take anything they do or say seriously. Terrified by the plurality of freedom in the West ("Looking for freedom, we found slavery"), Komar and Melamid have created a totalizing picture of the world outside the enclosed system that once coddled their sense of their own importance. It is cheap and easy world, like prostitute who leaves you with best feeling of whole life. It is free world, which is pathetic world ready to give hug to fraudulence. What is this bullshit? What's the problem? What are you solving? What freedom? Communism dead, falsely optimistic capitalism dying. Only ism left is solipsism, I-State, where artist is tyrant. You hope for good, for true, for beautiful life? Please, do us favor. Go fuck your mother. Call us, too, so we talk about project for future. And excuse please ironical nature of two of us. Stalin made us nuts.

Barbara Kingsolver's Icy Virtue

I.

BARBARA KINGSOLVER is the most successful practitioner of a style in contemporary fiction that might be called Nice Writing. Nice Writing is a violent affability, a deadly sweetness, a fatal gentle touch. But before I start in on Kingsolver's work, I feel I must explain why I feel that I must start in on it.

I do so for a younger version of myself, for the image that I carry inside me of a boy who was the son of a sadistic, alcoholic father, and of a mother who was hurt but also hurtful, and abusive. And I do not feel the need to make a pretense of sweetness or gentleness as I confess this.

"She told me that maybe one out of every four little girls is sexually abused by a family member. Maybe more," says Taylor, the protagonist of Kingsolver's first novel, *The Bean Trees,* reporting her conversation with a social worker; but in her "Author's Note" to *The Poisonwood Bible,* Kingsolver writes that she herself was "the fortunate child of medical and public-health workers, whose compassion and curiosity led them to the Congo. They . . . set me early on a path of exploring the great, shifting terrain between righteousness and what's right." It is easy for Kingsolver, then, to spin such tragic conceits. But I remember my father's heavy hand on my face and the door slamming behind him, as if the slap were a firecracker and the slamming door its echo in some grotesque celebration of violence.

The flesh has its own memory, and sometimes my skin heats up before the flashback lays its heavy hand across my consciousness. It is the opposite of when you touch something hot and it takes a second to feel the pain. I cannot really talk about all the ways my father hurt me. Later, when the door slammed for the last time, and my father left for good, I lay in the dark with my older brother and younger sister and listened to my mother and her boyfriends. Sometimes the men she brought home stayed the night, and sometimes they didn't. I can remember my little sister, Mandy—my brother and I called her "Ostrich" because of the way she buried her head in the bedclothes when she heard the strangers' voices, crying herself to sleep.

I also remember my mother storming into the bedroom that we shared, and screaming at Mandy to shut up. Sometimes my mother kissed me very hard on the mouth, a kiss that no mother should ever give to a son. Then she returned to the bedroom where her boyfriend of the hour, or her crazy solitude, waited for her. Those nights are like sudden breaks in a film at a dingy porn-house. They are desolate lapses in a desolate movie that no one should ever have to see.

Since she was born with Gibson's syndrome and was mentally impaired, Mandy might have had in her unlucky brain an avenue of escape from all the pain. I don't really know. She went to live in a special place when I was fifteen. As Gibson's got worse and worse, she lost all recollection of me. I remember a strange girl-woman sitting in a big chair, wearing a white blouse, a pleated navy blue skirt, and a plaid bow tie. She would stare for hours at art books that she held upside down in her lap. Her small bare legs hung motionless off the chair and looked like skittles. They made me wince.

The plaid bow tie had belonged to my maternal grandmother. It was the only one of her husband's things that she was able to bring to this country. David Schnorr, my grandfather, died in a concentration camp. So when I read the portrait of a Native American woman named Annawake in Kingsolver's *Pigs in Heaven,* I think of my mother's father, because Kingsolver approvingly has Annawake make a historical analogy: "That's us. Our tribe. We've been through a holocaust as devastating as what happened to the Jews." (David Schnorr had been a minor literary figure in Odessa. He was not as lucky as Barbara Kingsolver.) And when I read no less than two novels by Kingsolver centered on a cringingly cute little girl named Turtle—*The Bean Trees* and *Pigs in Heaven*—I think of the real little girl we called Ostrich.

This hurts me. I really don't want to use my family to make a point. But when Kingsolver writes so facilely about lost people, I think of my brother's drug addiction, and the hand that he lost in Nicaragua to the machete of a contra, and his psychotic breakdown in the offices of *The New Yorker,* where he was a frequent contributor. And I think of my father coming back to live with us after a car accident left his entire right side paralyzed. Once I cried from rage and shame after he hit me; now, whenever I saw him in his wheelchair, I cried from rage and guilt.

That was during my first year of college. In my third year, my mother became gravely ill. Fortunately, my brother had straightened his life out, and he returned home with Luisha, his black wife, who had been his nurse in the psychiatric hospital. Together they tended to my mother. It was Luisha, having grown up hearing stories about the lynching of her great-grandfather, who taught my reckless brother lessons about dignity in adversity. She had seen her own teenage daughter shot dead before her eyes by drug dealers in her neighborhood. We were all very proud of Luisha.

After a while, my uncle Jeremiah came to help out with Tobey, who had been his lover and was now his friend and companion. Jer had been in jail in the sixties and had the soles of his feet beaten so badly by prison guards that he could barely walk. Tobey was HIV-positive and too depressed to work. I admired Jer, and I loved Tobey's spirit. Eventually I took a couple of years off from school and came back home to look after people who had so injured my young life. At night, my mother cried out, my father whimpered, my brother banged his fist against the wall, Luisha screamed in her sleep, Jeremiah sobbed, and Tobey wept. Sometimes I could not make sense of what I was doing there. But somehow I stayed.

I have a pretty good life now, but I cannot forget those nights. They, and all the history behind them, are why I write criticism. I write for the little boy that I was, the little boy crushed by untruth. He was surrounded by facts, but they were inaccurate facts. They did not correlate with the reality of human freedom. They were not true, or beautiful, or good. So these facts might just as well have been fiction; and any fiction that preserved their raw unreality would be an emaciated lie. It would not be true fiction at all.

Thus whenever I see the promulgation of such illusions by two fraudulent Russian artists, or by sanctimonious academic theorists, or by icily virtuous novelists, I sit down and I write for the little boy who craved the truth. I write for all the young boys and young girls who crave the truth. I strike for the children, and for their children's children. And I hope that anyone who takes exception to the ferocity of my tone will think of my father's hand across my face, and of my cruel mother, and of my dying mother, and of poor Ostrich, and of what the Nazis did to David Schnorr. And I hope, cherished reader, that you will not be angry about what I have to confess to you next.

II.

By now you will have realized, I hope, that nothing that I have written here is true, except for the quotations from Kingsolver and the references to her work. I made everything up; I meant it to be satire. I have passed beyond the boundary of good taste, and I apologize to anyone I have offended, since I know that the situations I described happen, and I know how much pain and sadness they bring. And though I have my own portion of pain and sadness, I also know that there are degrees of suffering. But the actuality and the complexity of suffering: that is precisely my point.

For at least the past decade, American writers have been pouring forth a cascade of horror stories about their condition or the condition of their characters. The Holocaust, ethnic geno-cide, murder, rape, incest, child abuse, cancer, paralysis, AIDS, fatal car accidents, Alzheimer's, chronic anorexia: calamities drop from the printer like pearls. These are elemental events of radically dif-ferent proportions, and the urge to make imaginative sense of them is also elemental. Some contemporary writers treat these subjects strongly and humbly and insightfully, but too many writ-ers engaged in this line of production turn out shallow and dis-torted work. They seem merely to be responding to a set of opportunities created by a set of social circumstances. In their hands, human suffering goes unimagined, and the imagination goes hungry and deprived.

There are a handful of reasons behind this trend. For a start, we live at a uniquely prosperous time in a uniquely prosperous society, a moment in which tragedy and catastrophe seem all the more confusing and inexplicable, and so their depiction is all the more gripping. Also, we are fortunate to inhabit a culture in which practical techniques for mastering life's hardships have become so successful that it is perhaps natural for writers to develop a technique—a Calamity Style—for the conceptual mastery of life's inevitabilities.

Maybe we also feel, in our increasingly freewheeling culture, less protected as the forms of gratification multiply. The more gratification you seek, after all, the less stable and constant you are, whether you consciously feel yourself shifting or not. In this sense, these catastrophic tales are the emblems of a faintly enveloping anxiety. Then, too, since we live in such flush and tranquil times, more and more people have the privilege of shunning conventional work-routines and taking up creative labors. Writing, which requires no special training, holds out the promise of the freest kind of life. The problem is that not everyone who takes up the occupation of writer has the writer's gift. Thus extremity becomes an aid to straining imaginations.

But I think there is one reason for Calamity Writing that looms much larger than the others: it advances the amoral pursuit of a virtuous appearance. This is where Calamity Writing blossoms into the plastic flower of Nice Writing. The portrait of people doing evil things to each other, or of someone sick and dying, or of a person psychologically hurt, flatters the portraitist. It can enfold the writer in a mantle of invincible goodness. The artistic worth of the portrait fades away as an issue. What remains is the invaluable appearance of goodness.

I am not talking about hypocrisy. I am talking about the mere appearance of goodness as a substitute for honest art. The trend is everywhere. It is to be found, for example, in Lorrie Moore's short stories, especially "People Like That Are the Only People Here," the longest tale in *Birds of America,* her acclaimed new collection. The story is about a newborn baby dying of cancer. That is, the story's emotional register begins, from the very first paragraph, far beyond the reader's capacity to develop his or her own response to it. The effect is to place the supremely empathetic author in a protected niche, far beyond the reader's capacity to criticize. In this way Nice Writing fosters Nice Criticism. Anyone who writes nice writes with impunity.

BARBARA KINGSOLVER can be a very funny writer; her infrequent outbursts of humor make up her best quality. And those plots: when they do not hit patches of dense cuteness and saccharine emotion, they unfurl swiftly and engagingly, as the newspaper reviewers like to say. Still, if it were not for professional purposes, I would never read her. The loveliness becomes unbearable. From *The Bean Trees:*

> But it didn't seem to matter to Turtle, she was happy where she was. . . . She watched the dark highway and entertained me with her vegetable-soup song, except that now there were people mixed in with the beans and potatoes: Dwayne Ray, Mattie, Esperanza, Lou Ann and all the rest. And me. I was the main ingredient.

From *Animal Dreams:*

> "Sure I remember when we almost drowned in a flood. Plain as day. God, Codi, don't you? We found those abandoned coyote pups, and the river was flooding, and you wanted to save them. You said we had to."

From *Pigs in Heaven:*

Taylor puts up her hand, knowing what's coming. "Mama, I know I wasn't nice, but she's a kook." She glances at Turtle, who is using Alice's ballpoint carefully to blacken the entire state of Nevada. "A kook in need of kindness."

From "Paradise Lost," an essay in the collection *High Tide in Tucson:*

I went to the Canaries for nearly a year, to find new stories to tell, and to grow comfortable thinking in Spanish. Or so I said; the truth is closer to the bone. It was 1991, and in the U.S. a clamor of war worship had sprung like a vitriolic genie from the riveted bottles we launched on Baghdad. Yellow ribbons swelled from suburban front doors, so puffy and ubiquitous as to seem folkloric. But this folklore, a prayer of godspeed to the killers, allowed no possibility that the vanquished might also be human. I grew hopeless, then voiceless. What words could I offer a place like this? Five hundred years after colonialism arrived in the New World, I booked a return passage.

"An easy book to enjoy," *The New Yorker* said about Kingsolver's first novel, *The Bean Trees;* "rich fodder," said *The Denver Post,* meaning well, about her second novel, *Animal Dreams;* full of "issues that are serious, debatable and painful," said *The Los Angeles Times Book Review* about *Pigs in Heaven,* her third novel; "delightful, challenging, and wonderfully informative" wrote the *San Francisco Chronicle* about *High Tide in Tucson.* The standard congratulations are especially appropriate for Kingsolver's work, for they echo her work's self-congratulatory quality. Still, if these smug and trivial books do any violence to clarity or to reality, it is a minor aesthetic crime. It is a case for the local authorities. Let *Elle* or *Allure* handle it. When they are praised for their seriousness, well, that is another matter.

III.

Kingsolver does not exactly outrage me, because she is so damn nice; but she is becoming outrageous. With the publication of *The Poisonwood Bible,* this easy, humorous, competent, syrupy writer has been elevated to the ranks of the greatest political novelists of our time. *The New York Times Book Review* praised *The Poisonwood Bible* as a "profound work of political, psychological, and historical understanding." An obtuse profile of the writer in *The New York Times Magazine* declared that "perhaps only Kingsolver, of all contemporary novelists, has the expertise to pull off *The Poisonwood Bible*'s portrayal of white Europeans and Americans confronting black Africans in the 1950s and 1960s." In *The Nation,* John Leonard anointed Kingsolver as "our very own Lessing and our very own Gordimer."

Nearly all the reviews that I have read of *The Poisonwood Bible* have praised it in approximately the same lofty terms. Those who found something to criticize in the best-selling novel couched their criticism in the most anguished idiom, as if they were forced by circumstance to leave litter in a national park. Writing in the *Washington Post,* Jane Smiley rightly observed that Kingsolver's portrait of Nathan Price, an abusive father and fanatical Baptist missionary, is so flat and one-dimensional as to be totally implausible as a fictional construction. But this is not, Smiley adds, Kingsolver's fault. No, Kingsolver's admitted "failure" is the fault of American culture.

And yet. Nathan's enigmatic one-sidedness reflects our culture's failure to understand the humanity of those who seem to be the source of evil. . . . The author loses interest in Nathan, tries to compensate by giving him a dramatic death that seems pale in the telling. This failure goes right to the heart of who we are as a culture and how we look at ourselves: Yes, there are those who hurt others and show no remorse, who do not acknowledge the damage they have done. But they, in the end, are us. They should be acknowledged, allowed to say who they are, recognized. Loved, even, if not by readers and citizens, then at least by their own creators.

Smiley's peroration on self-abnegating goodness is the bonus of virtuous appearance that Nice Critics instantly reap when they nicely review Nice Writing. Since Kingsolver is the queen of Nice Writing, she has been the constant beneficiary of this kind of criticism. You can find a representative example of her niceness in a talk that she gave in 1993 called "Careful What You Let in the Door." It appears in *High Tide in Tucson,* which came out that same year.

Three years earlier, Kingsolver had published *Animal Dreams,* a novel that was partly about American involvement in the Nicaraguan civil war during the 1980s. Its dedication reads, "In memory of Ben Linder," a reference to Benjamin Linder, a young American engineer working in Nicaragua whom the contras killed in an ambush. In her talk, Kingsolver says:

It matters to me . . . that we citizens of the U.S. bought guns and dressed up an army that killed plain, earnest people in Nicaragua who were trying only to find peace and a kinder way of life. I wanted to bring that evil piece of history into a story, in a way that would make a reader feel sadness and dread but still keep reading, becoming convinced it was necessary to care.

There is something characteristically fishy about Kingsolver's language here. Why are all the good, murdered Nicaraguan people "plain" and "earnest"? If some of them had been complicated and ironic, then would caring readers have regarded them as expendable? And if the Nicaraguan peasantry really had been behind the Sandinista revolution, would it have been because they were trying to find "a kinder way of life," and not because the revolution offered peasants ownership of their land and the freedom to decide for themselves whether to be kind or unkind? The surfeit of sentiment rings with an absence of true conviction.

This does not bode well for fiction. You can fault Kingsolver for not knowing—or refusing to know, or not caring—that the mass of impoverished Nicaraguans astutely saw the Sandinistas as elites trying to steal their land and impose their will; or for not acknowledging that the Sandinistas were displacing and murdering Nicaragua's Miskito Indians; or for not knowing—or not caring, or not being convinced of the fact—that "Ben" Linder, whom Kingsolver never met, was carrying a rifle when he was cut down. But the writer has her politics, and she is entitled to believe that her advertisement of virtue is sufficient for her politics. In politics, certainly, rhetoric can be very effective. Yet the novelist's politics are insufficient for her art.

Gordimer or Lessing—for all their differences—would have so complicated a novel about Nicaragua that the truth about the revolution, when it finally unfolded, would have been already embedded in the novel's multilayered psychic and social world. And they would have retained, as they do, their political values. Yet *Animal Dreams* is not about character or society. It is about "serious, debatable, and painful issues": a father with Alzheimer's;

a corporation's health-threatening exploitation of a small town; class prejudice; ethnic prejudice; cruelty to animals.

Its sub-subplot of a young woman agriculturist from America named Hallie—whom we never meet—doing volunteer work in Nicaragua—where we never go—is just one heart-tugging flourish among all the others. It clinches the novel's principal plot, which is the not-terribly-gripping saga of Hallie's sister, a thirty-two-year-old woman named Codi, who goes back to her hometown to figure out who she is and what she should do with her life. (Kingsolver's books are self-help books disguised as novels.) When Codi learns that the contras murdered Hallie, she suddenly matures. Hallie's murder, she tells us, is like a "flower in the soil of another country." One woman's political assassination is another woman's step toward personal growth.

There was once an American president whose cloying promise to Americans of a "kinder, gentler nation" was a gift to anyone who wanted to prove his or her principles without acting on them. The simple derisive repetition of the phrase guaranteed the right adversarial status. Kingsolver may be a favorite figure on the left, but in truth her "kinder way of life" rhetoric spans the ideological spectrum. Who, really, is for evil corporate interests or for class or ethnic prejudice? Is there anyone who would like to go to bat for cruelty to animals, or for Alzheimer's? Kingsolver's novels are filled with indictments of people and forces that make children suffer. They are bursting with tender affirmations of motherhood. In the acknowledgments to *Pigs in Heaven,* she thanks Nancy Raincrow Pigeon and Carol Locust, among others, "who helped me understand the letter and spirit of the Indian Child Welfare Act." I dare you to give that novel a negative review.

Such a guaranteed universal appeal is why, Kingsolver might be surprised to know, she has been referred to enthusiastically in places such as the Federal Reserve Bank of New York's *Economic*

Policy Review and Management Review. According to the *ABA Journal,* a judge ordered women offenders to read *Animal Dreams.* They love Kingsolver even in the *Washington Times,* and they like her fiction even in the *Weekly Standard* ("a gentle allegorist . . . easy, flowing prose, engaging characters, and a biting wit"). And there is no reason why they shouldn't. Under the guise of a strong political stance, Kingsolver purveys a potpourri of tried-and-true soppy attitudes that are attached, with demographic precision, to an array of popular causes. She is something new: a political novelist who is careful not to step on anyone's toes. There is not a single sentiment expressed in her fiction that you could not express in an exchange with a stranger at a convention, or during a job interview, or on a first date.

But this seamlessness with the superficial rhetorical conventions of everyday life is actually a terrible disjunction from life. It is why Kingsolver's working-class characters look and sound like the idea of working-class people held by a professional couple's privileged daughter who studied music and languages at DePauw. (I mean Kingsolver.) Her working-class characters are dumb or saintly, and her young working-class women—except for her brilliant, confident, heroic fictional personae—are almost always stupid and selfish and reckless with the nail polish and mascara. They are literary tautologies: they are so much like themselves that they bear no relation to who they really are.

Kingsolver is so committed to keeping up the appearance of conventional morality that she sometimes mixes up her molasses-sweet descriptions of animals with her molasses-sweet condescension to the downtrodden. Seeing some pigs wander into her yard, the elderly Alice in *Pigs in Heaven* thinks: "The poor things are just looking for a home, like the Boat People." Underneath all the whispering of sweet nothings into the reader's ear, Kingsolver doesn't really seem to like human beings. She is sweetly lethal. It is the obverse side of her unremitting Niceness; perhaps it is the source of her Niceness. She describes her characters with an air of haughty repulsion, the way adolescents will stand in a corner at a party and quietly annihilate the other people there, until the other people come over and reveal that they do not have the power to hurt:

He was bald and red-faced and kind of bossy.

Otis is very old and bald with bad posture and big splay feet in white sneakers.

Her eyelashes were stuck together with blue mascara and sprung out all around her eyes like flower petals.

The woman has colorless flippy hair molded together with hairspray so that it all comes along when she turns her head.

Her doughy breasts in a stretched T-shirt tremble.

The manager has fat, pale hands decorated with long black hairs.

They look strange: one is shrunken-looking with over-blown masses of curly hair; another is hulky and bald, the head too big for the body.

The cousin she's just met is a thin, humpbacked woman in canvas shoes and a blue cotton dress that hangs empty in the bosom.

The woman has swollen knuckles and a stained red blouse.

This is perhaps the same icy indifference to humanity that is behind Kingsolver's portrayal of a retarded character who speaks perfect English. It is a safety measure for the preservation of the Nice Appearance of respecting retarded people: "Mom, I accidentally walked on the railroad tracks to Havasu." (The retarded character is named Buster; and Buster happens to be, Kingsolver tells us in her essay "High Tide in Tucson," the name of a real-life hermit crab she keeps as a pet.)

It is the same polar numbness, this time to social reality, that lets Kingsolver depict the evil corporation in *Animal Dreams* as leaving its lucrative position in the small town without a legal challenge. And a cognate authorial glacialness has the lower-class Native American man in that novel, Loyd Peregrina, immediately decide to abandon his decades-old business enterprise of investing in fighting cocks. Why? Because the heroic Codi, his new girlfriend from a higher social stratum—and Kingsolver's fictional persona in this novel—thinks that the spectacle of battling birds is mean and icky. Even if the income from training the birds helps Loyd to survive. This is the sort of cruelty of which the saintly-in-their-own-eyes are especially capable.

And what cold-heartedness lies behind *The Bean Trees'* subplot of a Mayan couple from Guatemala, with connections to the left-wing guerrillas, escaping from the death squads to the United States. The Guatemalan soldiers, the narrator tells us, wanted information from the couple. So the army abducted their infant child—for Kingsolver, political violence is not political violence unless it affects the adorable Turtles of the world—and threatened to give her to a presumably upper-class family unless the couple told the army what it demanded to know about their rebel comrades. This, miraculously, gave the couple the time and the opportunity to flee.

In the real Guatemala, however, during the army's onslaught against the Indians in the eighties, the army simply tortured people from whom they wanted information. They raped the wives in front of their husbands, they beat the husbands to death in front of their wives, they killed the children in front of their parents. In *The Bean Trees,* Kingsolver introduces us to a relatively

Nice death squad. For Nice Readers must not get the idea that politics has other features besides Nice Attitudes. Otherwise they might stop singing the vegetable-soup song, and get real.

IV.

From the terror in Guatemala in *The Bean Trees,* to the revolution and the counterrevolution in Nicaragua in *Animal Dreams,* to the plight of Native Americans in *Pigs in Heaven,* Kingsolver has, as she would say, "booked a return passage" to Africa and produced *The Poisonwood Bible.* Of all her books, though, her new book most closely resembles *Animal Dreams.* They both embody the full flowering of the Quindlen Effect.

I date the Quindlen Effect from December 13, 1992, though other readers might have their own favorite moments from the newspaper career of Anna Quindlen, the former *New York Times* columnist and one of the original Nice Queens. On that December day, Quindlen published a scathingly indignant editorial comment on the Glen Ridge sex assault trial, in which four male high school students were accused of sexually assaulting a twenty-one-year-old retarded woman.

True to her niche, Quindlen attacked with scathing indignation actions that no sane *Times* reader would ever defend. No neutral observer would defend four boys who manipulated a retarded girl into performing oral sex on them and inserted a broomstick and then a bat into her vagina; no more than any neutral observer would defend death squads or evil corporations. But Quindlen went on. She displayed a surfeit of sentiment ringing with an absence of true feeling that was downright Kingsolverian: "Most neighborhoods are divided into three kinds of children: those who torture the slow kid, those very few who defend her, and the great majority, who stand silent." But the great majority of teenagers in Glen Ridge, New Jersey, did not stand silent as the assault took place. The assault took place in a basement, and the great majority knew nothing about it. And most neighborhoods are really not like that.

During that time, though, there was a place where the neighborhoods really had deteriorated. Right next to Quindlen's commentary, the *Times* published an essay by the Croatian writer Slavenka Drakulic exposing the mass rapes of Bosnian Muslim women by Bosnian Serb men. Drakulic was not attacking actions that everyone already despised; she was exposing actions that few Americans knew were happening. Her essay included chilling first-person descriptions of rape and mutilation and murder in Bosnia. The last account, given by a sixteen-year-old girl, ended with a paragraph that was also the final paragraph of Drakulic's piece: "I would like to be a mother some day. But how? In my world, men represent terrible violence and pain. I cannot control that feeling."

Looking at the op-ed page that morning, it was hard to avoid the implication that it had a theme. With Drakulic's article right there alongside Quindlen's article, the point was made that the male violence in Bosnia and the male violence in that suburban basement were phases of the same moral phenomenon. The analogy was appalling, and not only owing to its childish moral equivalence. It was appalling also because the moral equivalence promoted the idea that condemning the male violence at home would suffice as a response to the male violence abroad. (And of course we never did fight the violence in Bosnia, not until it was too late.) In the hands of monsters of empathy such as Anna Quindlen, the immediate preoccupations of the American self subjugate and domesticate and assimilate every distant tragedy.

Lenin famously declared that imperialism was the final stage of capitalism. He was wrong. A narcissistic capitalism, in fact, is the final stage of imperialism. Kingsolver is the bold anti-imperialist who fled to sunny Spain in order to escape government repression in Arizona during the Gulf war. And she is also the narcissist-imperialist par excellence. For the conclusion of *Animal Dreams* depicts an inversion based on a Quindlen-like connection. Kingsolver transforms the contra helicopters that mow down plain, earnest people in Nicaragua into the helicopter in which Codi's mother died after giving birth to Hallie. If it had not been for Hallie's letters describing those helicopters, we learn, Codi would never have remembered seeing her mother taken up in the helicopter. This was a memory that she needed to recover so that she suddenly could become an adult. Thus Hallie's death is redeemed by Codi's finally getting a life. Black night in Nicaragua; morning in America.

Kingsolver has perfected the Quindlen Effect in *The Poisonwood Bible*. The novel's cartoonish mainspring is a tyrannical Baptist missionary named Nathan Price, who takes up residence in the Congo in the late 1950s with his wife, Orleanna, and their four daughters. Told by Orleanna and each of her daughters in turn, *The Poisonwood Bible* portrays Nathan's fanatical insensitivity to the Congolese, which alienates his small congregation, resulting in the death of his youngest daughter, Ruth May (the children again), and in his own madness, and in the disintegration of the family.

The novel has a silver lining, though. The silver lining is the indignant Kingsolver's most characteristic device. The other daughters—the bigoted right-wing Rachel; the sensitive and conscientious Leah; Leah's twin, the hemiplegic clairvoyant genius and verbal prodigy Adahall—come into their own by novel's end. In the course of all this, we also enjoy saintly glimpses of Patrice Lumumba, Congo's first democratically elected prime minister, whose probable murder by Mobutu's men got an enthusiastic green light and support from an Eisenhower worried about Lumumba's alliance with the Soviet Union.

"There is wisdom in every sentence," wrote the editors of *The New York Times Book Review* about *The Poisonwood Bible*. I hope they are not referring to the analogy that Kingsolver makes between Nathan's harshness toward the women in his family, and Belgium, whose King Leopold annexed the Congo in 1901, and cold-war America. As Orleanna puts it, again and again:

And where was I, the girl or woman called Orleanna, as we traveled those roads. . . . Swallowed by Nathan's mission, body and soul. Occupied as if by a foreign power. . . . This is how conquest occurs. . . .

Nathan was something that happened to us, as devastating in its way as the burning roof that fell on the family Mwanza; with our faces scarred by hell and brimstone we still had to track our course. . . . But his kind will always lose in the end. I know this, and now I know why. Whether it's wife or nation they occupy, their mistake is the same: they stand still, and their stake moves underneath them. . . . A territory is only possessed for a moment in time. . . . What does Okinawa remember of its fall? Forbidden to make engines of war, Japan made automobiles instead, and won the world. It all moves on. The great Delaware moves on, while Mr. Washington himself is no longer even what you'd call good compost. The Congo River, being of a different temperament, drowned most of its conquerors outright. . . . Call it oppression, complicity, stupefaction, call it what you like, it doesn't matter. Africa swallowed the conqueror's music and sang a new song of her own.

Wisdom in every sentence. And here is Leah on the same theme:

> Anatole explained it this way: Like a princess in a story, Congo was born too rich for her own good, and attracted attention far and wide from men who desire to rob her blind. The United States has now become the husband of Zaire's economy, and not a very nice one. Exploitive and condescending. . . .
> "Oh, I understand that kind of marriage all right," I said. "I grew up witnessing one just like it."

The reduction of history to an afternoon with Oprah is bad enough. But it is really extraordinary, is it not, that our very own Gordimer has written a "political novel" about Africa that does not refer to the present-day shattering events in Africa. In *The Poisonwood Bible,* we hear a lot about how American men, especially bad American Baptist missionary men, physically abuse their wives and daughters (though, as ever, Kingsolver is too nice to portray the abuse). Yet we do not get the slightest reference, or the most veiled allusion, to the Rwandan genocide and its ongoing blood-drenched aftermath, one of the least nice events in modern history, in which even the children were killed. For Kingsolver, Africa is happily singing "a new song of her own." Something like the vegetable-soup song.

In *The Poisonwood Bible,* instead of the momentous present, Kingsolver scavenges for heart-rending bulletins from the past. It is all so easy, this sentimental carpetbagging of a far-away history. We hear about how Belgian overseers on the rubber plantations disciplined their Congolese workers by cutting off their hands. About how the Belgians jailed Lumumba at one point, and how he miraculously "got out" in time for the elections. What King-

solver doesn't tell her readers is that by 1959, when her novel begins, such cruelty had been defunct for over fifty years. (For the
amputation of hands as a widespread instrument of torture, you
must look to contemporary Sierra Leone.)

In 1908, the Belgian parliament bought the Congo from King
Leopold as a response to the international outcry against the
atrocities that Belgian companies had been committing on the
Congolese. By 1959, the Belgian Congo had the highest literacy
rate and the most widespread health care of any European colony.
Almost all of those improvements had to do with the work of
missionaries. Most of the missionaries were Catholic, but some
were Protestant like Nathan Price. And Lumumba did not magi-
cally "get out" of jail in time to get elected prime minister. The
Belgians let him out, knowing full well that he was going to win.

This is not to say, this is really not to say, that the Europeans
did not do atrocious things in Africa right up to decolonization,
or that Belgium did not display calamitous self-interest in rushing Congo's independence when the colony was completely un-
prepared for it. (The Belgians had prohibited the Congolese from
obtaining a university education, and when independence came
there was not a single trained administrator or military officer.) It
is also not to say that Europe and the United States do not have
to answer for some portion of Africa's ordeal. But it is Kingsolver
who is not playing fair with her readers.

For again she substitutes the image of goodness for honest
representations. Almost every reviewer has rightly praised her
beautiful evocation of the African landscape and her vivid treatment of African life; but not a single reviewer I read mentioned
the twenty-eight-book bibliography that Kingsolver obviously
felt obligated to include at the end of her novel, a list with books
such as *The Accidental Anthropologist, Congo Trails, Congo Cauldron,
The River Congo, Back to the Congo, Travels in West Africa, Swimming*

in the Congo, On the Edge of the Primeval Forest. Many of these books are travel books containing beautiful evocations of the African landscape and exhilarated treatments of African life. The influence of this apolitical, upbeat ethnography accounts for the difference in the style of Kingsolver's new novel. And it is why *The Poisonwood Bible* is so distant from its subject.

Still, the Nice Writing has not disappeared, and it extends its usual protections. You would not know from any of the reviews also that all the women in the family express the same tough ironic contempt for Nathan. Here is Ruth May: "'Africa has a million souls,' is what Father told him. And Father ought to know, for he's out to save them all." This is presented as the thought of a five-year-old girl, who is supposed to be brutally suppressed by her authoritarian father.

"Ultimately," the *Times* editors wrote, summarizing John Leonard's review in their "Editor's Choice" citation of Kingsolver's novel, "this is a novel of character; the women discover themselves as they lose faith in Price." But the women in *The Poisonwood Bible* are onto their father's hypocrisy from the very beginning of the book. They express their skepticism in the same jaunty sarcastic tone, which is the identical tone Kingsolver used for her earlier fictional personae, Taylor and Codi. This is the fifteen-year-old Rachel: "[Father] was getting that look he gets, oh boy, like Here comes Moses tromping down off of Mount Syanide with ten fresh ways to wreck your life." This is the fourteen-year-old Leah, supposedly in her father's thrall more than her sisters: "'Heavenly Father, deliver us,' I said, although I didn't care for this new angle . . . what was this business of being delivered through hardships?" This is the fourteen-year-old Adah, who refers sardonically to Nathan as "Our Father" and "Reverend": "When the Spirit passed through him he groaned, throwing body and soul into this weekly purge. The 'Amen enema,' as I call it. My palindrome for the Reverend." If this is the story of women struggling for psychic autonomy, they do not have all that much work to do.

V.

Barbara Kingsolver does not finally give a hoot about Africa. She does not care about Africa (I mean, intelligently and respectfully care, with a sense of its otherness and its complexity) any more than she cared about the simple folk of Nicaragua. That is why the penultimate climax of *The Poisonwood Bible* is not about Africa. It is about our very own Gordimer's favorite domestic themes: cruelty to children and cruelty to animals. Thus her novel begins its climax in a scene depicting the Congolese villagers engaged in a hunt. They set the brush on fire and herd the animals inside the flames.

> For every animal struck down, there rose an equal and opposite cry of human jubilation. . . . Of the large animals who came through the fire—bushbuck, warthog, antelope—few escaped. Others would not come out and so they burned: small flame-feathered birds, the churning insects, and a few female baboons who had managed against all odds to carry their pregnancies through the drought. With their bellies underslung with precious clinging babies, they loped behind the heavy-maned males, who would try to save themselves, but on reaching the curtain of flame where the others passed through, they drew up short. Crouched low. Understanding no choice but to burn with their children.

This breaks new ground in monster empathy. Abusive husbands are like conquering countries; mothers and children are the same whether human or animal. Killing is killing. And although, as Kingsolver herself tells us, the villagers are starving, she goes on to explain that this massacre was so cruel that it brought down upon the village a streak of terrible luck.

It is an icy marvel, this spectacle of a writer who can manipulatively wax so emotional and with such impressive virtue over the killing of animals by starving villagers in a place where, in reality, hundreds of thousands of people had just been exterminated. In a place where, perhaps at the very moment Kingsolver was writing her book, men were raping and murdering wives in front of their husbands (those selfish "heavy-maned males"), and beating the fathers to death in front of the mothers, and killing the children in front of their parents.

But Kingsolver has too much respect for other cultures to refer to the bad things that happen in them. Other cultures have different attitudes toward life and death. Through Adah, who later becomes a medical researcher—she works on the AIDS virus *and* the Ebola virus!—Kingsolver guides us through African values:

> People are *bantu*; the singular is *muntu*. *Muntu* does not mean exactly the same as person, though, because it describes a living person, a dead one, or someone not yet born. *Muntu* persists through all those conditions unchanged. . . . The transition from spirit to body and back again is merely a venture.
>
> In the world, the carrying capacity of humans is limited. History holds all things in the balance, including large hopes and short lives. . . . Africa has a thousand ways of cleansing itself. Driver ants, Ebola virus, acquired immune deficiency syndrome: all these are brooms devised by nature to sweep a small clearing very well . . . the race between predator and prey remains exquisitely neck and neck.

In Africa, then, death is a state of mind. There they are used to dying, and dying is so exquisitely good for them. The *Times* editors enthusiastically took this up in their citation: "Perhaps [*The Poisonwood Bible's*] greatest character is collective, the Congolese, whose perfect adaptation to the harshness of their lives amid drought, hunger, pests and diseases is simply beautiful." What a ravishing, talented, instinctive, unself-conscious race of people. And how beautiful is their extinction!

In Kingsolver's Africa, only her intrepid heroines, not the Africans themselves, get the burdensome dignity of moral struggle, confusion, and anguish. Here is Leah, who has chosen to live in Africa with her Congolese husband:

> I rock back and forth on my chair like a baby, craving so many impossible things: justice, forgiveness, redemption. I crave to stop bearing all the wounds of this place on my own narrow body. But I also want to be a person who stays, who goes on feeling anguish where anguish is due. I want to belong to somewhere, damn it. To scrub the hundred years' war off this white skin till there's nothing left and I can walk out among my neighbors wearing raw sinew and bone, like they do.

But enough of this frigid treacle. Let me tell you a story about my family, and this time I am writing the truth. My grandfather, Saul Siegel, who died a few months ago at the age of ninety-two, was with UNICEF in the Belgian Congo in 1960, when Congo got its independence. He was there during the riots and the strife and the civil war, and he stayed for some time after the United States installed Mobutu. I could not even begin to describe the lives that he saved and the good that he did. He knew that true goodness is the virtue that dare not speak its name. He knew all about the cold, calculating phonies who spray their virtue into your eyes like mace, and also about the cowards and the fools who abet them to aid themselves. I loved him very much. I sat next to his bed and watched him die as he struggled to keep breathing. I saw the light start to fade from his beautiful green eyes, and I let him pull me toward him by my shirt with his trembling hands so that he could whisper to me his farewell. With my heart full of love and grief and terror, I leaned toward him, and he pulled himself up a little and he rasped softly, and then he screamed: "Get Kingsolver!"

I did it again. I lied. I am sorry, but I cannot resist the temptation. The rewards are so great. And the words are so cheap.

Television and the Pope

MANY CATHODE-ILLUMINATED YEARS have passed since the term "infotainment" settled into reality and started appearing without quotation marks. The devolution of the evening news into a hybrid sort of entertainment is an old tale. In its original form, it simply meant that hard news stories would still be broadcast, but that there would be fewer of them, and more segments about lifestyle issues, celebrity shenanigans, and the like. How quaint it all was. Now you almost long for the bygone sense of alarm that you felt when the networks started to be All About You; when serious reports about eroding coastlines started giving way to more serious reports about expanding waistlines. Consider the past few weeks, in which American television discovered God.

First you had the television newspeople popping up in Atlanta and transforming themselves into evangelical Christians in order to perform—not report—the story of Ashley Smith, who claimed that God had used her as a divine instrument in his (disconcertingly messy) plan to bring a sinner into the light. Then they all piled into their shiny, decaled, satellite-topped vans and sped down to Florida, where this time they didn't so much perform as sensationally stage—and again, not exactly report—the conflict between the husband and the parents of poor Terri Schiavo, and the conflict between the will of God and the will of the state court. And then it was off to Rome.

In the new world capital of sacred feeling, the television newspeople deftly began to assimilate, like Method actors studiously researching a character's circumstances and environment. It was not long before all these media sophisticates began to speak about John Paul II's life and death in the manner of Calabrian peasant women. For CBS's Harry Smith, ensconced in this ancient place renowned for its beautiful and sunny days, "it's been a kind of miraculous week in its own way, because it's been beautiful and sunny." Before the pope's dying, death, funeral, and entombment, you can bet your cable subscription that most, if not all, of the talking heads converging on the Eternal City thought that a pectoral cross was something you did at the gym. But they were all Catholics now.

Miracles abounded. With astonishing verisimilitude, the newscasters spoke sentimentally, reverentially, about every single thing, no matter how trivial or dogmatic or cloying or cunning, that the late pope had said or done. Despite the fact that this church had its institutional origins in the Middle Ages, the funeral was, they insisted, unprecedented. For CBS's Allen Pizzey, the sheer number of people gathered in St. Peter's Square was itself a "miracle" that would easily serve as one of the two wonders the pope had to knock out of the park if he was to gain admission to sainthood. For CNN's Anderson Cooper, looking at the crowds lingering in the square after the funeral mass was finished, the experience of being there was so, like, spiritual: "This is the kind of energy, the kind of passion, the kind of love which we have witnessed." Most of the experts who were paraded before the cameras were Catholic priests. All of them turned out to have loved and admired the pope greatly.

After nearly two weeks of obsessive round-the-clock coverage of the passing of John Paul II, it is clear that there is no longer a crisis in the ratio of hard news to soft news. Hard news has gone the way of "snow" at the end of a television channel's broadcast day. The delivery of the news is itself an event that now should be reported in some meta-news format. Maybe this accounts for the popularity of Jon Stewart's real-but-not-real send-ups of the news.

The talking heads are no longer content to sit back and report. Like the reality-show participants who can't bear to sit back and watch TV drama but have to be part of it; like the bloggers who broadcast their days and nights; like the memoirists; like the self-dramatizing performance artists; like that friend of yours who responds to every comment you make about world affairs with a story from his own life that illustrates each international event—like so many people nowadays who live inside their heads, the talking heads are trapped in the belief that they are experiencing what they are merely covering. They report the news as if they are making it.

Say what you will about the inaccuracy or the slantedness of mainstream print organs, a schism yawns between print and television news that gapes even wider than the split between the Roman and Eastern churches. Maybe because we take for granted the sharp differences between the two mediums, we no longer see that the differences are becoming more extreme. But the coverage of the pope depressingly demonstrated that television news has mutated from viewer-centered stories to reporter-centered stories. The anchor is dead. Long live the anchor!

We get uncomfortable and occasionally outraged when we feel that some public figure has been "acting," or that a resonant public event has been "staged" in order to manipulate our feelings, in the manner of Bush's "Top Gun" landing on that aircraft carrier. We hear Reagan described as the Great Communicator and some of us roll our eyes, because we know that "communicate" is often a sunny synonym for "obfuscate." At the pope's funeral, however, you could tune in to CNN and hear international correspondent Jonathan Mann enthusiastically seconding an archbishop's shrewd counsel that "the next pope is going to have to be a communicator." The elementary journalistic response to such a prescription should have been either to let the statement stand by itself or to let viewers know that Mann knew—in his journalist's role as the vicar of common sense—what contrapuntal possibilities were lurking behind the term "communicator." But media submission came to the archbishop as Mann endorsed his sentiments.

Later we heard Alessio Vinci, CNN's Vatican correspondent, celebrate the fact that "this is a pope who uses symbols and symbolism in order to bridge those churches and those religions together." A slight inflection of integrity and professional skill, and you could hear a different kind of journalist carefully creating a space for the possibility that this was a pope who used symbols and symbolism as pretexts for virtuous inaction. Anderson Cooper, through whose body the funeral "sent chills," conceded that many people disagreed with the pope's teachings, "but they see him as a man who preached compassion, who preached tolerance and love." But was the fact that the pope preached these virtues enough to make his critics satisfied with his "teachings"? Cooper didn't create a space for that possibility. These days a television correspondent's main qualification is the ability to give the impression that he or she is feeling deeply.

This was an insult not just to non-Catholics, but also to Catholics who cherish their faith but also prize their critical stance toward the church (a stance that some traditions of Catholic thought have nourished). There was something chilling about CNN's sudden cessation of professional detachment. It covered the death of the pope as I imagine the media of Eastern Europe covered the death of Stalin. (No, I am not comparing the great enemy of communism to the great hero of communism.) For Mann, a supposedly secular representative of an allegedly secular news organization presumably dedicated to the presentation of unaffiliated facts, the totalizing worldwide broadcast of the pope's death and its aftermath meant that Catholic "themes are being taught to the world that doesn't know it," the main theme being that "Christ is available to all, and that man is mortal but has the promise of everlasting life." You yearned for a commercial break, which in this context would have had the liberating effect of an aria by Mozart. But Mann pressed on. In a state of near rapture, he suddenly related his own epiphany: "If you wanted . . . a moment and experience that would spread what the Catholic Church has been teaching for two thousand years to people who don't normally hear it from the church, this is the ceremony, this is the event, this is the message." Hallelujah.

THERE HAS BEEN SOME CRITICISM of how news organizations exploited the occasion in Rome, but I have yet to see anyone remark that the trinity of recent events—Saint Ashley, Saint Terri, and the pope—exemplified a new reality in the delivery of the news in general. The television newspeople's fluid inhabiting of the story, which is by definition always other people's story, was not merely pandering to a newly discovered religious market, or a nervous response to charges of "liberal" bias against religion. (Nobody had better make that accusation again.) Above all, it meant that stories About You, once intended to bring the news to more viewers, had been usurped. Now the television people were reporting real news in a way that made every event, no matter how "hard," a story that you experienced through the vicarious empathizing of the anchors and their cast of dozens. They were Us. And we were Them.

Call it newsaoke—karaoke with deadlines. The worst—or most gifted, depending on what qualities you are measuring—practitioners of newsaoke are to be found on CNN. The networks had their share of oozing credulity, but nothing could surpass the Cable News Network, which for the duration of the ceremonies in Rome transformed itself into the Catholic News Network. This was perhaps inevitable, given the fact that a round-the-clock station devoted exclusively to news would inevitably try to adapt the news to all the genres it was competing against: drama, comedy, action-adventure, confessional talk show, and so forth. And maybe the network's mandate of eternal watchfulness had gone to its head, causing it to imagine that it was doing God's work in a godless world: according to CNN correspondent John Allen, "CNN and the papacy of John Paul II, in a sense, grew up together."

Some print journalists pointed out the irony (if not the offense) of the pope spending so much of his reign traveling the globe apologizing to everybody for centuries of church intolerance, stupidity, and slaughter. But the talking heads represented the apologies as crescendos of authentic feeling that actually accomplished the goals the church hoped to achieve by making them. Christiane Amanpour earnestly related that the pope had apologized to the Muslims for the "excesses of the Crusades"—though not for the Crusades themselves—and also to the Jews for the Holocaust. She then solemnly intoned that during John Paul's pontificate the Catholic Church had apologized to the Eastern Orthodox Church, and the Eastern Orthodox Church had apologized to the Catholic Church, for the schism that had occurred between them in the eleventh century, though neither set of apologies had closed the schism. This persistent discord between Catholicism and Eastern Orthodox Christians was, she said, "the great sorrow of the pope's life," but neither she nor anybody else on television bothered to explain what the schism was really about, or what steps the pope might have taken to defy church doctrine and overcome it. There was little time for such nuances. There were still the matters of the Inquisition and the historical anti-Semitism that led to the Holocaust, and John Allen eagerly reminded us that this pope made sure to apologize for them, too. Also for the *tsuris* with Galileo.

Meanwhile, an archbishop working as a consultant to CNN—there's a phenomenon—was able to show that the injuries were not all one-sided. Gerhard Schroeder himself had apologized to the Catholic Church, and also to the Polish people, for Germany's failure to come to the aid of Solidarity during the revolt against Soviet rule. All these apologies, the CNN theatrical troupe assured us, were "amazing" and "extraordinary" acts of reconciliation on the part of this pope, who also, we were told reverentially, had the courage actually to set foot in a synagogue, and also in a mosque. You almost felt like you should apologize to the church for making it feel so guilty that it had to do so much apologizing. Was the thing with Galileo really *that* bad?

There were moments of sanity, or at least an occasional recognition that the performance had gone too far. Toward the end of CNN's run in Rome, the network even brought in someone whose very presence might imply a criticism of this pope's attitudes toward women and human sexuality, one Claudia Spadazzi, an Italian gynecologist. Spadazzi assured viewers that far from being in thrall to the church, Rome was a great city "where there are many different realities." Of course, she couldn't have been directly critical of John Paul. (That would have been a pope smear.) And any such old-fashioned journalistic independence quickly collapsed under the weight of having to turn in the most maudlin reading of events possible. When Jeff Greenfield tried to make the point that the massive demonstration of affection in St. Peter's Square did not necessarily signify broad support for the pope's more intransigent positions, Wolf Blitzer reined him in: "And yet at the same time, Jeff, the outpouring of emotion that we saw today involving the pope's funeral does involve an extraordinarily strong bond. You have to, I think, agree with that." You just have to.

By that point, only Christ himself could have harrowed the CNN crowd into some semblance of rational skepticism and detachment. For the pope had barely arrived in heaven when he seemed to swing into action. Amanpour credited him with the handshake between the Israeli president and the Syrian president: "Maybe it's the spirit of John Paul." "Amazing," agreed Cooper, who asked the archbishop-consultant if the pope was watching from heaven. "Certainly," said the archbishop, pleased to offer his expertise in the afterlife department. And the archbishop added that the pope watching from the sky "is pleased at the great number of young people who are here." But what about Schiavo, Sontag, Bellow, Hunter Thompson, Grace Kelly's husband, and all the other new arrivals? What about a special two-hour "edition" with the dead on *Larry King Live*? It would be, as they say in the kingdom of television, ratings heaven.

Updike's Bech

EVERYONE DOES EVERYONE ELSE. Gay men wrote the classic boy-girl love songs; Jewish screenwriters modeled the ideal American type on their notion of the ideal WASP. Blacks supplied Jewish songwriters with their rhythms; Jewish songwriters gave black jazz musicians their standards. White suburbanites do black ghetto kids; black college kids do the white middle class; professional women mime the manner of executive men; executive men copy the empathetic style of successful women—and on and on and on. After all the historical brutalities and injuries, our national heart is ultimately a miscegenating organ. A kind of spiritual transvestism is woven into our daily existence. No wonder the word "celebrity" is almost synonymous with the word "actor."

Interestingly, in American speech, the verb "to do" means not only to impersonate but to have sexual intercourse with and to kill, as if sex and murder were different phases of the desire to be another person. Perhaps the very act of impersonation is a mastery of the homicidal impulse or a sublimated lust. These verbal echoes are significant because the true Other is never safe in America. Our assimilations of race, religion, ethnicity, gender, sexuality repress the profoundly alien element in life.

For the true Other is we ourselves, we who are so different and other than what we expect. This incalculable us-ness persists through all our hearty embraces of seemingly alien identities. It's our own strangeness that makes us fear alienness in the first place and, although popular culture has been the gratifying treasure house of commingling othernesses, literature is the place where the act of impersonation goes beyond superficial inhabitings into the impersonator's own perplexing and perplexed nature.

There have not been many memorable impersonations in classic American fiction: Jim in Mark Twain's *Huckleberry Finn;* the multiple personalities in Herman Melville's "The Confidence Man"; Theodore Dreiser's Sister Carrie; arguably, J. D. Salinger's Holden Caulfield (the adult doing the adolescent); the Jewish Saul Bellow's WASPish Henderson. Of course, more and more novelists try their hands at inhabiting figures in extremis: Siamese twins or explorers dying on mountain peaks, for example. But these characters are often bloodless exotic essences. A real impersonation requires a palpable everyday existence.

John Updike's impersonation of an American Jewish writer named Henry Bech, an authentic impersonation if ever there was one, has been going on for almost forty years. It is the WASP version of blackface. The twenty previously published Bech stories, now collected in one volume—not to mention the several "interviews" of Updike by his creation not included here—make up one of the weirdest, most audacious and provocative occasions in American literary history. And yet these stories, bound into a totality, have attracted little attention to Updike's singular enterprise.

There are a few possible reasons for such neglect, the first simply being that a WASP author semisatirically inhabiting a Jewish character doesn't have the same daring piquancy that it did when Updike published his first Bech story, "The Bulgarian Poetess," nearly forty years ago, in 1964. Besides, with American Jewish books like *The Talmud and the Internet,* with an American Jewish novelist recently comparing Israel to a lost wallet on the

New York Times op-ed page, where is the satirist who could outdo the often ridiculous American Jewish literary reality of our day? Now if a gay author were to semisatirically inhabit a straight author, or vice versa; or a male author send up contemporary feminist and postfeminist attitudes in the person of a female character; or a female author adopt the soft, sensitive, virtue-conscious persona of the new Machiavellian male—these literary feats would attract attention. What a blessing they would be. But everyone seems too careful nowadays for such imaginative improprieties.

There is also, with regard to the stunning indifference with which *The Complete Henry Bech* has been received, the question of literary reputation. Updike puts it well in the short story "Bech Presides," in which he describes the curious literary dynamic that attends authorial duration. The longer an author lives and the less he publishes, the more burnished his or her reputation becomes: "the mud of a clinging fame. . . . Such an honorable retreat could go on forever, thanks to modern medicine." Updike, like some other aging American literary giants, continues to flourish, and unlike the famously fallow Bech, he publishes a great deal. Rich, famous, much-laureled, Updike continues to be so much with us that it is easy to take him for granted.

The necessity for the artist to remain unappeased by fame and wealth: this is one door Updike knows well, and it is the door through which Bech makes his entrance. "The Bulgarian Poetess" appeared immediately after Updike's *The Centaur* won a National Book Award in 1963 and made famous its thirty-one-year-old author, already widely acclaimed for two wonderful volumes of short stories. Fame is a (cherished) calamity, especially for artists. Hapless, blocked, desublimated Bech, who at one point receives "the Melville Medal, awarded every five years to that American author who has maintained the most meaningful silence," seems to have provided his creator fame-therapy. Bech has kept Updike down in the foul rag-and-bone shop of existential toils.

Yet Bech prevails, becoming more and more distinguished, finally in "Bech and the Bounty of Sweden" (probably the worst story in this series) winning the Nobel Prize ("'BECH WHO-DAT???' was the *Daily News'* front-page headline"). In Yiddish literature, the schlemiel performed the identical cathartic function of turning chronic failure into a weapon of ultimate success. With Bech, Updike stole from Yiddish culture one of its star figures and appropriated one of that culture's driving engines: the hardship at the heart of things.

Of course, the impulse to savor, even exaggerate, the Other's ordeal is partly behind such a cultural appropriation. Bech almost theologically keeps Updike's mortal coils warm through the reminder of ultimate human failure: love ebbs, life ends, the work of art always falls short of its conception. But Bech also represents, through the decades of his existence, the wish of his triumphant creator for the failure of Updike's rivals. It might seem like an obscure footnote now, but by 1964, American Jewish authors like Norman Mailer, Bernard Malamud, and Philip Roth were seizing the ground once occupied by Ernest Hemingway, F. Scott Fitzgerald, and William Faulkner. Leading the pack was Bellow, and it's no coincidence that "The Bulgarian Poetess" came out in the same year as *Herzog,* Bellow's own satire on, but also celebration of, the urban Jewish male intellectual.

In *Herzog,* Bellow patented one of the saliences of his style: the casual philosophical generalization as a storytelling springboard. And here in "The Bulgarian Poetess" is Updike, beginning sections of the story with "Men traveling alone develop a romantic vertigo" and "Actuality is a running impoverishment of possibility." Strangely, marvelously, these ploys poke fun at Bellow's style while reiterating Bellow's satire on just such a mode of intellectualizing, and they duplicate Bellow's habit of, at the very same time, intellectualizing in a serious, poetic way. There is a modest truth and beauty to both of Updike's poetically stated propositions. Bellow begins as his target and grows into his inspiration.

Is there a writer at work today who has read his rivals as viscerally and intelligently as Updike once did his and then acted on it? Is anyone having serious literary fun anymore? These Bech stories, uneven, though usually sharp and witty, sometimes profound and always original, seem on the surface to be the *divertissements* of an author blowing off extra steam, but Updike is also out to accomplish some meaningful business. In his warm, though somewhat nonplussed introduction to this volume, late novelist and critic Malcolm Bradbury writes that for Updike, Bech has represented the alienated counterpoint to the mainstream average American Rabbit Angstrom, the hero of Updike's most famous series of novels. Updike, according to Bradbury, "needed a second alter ego, rather less wholesome." Bech, Bradbury goes on to say, "comes from the counter-strand of American fiction, the dissenting, immigrant, anguished and extreme."

Maybe someone should have pointed out to Bradbury the word "angst" in Rabbit's last name. Bradbury seems to have been guided by a prejudice; he seems to have some British writers' idea of the Jewish writer as a kind of two-legged id, dashing around in plaids and dark glasses, flicking cigar ashes on all the conventional consolations. "Dissenting," "anguished," and "extreme" describe just about every great American writer from Nathaniel Hawthorne and Twain and Melville up through Stephen Crane, Dreiser, Hemingway, Fitzgerald, and Faulkner. And great artists are always immigrants. They are not born in a literal place; they are born again and again in their daily immigrations. Certainly postwar American Jewish writers introduced into American fiction a special style of dissent, of anguish, of extreme imaginings, but Updike pilfers these energies and gives them his sensibility. He turns the American Jewish writers of his generation inside out. He assimilates them to his own WASPish, northeastern, suburban sensibility.

THE COMPLETE HENRY BECH comprises three previously published collections of Bech short stories with a kind of coda, "His Oeuvre," the final tale in this volume. Updike takes Bech through a rough comic spectrum of worldly encounters: smoking pot with a former WASP student who reintroduces himself to the wry Jewish author one summer's day on Martha's Vineyard ("I bet you don't remember who I am"; "Let me guess. You're not Sabu, and you're not Freddie Bartholomew"); touring what was once known as the Third World ("in his role as ambassador from the kingdom of stupid questions"); exchanging rapid-fire ripostes with his hip upper-class British girlfriend in the "swinging" London of the seventies ("Merissa: 'I'm terribly tired of being white'; Bech: 'But you're so good at it'").

We find him in Israel with his WASP wife, where he resents her awkward Christian ardor and its ebullient assimilation of the Holy Land ("'Jerusalem,' Bea said, 'belongs to everybody'"); we find him in Scotland with his WASP wife, where she resents his cheerful Jewish gloom and its ebullient assimilation of her ancestral home ("'That's the point,' Bech said. 'They moved the poor crofters out and then burned their cottages'"); and we encounter him in numerous other outlandish situations. But as the Bech stories proceed, Bech's American Jewish style of dissent, anguish, and extremism shades poetically into Updike's special turf of domestic crises, of transcendental longings, of adultery as the apple in the modern Eden. Bech is Updike's answer to the charge of suburban complacency and empty aestheticism first leveled against him almost forty years ago by—you should pardon the expression—the Jewish literary establishment at the time, headquartered in the offices of *Commentary* magazine, among other places.

Updike's revenge is as diabolically ingenious as Shylock's. "You want complacent?" he seems to be saying; "Here's complacent." "You don't like my lavish style? Then choke on it." The first Bech stories have Bech touring communist Russia and Eastern Europe for the State Department, as if Updike wanted to send his Jewish writer back to where the parents of his rivals (Bellow's, for example, and Herzog's) came from, as if he wanted Bech to begin in the high-modernist land of radical skepticism from which the hanging judges of *Commentary* had once condemned Updike himself. Bech finds no occasion for political reckoning or metaphysical irony in these extreme circumstances. He ends up falling in love, betraying someone's heart, witnessing adultery, longing for a familiarity of feeling that he has never experienced as familiar. He is like Rabbit, but from the Bronx and with a City College education. (In fact, Bech attended NYU on the GI Bill.)

What evocation of dark conditions there is in these Eastern European stories comes obliquely, captured in a net of domestic emotions, soaked in shimmering poetic details, and under absolute literary control. Soviet Russia "must be the only country in the world you can be homesick for while you're still in it." In Romania, Bech feels that "there had been a tough and heroic naiveté in Russia that he missed here, where something shrugging and effete seemed to leave room for a vein of energetic evil." One can imagine Irving Howe or Norman Podhoretz— two of Updike's most dismissive critics—pouncing on the taming literary superfluity of "energetic." How could evil ever be anything but energetic? The qualifying addition seems like a sunny subtraction.

Tug on "energetic" and the whole sentence appears to unravel, like the balding fabric on a comfortable old armchair. It descends by stages into cushy nuance: "a vein of"; "seemed to leave room for"; "something shrugging." But what might seem like a self-satisfied optimism is a refraction of Updike's true sympathetic voice. It is the voice of a country that pushes its lucky, capacious idiom into the history-scarred world. It is the voice of an author whose seeming complacency is actually his country's invincible innocence, which measures evil on its own scale of pain and therefore has had less tolerance for the mass organization of evil.

This voice also has its own sadness, not to say its anguish. A troubling tension tears quietly at Updike's prose. In the lush miracle of his physical details, you glimpse the American dream that often succeeds in protecting happiness from history; in his patterns of lust and possession and disintegrating loss, you feel the widening depression induced by the American illusion of unbroken happiness. Updike titled his second novel *The Centaur,* and his fiction is centaur-like: one half of the creature is the immanence glowing at the heart of American expectations, the eternity in a grain of quotidian detail; the other is the harsh, chilly psychology of blown expectations, of an immanence that never arrives. This is why critics react so acidly to Updike: encountering his artistic tensions, they find themselves confronted with American paradoxes.

Assimilated to a defiant, middle-class voice, Bech turns up in the affluent suburb of Ossining, New York, the fictional domain and actual home of John Cheever, where he meets Johnny Hake, one of Cheever's most famous characters, and commits adultery, the metaphorical quiddity of Updike's fictional world. In a much later story, Updike even appropriates the theme of the Holocaust.

This is from the opening pages of "Bech in Czech," which finds Bech visiting communist Czechoslovakia.

> The Americans had acquired the building [the American ambassador's residence] and its grounds after the war, before Czechoslovakia went quite so Communist. . . . For a Jew, to move through postwar Europe is to move through hordes of ghosts, vast animated crowds that, since 1945, are not there, not there at all—up in smoke. The feathery touch of the mysteriously absent is felt on all sides."

Similarly, in Prague's old Jewish cemetery, Updike describes "the tombstones jumbled together like giant cards in a deck being shuffled."

"Quite so Communist"; "the feathery touch of the mysteriously absent"; "like giant cards in a deck being shuffled"—this detached domesticating rhetoric, this irritating fluency amounts to an extreme, dissenting assault on a Jewish passion and obsession. As if all that were not irreverent enough, Updike inserts a Jewish *bête noire*, T. S. Eliot, the anti-Semitic WASP literary doorkeeper, into Bech's visit to the site of the central event of modern Jewish history. "Are not there, not there at all—up in smoke" echoes Prufrock's famous lines: "That is not it at all/That is not what I meant, at all." Through Bech, Updike attempts to assimilate his Jewish rivals with the same subversive friction as his Jewish rivals mocked the suburban assimilation of their parents. He wants to undercut Jewish adversarial energies by adopting them himself, in his own antithetical idiom.

This is caustic stuff. It is admirably caustic stuff. All's fair in love and literature, even the ugliest of the fair. Updike describes a Jewish woman who is coming on to Bech: "She looked up into his face like a dentist who had asked him to open his mouth. She was interested. If he had said he had hemorrhoids, she would still be interested. A Jewish mother's clinical curiosity. Abigail Bech [Bech's mother] had always been prying, poking."

This is in truly bad taste, nor does it rise from crude caricature to genuine satire. A memorable caricature first generates its own qualities and then becomes a type, like Mr. Micawber or Tartuffe, but Updike's Bech, his Jews, and even his WASPs and his Third World radicals are frequently stereotypes that tumble straight into caricature without first ripening into their own particularities. Bech himself, insofar as he does acquire a real satirical weight, is a passé figure, a first-generation American Jewish intellectual whom few younger American Jews, let alone anyone else, will now recognize. Updike, in a startling intuition, has Bech thinking that "nothing in history sinks quicker . . . than people's actual motives, unless it be their sexual charm." The motives of a Bech are, for satirical purposes, now lost to us.

What remains in these stories is the dynamism of a satirical libido unafraid of bad taste, the presence of which, after all, is the liberated excess of true satire. And what will last in the desultory Bech saga is the drama of an author reclaiming his own otherness to himself—the source of all art—through the not-always-good-hearted impersonation of another type of person. By the end of this series, Bech and Updike are together writing the kind of satire that a new generation of Bechs, Jewish or not, should be producing but isn't.

In the sidesplitting "Bech Noir," Bech goes around knocking off his most vituperative critics, one of them an embittered academic from Seattle who has written three children's books: *Jennifer's Lonely Birthday, The Day Daddy Didn't Come Home,* and *A Teddy Bear's Bequest.* "Bech Presides" is a marvelously mordant jab at the mingling of art and money, in which the villain is in real estate, a WASP who ignobly tricks the noble Bech. Imagine that, a satire on art and money in which a real estate developer is the bad guy! Perhaps you have to be a rich and famous seventy-year-old author to have the courage to lance our current pieties without fearing charges of sour grapes.

Just as Cervantes came to love and then inhabit Don Quixote—the author jealously repossessing his autonomous creation—Updike does not come just to love Bech but to pass into him. Author and character become a composite creature, a WASP Jew—the beast with two Bechs. In the gorgeous coda, "His Oeuvre," Updike and Bech disappear into a world composed of each author's spiritual and aesthetic values. Lecturing around the country, the famously randy but now aging Bech characteristically sees a former lover at each talk. The visitations prompt an odyssey of characteristically Updikean memories, a chain of sensuous associations that ends with Bech recalling nights of love with a married woman on a train speeding from one end of the country to the other. While lecturing, Bech even spies a "magic lantern" illuminating the ladies' room, as if Updike was invoking the famous magic lantern in *Swann's Way* and then replacing Marcel Proust's memory-inducing madeleine with Bech's memory-inducing women.

The stories end with Updike/Bech submerged in another hybrid personality: that of Proust, the Jewish homosexual whose art has shaped the sensibility of both the real author and—Updike has told us—his creation. Appropriately, Updike evokes Bech's lover with a Proustian fluidity: Bech experiences "his companion's supine beauty as a continuous, calm, exultant entity, with rises and swales and dulcet shadowed corners. The curious silvery light of her eyes now lived all along her skin." About the pair's lovemaking in their small sleeper on the train, Updike writes, "The couple's closet of satisfied desire became nicely rank with a smell that was neither him nor her." The same consummating fusion could also be ascribed to Updike and his character. It is the greatest instance of cross-dressing and identity-swapping in American literature. But centaurs, like great impersonators, always take themselves by surprise.

The New King of Irony

In America, the movies are always wanting to become life and life is always wanting to become a movie. Maybe that's why we're so attached to our iPods: they provide a score of background music that lends to our ordinary days something like the cohesion of a meaningful plot. And once we have a plot, we can anticipate that cinematic event in which America's very promise is captured.

That is the moment when an actor stops playing his or her particular character and starts playing his or her persona as an actor. Take an extreme example: In *The Shining,* Jack Nicholson's deranged character—whose name also happens to be Jack—breaks through the bathroom door with an ax, sticks his head in, and says, in demonic parody, to his cowering wife, "Wendy? I'm home!" This is the over-the-top culmination of an entire lineage of Nicholson characters, seen in movies from *Easy Rider* to *One Flew over the Cuckoo's Nest,* characters who are at odds with conventional morality, with the very idea of "home." The larger-than-screen persona suddenly towers over the specific role. Or to put it in different terms, the authentic self triumphs over shifting circumstances.

Such a moment is a vicarious fulfillment of the American Dream, for the talk about self-reinvention in American life is a lot of trite gibberish. What we truly desire is that our original identities persist through all the pressure to reinvent ourselves along prescribed social lines. Authentic, clear-sighted Nick Carraway survives; the permutating Gatsby does not. Playing one's persona has tended to be the rule among American film actors—as opposed to their British counterparts, who submerge themselves in their roles—but no two actors have done it more completely, and more artistically, than Jack Nicholson and now Kevin Spacey.

This is how it works: Nicholson, whose first important role was the alienated, ill-fated passenger on Peter Fonda's motorcycle in *Easy Rider,* went on to play the alienated, ill-fated protagonist in Antonioni's *The Passenger.* Spacey, whose breakout role was Keyser Soze—note the initials—in *The Usual Suspects,* a master criminal who abruptly and without remorse slays his family, went on to play in *American Beauty* a man who abruptly and without remorse jettisons his middle-class morality and cuts his ties to his family. The trajectory of these two actors' personas tells a story about what's been happening in the culture. It's a tale about a sea change, and it has to do with the twilight of Nicholson and the ascendancy of Spacey.

Consider Nicholson's persona first. His disaffected, iconoclastic lawyer in *Easy Rider* evolved into the disaffected, iconoclastic concert pianist-turned-drifter in one of his next films, *Five Easy Pieces.* And so it went with Nicholson's roles throughout the 1970s, as he inhabited detached, unaffiliated characters in one film after another: *Carnal Knowledge* (with the emphasis more on disaffection than iconoclasm); *The King of Marvin Gardens; The Last Detail; Chinatown; The Passenger; Cuckoo's Nest.* It was as if, his character having been murdered in his sleep by rednecks in *Easy Rider,* Nicholson played his subsequent roles as a ghostly presence never at home in the world.

During the 1970s the Nicholson character was usually a guy with working-class origins, seething with frustrated aspirations toward a more meaningful existence—in love with women, at war with women, always trumped by women. He broke the rules, as in *The Last Detail, Chinatown,* and *Cuckoo's Nest;* he exploded with helpless rage in just about every film but *Marvin Gardens;* he used irony, mimicry, parody as weapons of defiance. Indeed, a supreme ironist, Nicholson allowed his persona to obtrude from his roles the way the characters he played obtruded uneasily from life. By the time—in 1975—that Nicholson appeared in *The Passenger,* he didn't have to say a single ironic word. His mere presence on the screen unmoored every stable meaning around him.

Nicholson's lunatic blocked writer in Stanley Kubrick's *The Shining* was a turning point for him. It seemed that his persona had become so powerful that he could no longer harmoniously fuse it with the kinds of characters he'd been playing. So the characters he chose became more outsize and extreme, as though to fit the proportions of his persona. In the 1980s and 1990s the conscientious outsiders Nicholson had brought to life metamorphosed into campy or comical menaces to society in movies like *Prizzi's Honor, The Witches of Eastwick, Batman,* and *Wolf.* Just as the Nicholson-outsider's subversions grew more violent, weird, and outrageous, the role of the outsider in American society—the beat, the bohemian, the punk—grew more attenuated. In the 1980s the business culture gained a foothold in American society that it hadn't had since the 1920s, and the Nicholsonian rebel lost the status of a hero and acquired the qualities of a freak.

The passionate explosions, the angry combat with women, the insolence and rawly explicit irony as instruments of dissent—they all got transformed in many of Nicholson's later films into what amounted to social pathologies. No coincidence, then, that Nicholson's most brilliant recent performance was as the writer in *As Good as It Gets,* a character who's emotionally crippled by obsessive-compulsive disorder. It was as if the erstwhile passion had reemerged as a clinical condition, the stuff of recovery movements and lugubrious memoirs.

As Good as It Gets was a significant event in the story of overriding film personas. The film reflected the transition from the Age of Nicholson to the Age of Spacey. His psychic stuffing knocked out of him, the Nicholson persona finally (sort of) gets the girl instead of being defeated by her. The movie itself ends with a stunning image of cinematic upheaval. The tranquil, reassuring shot of an empty, urban, matinal street on the right side of the screen and a warmly glowing bakery on the left side reverses a classic American scene: Edward Hopper's *Nighthawks,* with its unsettling view of an empty, urban, nocturnal street on the left side of the canvas and a lonely, anomie-ridden diner on the right side. In *As Good as It Gets,* the romance of the explicitly alienated outsider comes to an end. And when, in that film, the ur-heterosexual Nicholson character comes to accept the film's gay character, the baton of ironic outsiderness passes to Kevin Spacey.

Rumors that Spacey is gay have been around for some time, though Spacey has vigorously denied them, especially after an *Esquire* article all but attempted to out him a couple of years ago. Spacey's sexual orientation should have nothing to do with his work as an actor, but the persona he's developed for himself is constantly playing with the possibility that Spacey—Spacey the persona—is gay.

The Usual Suspects is full of references to anal intercourse and "cocksucking." At one point, one of the men in Verbal Kint's (the Spacey character's) gang looks at another gang member and says, "Do you wanna dance?" The men draw close and tilt their heads as if to kiss. In *Glengarry Glen Ross,* the Al Pacino character verbally attacks Spacey, calling him a "fairy" and taunting him by saying, "I don't know whose dick you're sucking on." The Spacey character in *Seven,* a psychotic killer, adopts a stereotyped tone of snippy, petulant sissyness, as so many of Spacey's characters do— the sadistic Hollywood executive in *Swimming with Sharks* is the most vivid example. Spacey's corrupt cop in *L.A. Confidential,* Jack Vincennes, decides to go straight, as it were, only when the killing of a gay character sickens and outrages him: The way the camera closes in on the expression of grief and pain on his face as he looks at the murdered boy is extraordinarily pointed. In *Midnight in the Garden of Good and Evil,* Spacey plays an explicitly gay character. And *American Beauty,* a kind of parable of dysfunctional heterosexual life, has the Spacey character dying at the hands of a homophobe.

Why is Spacey constantly toying with gayness on screen? It's tantalizing to think that it has something to do with the defeat of Nicholson's rebellious, vexed, working-class heterosexual heroes. Whereas the Nicholson character's passionate openness spelled his doom, Spacey refuses to be open about anything. It's as if he's learned his lesson from Nicholson. His insolence, his defiance come from within. Nicholson's persona was fire; Spacey's is ice. (Spacey has even written the introduction to a book about an Eskimo.) Nicholson's explosions did him in: They cut him off from humanity in *Five Easy Pieces,* made him impotent in *Carnal Knowledge,* killed the woman he loved in *Chinatown,* earned him a lobotomy in *Cuckoo's Nest.* In *The Passenger,* his emotional candor brought his life to an early end. Spacey, on the other hand, almost never blows up, and when he does he combusts coldly, calculatedly, cerebrally.

He has a secret, he seems to be saying, and his power lies in the way he discloses his secret without actually revealing it.

Rather than explode, he gets exploded against, by angry heterosexual guys who might once have been fine Nicholsonian rebels but now are just angry heterosexual guys. He's verbally abused by Pacino and Jack Lemmon in *Glengarry Glen Ross,* grilled and bullied by Chazz Palminteri in *The Usual Suspects,* taunted and then killed by Brad Pitt in *Seven,* tortured by his vindictive assistant in *Swimming with Sharks,* bullied and threatened with violence by Palminteri in *Hurlyburly,* slain by the homophobe in *American Beauty.* Yet, unlike the Nicholson character, the Spacey character always wins.

He sends Lemmon to jail and cows Pacino in *Glengarry,* humiliates Palminteri in *Suspects,* makes Pitt a murderer in *Seven,* spiritually extinguishes his assistant in *Sharks,* strips society bare in *Midnight,* delivers sarcastic quips about Palminteri's suicide in *Hurlyburly,* deranges and destroys his killer in *American Beauty.* His passivity and mystery drive his antagonists to reveal themselves. They seem to lack the feline intelligence to get what they want. Playing at maybe being gay, Spacey outs other men's rage. Rather than explode as a sign of weakness, he dies in a display of power. No wonder he played Hickey in *The Iceman Cometh* with such commitment. Hickey is a spinner of illusions.

The really striking thing is that Spacey turns the Nicholson persona on its head while assimilating that persona's principal traits. (Spacey's first feature film was *Heartburn,* with Nicholson, and he has spoken of his admiration for Nicholson.) Like his forerunner, Spacey plays his roles as if his characters were sticking out of the screen at an angle. He speaks his lines with Nicholsonian irony, parody, and mimicry; in fact, no one since Nicholson himself has detached words from their contexts as jarringly as Spacey. Spacey's characters, like Nicholson's, are detached and unaffiliated. But they're not alienated, destabilizing outsiders. They're alienated, destabilizing insiders.

Nicholson's alienated outsiders turned detachment into defiance of a dominating money culture; Spacey's alienated insiders turn detachment into an indispensable mode of survival in a dominating money culture. The master criminal Soze in *The Usual Suspects* is everywhere and nowhere, invincible and indestructible, like a malevolent god. The husband and father in *American Beauty,* who tells the tale from beyond the grave, is everywhere and nowhere, like a benign storytelling god. The Spacey character's vices are simultaneously his virtues. Even in *Suspects* and *Seven,* where he plays psychotic villains, Spacey portrays social pathology coolly and rationally, as if it were a respectable character trait—as if he were playing the amoral smoothies in *Glengarry* and *Sharks* and *Hurlyburly* and *L.A. Confidential.*

Things have certainly changed. Perhaps, as this remarkable actor's performances seem to imply, present-day society itself is in rebellion against true social life.

PART THREE

Love Me Tonight?

D. H. Lawrence and the
Romantic Option

W E A R E A C I V I L I Z A T I O N awash in choices, in romance just as
much as in the realms of food and fashion, of cars and financial
services. But where many choices exist, great love stories are absent. For a great love story depends on an inevitable choice followed by inexorable consequences.

The Lost Girl is such a tale. Lawrence's third novel, published
in 1920, and written between *The Rainbow* and *Women in Love* in
fits and starts and discarded drafts over a period of seven years,
tells the story of Alvina Houghton, a middle-class Englishwoman
who lives in a dour mining village called Woodhouse with her
widowed ne'er-do-well father and two elderly women housekeepers. Alvina has a fine, noble nature that elevates her above
her limited circumstances. But she is not merely burdened by her
circumstances. She is one of those people possessed of a special
destiny; or, rather, she has a heightened awareness of her destiny,
which makes her special. Her destiny weighs on her every bit as
much as her environment does. "Her own inscrutable nature was
her fate," Lawrence writes, "sore against her will."

Alvina either follows her nature and so thwarts her opportunities, or she fails to assert her nature and so thwarts her destiny. Her first beau arrives from beyond the sea, from Australia.

He is "dark in colouring, with very dark eyes, and a body which seemed to move inside his clothing." He proposes to Alvina, but the bitter Miss Frost, one of the housekeepers, protests. Alvina gives in to Miss Frost, despite the fact that her sexual instinct has been aroused for the first time and now becomes part of her conscious life. In pursuit of independence, she takes up maternity nursing—a beautiful touch: throughout the novel, Alvina is bringing her true self to birth—and goes to work in another town, at a hospital where several handsome doctors offer to fulfill her agitating sexual desire. Yet mere carnal satiety is not what Alvina's nature demands, even though it is part of what her nature craves. And these doctors lack the dark vitality of the Australian, whom she yearns for most profoundly, beyond sex. She rejects the men's advances, nevertheless regretting that she rejected them, sorry that "fate had been too strong for her and her desires: fate which was not an external association of forces, but which was integral in her own nature." That is what Yeats meant when he wrote that destiny comes from within.

So Alvina returns to Woodhouse, thinking that she might marry to escape her failing father and oppressive housekeepers. But once again, her true self prohibits her from accepting the men she meets, stable and affluent and eligible as they are. And, once again, destiny knocks from deep inside her. Her father, James Houghton, has bought an old theater in a last attempt to make money, and a troupe of actors called the Natcha-Kee-Tawara come to perform. Though the little company consists of a Frenchwoman who runs it, a Swiss, a German, and an Italian, its specialty is the pantomimed dramatization of a scene set among American Indians, something involving a hunt, the capture of a bear, the escape of the bear, and the death of a squaw's husband. (The Natcha-Kee-Tawara are Lawrence's delightful satire on his own exaltation of the American Indian's primal powers, as well as his stubborn insistence on the American Indian's primal powers.)

The Italian is a Neapolitan named Ciccio; like the Australian, he is dark and sensuous, and he arrives from beyond the sea. By now, death has thawed Miss Frost into oblivion, and Alvina has fastened her self-knowledge more tightly onto her will. She falls in love with Ciccio, who leads her, step by fateful step, toward her special destiny, which is to become herself. Ciccio is an actor, after all, a half-imaginary being, and for Lawrence, the true self can only be reached by means of the imagination. But heeding one's imagination in the rational, calculating world is a hazardous undertaking:

> The inexorable in her nature was highly exclusive and selective . . . Hence men were afraid of her—of her power, once they had committed themselves. She would involve and lead a man on, she would destroy him rather than not get of him what she wanted. And what she wanted was something serious and risky. Not mere marriage—oh dear no! But a profound and dangerous inter-relationship. As well ask the paddlers in the small surf of passion to plunge themselves into the heaving gulf of mid-ocean. Bah, with their trousers turned up to their knees it was enough for them to wet their toes in the dangerous sea. They were having nothing to do with such desperate nereids as Alvina.

"A profound and dangerous inter-relationship"; "to plunge themselves into the heaving gulf of mid-ocean"; "the dangerous sea"—with a touch of the operatic, Lawrence made true loving the measure of authentic living, and he made the stakes for love very high. Born poor, the son of a coal miner in impoverished northern England, he believed that people should live essentially, with a joyous intensity rooted in full consciousness of death. He believed this perhaps because neither money nor social status can buy essentiality. And he offered eros as the occasion for this enactment of the high-stakes adventure of love because neither money nor social status has a purchase on erotic attachment. In the end, Alvina gets the man she wants, she attains her heart's desire, but she loses everything else, including the possibility of happiness with that very man. Such is the effect of a singular, exclusive choice. With *The Lost Girl,* Lawrence raised to the level of Greek tragedy our contemporary dilemma of the emotional "trade-off," our worrying over "settling" or not settling for the least unattractive romantic option. Over eighty years ago, Lawrence published the novel that everyone would be waiting for over eighty years later.

Lawrence composed *The Lost Girl* aiming for commercial success. "Let's hope my Lost Girl will be Treasure Trove to me," he wrote to a highborn benefactor (Lawrence loved rubbing the noses of his highborn benefactors in his dire financial straits). He padded his story with what he thought were comical set-pieces, and he overemphasized the Plight of Modern Woman to open the purses of women readers, though this latter impulse becomes transfigured early on in the novel into one of the most sympathetic inhabitings of a female character by a male author in the history of literature. *The Lost Girl* is not a masterpiece of form, which is partly why it has been forgotten; but it is a masterpiece of feeling and perception, which is why it needs to be restored.

One result of the academicization of literature is that literary people, when appraising fiction, consider feelings and perceptions to be the idiom of the amateur. Even beyond the university, in what passes for much literary criticism, one comes across interminable discussion of consciousness and irony, of character and caricature, of historical realism and psychological realism, et cetera. The reader begins to feel unauthorized to be reading, as though driving without a license. But there is nothing literary about an effective novel. It is not so much creative expression as natural respiration. Lawrence wrote as he lived and breathed; he repeats words and phrases as though he were stripping poetic cadence to biological rhythm, in the same way as, through the Natcha-Kee-Tawara, he wants to liberate the savage "red-Indian" heart from what he regarded as the desiccated corpse of European civilization.

It is easy, at our jaded, self-conscious point in history, to laugh at Lawrence's ideas about repressive civilization, about the necessity to retrieve the instinctual life. But we know, in our heart of hearts, that there are times when we must follow our instincts, obey our intuition, take advice from the deepest part of ourselves. There are times when we know that the way we are living is, in fact, preventing us from truly living. To heed your instincts when guilt, or fear, or habit, or other people are telling you to stay where you are requires a leap of the imagination. And such a leap requires an imagination. A belief in the power of imagination to change a person's life, not just an artist's but any person's life, is what lies behind Lawrence's animadversions against an enervating urbanity.

Alvina's bond to Ciccio is a bond of feeling, not primarily sexual feeling. It is feeling based in the imagination; this is why she herself becomes part of the acting troupe for a while. Indeed, Lawrence belies, as he often does in his art, his social elitism by embodying in Alvina, the lost maternity nurse, elements of artistic genius (these are preternaturally intuitive and visceral, as opposed to the Hollywood caricature of genius as being superlatively mental). And the bond of feeling between the dark man and the fair woman is decreed by a mutual intuition; this is what makes their love as inevitable as it is unlikely. Though sex is an essential part of the dynamic between them, their attachment extends far beyond sex. (Lawrence writes so beautifully about sex because, with the exception of *Lady Chatterley's Lover,* a dreadful potboiler, he never tries to describe sex; instead, he evokes the *feeling* aroused by sex, as if sex were really just a pretext for the sudden consciousness of being alive.) Ciccio gives Alvina peace out of the place sex comes from, out of sheer physical being. He is profoundly anchored in his physical nature. Since death is the most prominent fact of physical nature, Ciccio's ease in his element reassures Alvina that he can protect her from extinction.

One of the blessings of *The Lost Girl* is that it dispels the popular impression of Lawrence as an apostle of free sex, as a kind of Henry Miller with a penchant for Alpine hiking. It does this in a way that his more famous novels do not, packed as they are with dense cerebrations on the sexual instinct. Lawrence's purpose in such abstruse reflecting was to convey the idea of a primal, mystical force at the heart of human life that encompassed sex yet transcended it. Ironically, the reflections themselves are often so overheated and opaque that the reader flees all the arid conceptualizing and heads for the sex. Like a Buddhist confronted with the conundrum of having to use the ego to abolish the ego, Lawrence found himself straining his intellect to prove the futility of intellect.

The Lost Girl, however, unfolds its ideas about human life in the telling of its tale. It is the one novel by Lawrence that has the compact fatality, the terse purposefulness, of his short stories. Because Lawrence believed that civilization had turned the life force against itself, he turns the conventional, literary notion of a lost girl on its head. The unforgettable lost girls of literature are seduced, sometimes impregnated, and then abandoned, heroines like Richardson's Clarissa or Hardy's Tess;

or they are adulterous wives who follow their hearts and destroy themselves with society's nod of approval: Anna Karenina, Emma Bovary, Effie Briest. In every case, unhappiness, an ill-starred meeting, and illicit sex set in motion the plummet toward ruination and destitution.

But Alvina's ascent toward renewal begins with ruination and destitution. Society sins against her before she trespasses against society. Her father's business failures leave her in strangling debt. Isn't it absurd, Lawrence asks, for a person to have her precious mortal life suppressed by something as inanimate as *money?* That is the starting point for Alvina's embarkation into another, more fulfilling life, the first step of which is illicit sex between her and Ciccio:

> Well, despair was no good, and being miserable was no good either. She got no satisfaction out of either mood. The only thing to do was to act: seize hold of life and wring its neck.

Unhappiness, the bored, restless unhappiness of Karenina, Bovary, and Briest, is no catalyst either. Lawrence is very austere on the subject of happiness. He considered it a modern illusion, mostly fabricated by commercial society for the purpose of concealing unhappiness. In its place, he affirmed the existence of joy, which he believed sprang from the painful sacrifice of a lesser need for a greater desire. That is also what conventional sentiment calls unhappiness.

> Why should anybody expect to be *made happy,* and develop heart-disease if she isn't? . . . Happiness is a sort of soap-tablet—he won't be happy till he gets it, and when he's got it, the precious baby, it'll cost him his eyes and his

stomach. Could anything be more puerile than a mankind howling because it isn't happy: like a baby in the bath!

Isolated in the cold, harsh, impoverished, alien Neapolitan countryside with Ciccio, the love of her life, whom she can barely talk with but cannot live without, Alvina has sacrificed her lesser needs for a greater desire. She learns that happiness has nothing to do with joy; that, in fact, joy is attained at the price of pain and loss. The landscape's terrible beauty itself, sublimely evoked by Lawrence, both crushes her and transports her into states that border on mystic bliss. Alvina gets precisely what she wants but no more.

This is how Lawrence reversed the conventional idea of the lost girl. He was not content to allow Alvina to triumph morally by contriving her destruction at society's hands, in the manner of literature's previous lost girls. Lawrence's portrait of Alvina on her journey with Ciccio back to his mountain village in southern Italy is some of the most powerful and moving imaginative writing ever put to paper. Alvina thinks that she is

> quite, quite lost. She had gone out of the world, over the border, into some place of mystery. She was lost to Woodhouse, to Lancaster, to England—all lost.

Finally, it is not Alvina who is lost. How could she be, having reached a place of mystery. Rather, it is the hostile forms of life that are, through Lawrence's sudden, subtle inversion, "all lost" to Alvina.

The wonder in all this is that, even as he is enacting his gospel of feeling, Lawrence never lapses into sentimentality. Alvina chooses Ciccio when her other choices have fallen away for one reason or another, but this does not make Ciccio a *pis-aller*. On the contrary. Alvina's tight boundaries of escape give her the strength to obey her intuition of her fate. Yet she is undeniably galvanized by her dwindling choices. *The Lost Girl*'s characters keep their shadowy motives even throughout the fullest exposure of their magic potentiality as individuals seeking their particular, irreducible destiny. Yet Lawrence knew that, in the end, despite all your careful introspecting, you pay for following your instincts. And the more intensely and honestly you live, the more incessantly you pay. If you have become that particular, irreducible person, you get precisely what you want but no more. That is the unforgiving truth, and the revelatory beauty, of *The Lost Girl*.

Who Is Carrie Bradshaw
Really Dating?

SOME YEARS AGO, in magical New York City, a certain cable-television station began broadcasting from its Midtown head-quarters a weekly series about four single women who lived right there, in magical New York City. There was sunny, fair-skinned Charlotte York, with her dark eyes and shoulder-length dark hair, a WASP derived from New York high society who worked in an art gallery; Samantha Jones ("Sam" to her friends), a high-powered public-relations executive with her own firm, a caustic, bitter, formidable, all-of-a-sudden-masculine blond who had, like, lunar sex with every man in sight; Miranda Hobbes, a corporate attorney and graduate of Harvard Law School, with pale electric-blue eyes and copper-red hair, who alternated disastrous dates with calamitous relationships; and last but certainly not least, Carrie Bradshaw, the blow-dried, straw-haired sylph, who wrote a column for the imaginary *New York Star* called "Sex and the City," which happened also to be the name of the series, each episode of which is told in Carrie's voice, through Carrie's deep, almost viscously thick blue eyes, eyes that seem to look right through you, and through the character of Carrie herself, to Sarah Jessica Parker, the self-adoring actress who plays the self-adoring Carrie.

A fusion of soap opera, self-help commentary, therapeutic consolation, and prime-time porn, *Sex and the City*'s stroke of brilliance has been to address, week after week, the consuming obsession of every unmarried person, straight or gay, male or female, living in a big American city: the Relationship. Or as Carrie inanely puts it in her weekly question—she asks a different one in her column each week, an interrogative pseudoprofundity that the episode then seeks to answer—"Have relationships become the religion of the nineties?"

Having a "relationship," of course, is not the same as being together. Just as an attitude toward labor only hardened into an ideology called Marxism when the worker got cut off from the product of his labor, so erotic bonds only hardened into Relationshipism when people started, for a million familiar reasons, getting cut off from each other. A "relationship" is not to be confused with a union. It is an ongoing argument between two stubbornly sovereign selves about the possibility of a union.

About the infinite number of forms that this argument takes, *Sex and the City* can be very smart. If it is vulgar to judge high art by its effectiveness at reproducing "reality," it is myopic to approach television in any other way. Daily existence consists largely of putting out one little brush fire after another; and television is a fire extinguisher. No medium, even film, is as tied to everyday life as television. Everyone, or just about everyone, knows what's wrong, but who can say anymore with absolute certainty what's right, especially in the realm of emotion and desire? At the core of *Sex and the City* is a kind of crisis-center for bruised or befuddled hearts. It is appropriate that the series—now finished, and in reruns—aired on Sunday evening, in the choppy wake of Friday and Saturday nights.

The questions that Carrie asks are easy to deride, with their silly self-centeredness, their marketing-executive idiom, their coin-operated impersonality. "In a gravity-free world, where everything goes, what constitutes cheating?" "When it comes to relationships, how do you know when enough is enough?" "In a city like New York, with its infinite possibilities, has monogamy become too much to expect?" But Carrie's questions point to a world, our world, where everything seems allowed yet where it is hard to figure out the consequences of that illusion; to a world where possibilities seem infinite, yet where no one seems to know how to feel when those possibilities turn out to be unnervingly limited. In this sense, the Relationship—in which everything is not allowed, because there is the boundary of the other person; and in which possibilities are finite, because there is the problem of two distinct lives, each with its own limitations and vulnerabilities—is a laboratory for a lot of present-day quandaries that no social or cultural authority can explain, or even clarify.

So *Sex and the City* gets high marks for dramatizing these inarticulable dilemmas. Should Miranda stick with—which means, in worldly Manhattan, settle for—slight, bespectacled Steve, her working-class bartender boyfriend, with his outer-borough accent and the added authenticity of his basketball, who wants only to be a bartender, and who is cuddly, and funny, and kind, but also resentful, and thin-skinned, and intellectually desolate? They are ultimately mismatched, but she is so lonely, and it is so brutal out there. Should Aidan, a handsome, rough-hewn, sensitive guy who likes to work with his hands and doesn't know the difference between Condé Nast and Thomas Nast, stay with Carrie after she tells him that she betrayed him with another man? She loves him, but she lied to him; she is with him, but how will he know she isn't lying again? The significance of these emotional snafus is small, but their symbolic resonance—how do you live a good life?—is not small.

The problem is that *Sex and the City,* once it mustered a striking frankness on the tube about urban men and women, has gone about squandering it. Instead of plunging into all the strange new present-day configurations of sex and emotion, the series has proceeded to divide sex from emotion. There is an abundance of fucking in *Sex and the City,* but it is the sort of fucking you did years ago, when you were very young, lying on the bed and cavorting in the head. As the series rolled along, you became aware of a damning artifice, an unmimetic quality surprising in a series that was supposed to be a candid look at urban life: none of these women is hurt by sex.

IN URBAN AMERICA, you do not so much meet a romantic partner as inherit the product of someone else's romantic crimes. Someday someone will televise the real story of sex and the city and call it *Judgment at Nuremberg.* People get hurt, they become hard, they grow shrewd and wary. But these four women—a journalist, a public-relations executive, a corporate lawyer, and an art dealer, all high achievers, all in their thirties—are constantly humiliated, insulted, and embarrassed without the slightest effect on their egos or their self-esteem. The exception is Miranda, the show's token human being, wonderfully played by Cynthia Nixon, who, as the series has proceeded, has become more and more self-protective and withdrawn, an affecting protest against the show's indifference to the women's inner lives.

These are four single women in early middle age who appear to have been injured in just about every way a woman can get hurt by men, and they are not even on antidepressants. After Charlotte goes off somewhere at a wedding with a man whom she has just met and has sex with him, they return to the reception, where, angered by something she says about his father, he loudly barks that he never wants to see her again and stomps off.

Charlotte shrugs. Samantha meets for a drink a man who excuses himself for a minute; after half an hour goes by and he has not returned, Samantha goes looking for him and finds him in intimate conversation somewhere else in the bar with a younger woman. Even nymphomaniacs have feelings, but Samantha just rolls her eyes as though she were Lucy getting exasperated with Desi for the umpteenth time that evening. And before Miranda's transformation, she gets into a relationship with a guy who can only get aroused if he pushes her face out of the way and watches porn films over her shoulder while they make love. Another boyfriend, enraged by a mildly critical question Miranda had asked him—the men in this show are mostly angry creeps or mellow creeps—says to her as she is lying in his bed, "I'm going to take a shower. When I come out, I'd like it if you weren't here." Neither of these incidents upsets her much more than the breaking of a heel.

Every episode ritualistically has several scenes, usually set in restaurants over a meal, in which the women get together and talk about their romantic situations. But rather than talk about their adventures in terms of feelings or mental states, poignantly or angrily or comically, they speak about them almost exclusively in terms of sex. When they are not talking about "the classic dating ritual: the blow-job tug-of-war," or about "fucking your brains out," they are quipping, "If your friends won't go down on you, who will?" and discoursing interminably on anal intercourse.

It is not shocking to see women portrayed—though in comic caricature—talking the way women, when they are alone with each other, do talk sometimes (or so I assume), or to have part of the reality of female desire acknowledged on the small screen. What is odd is that for these smart, canny, emotionally alive women, pretty much every relationship comes down to the quest for sex—for perfect sex—as an end in itself. How many women, after years of dating creeps, would call off a relationship with a nice ophthalmologist because he doesn't always give them an orgasm? How many women have an orgasm just about every time they have sex with a man, a miraculous dispensation with which Carrie and her friends have been blessed? But breaking up with the nice ophthalmologist is exactly what Miranda does, she of the porn boyfriend and the angry boyfriend. Not much later she shuts up with a kiss a documentary filmmaker, who actually, finally, for once, is talking on their first date about something besides sex, and something interesting, too. "Miranda," Carrie enthuses in the voice-over, "was pleased to discover that Ethan was just as passionate between the sheets as he was about film."

It would be quite the opposite, one would think, for women as experienced, and intelligent, and reflective about what they need and want as the show's quartet should be. "Passion"—to use a euphemism—between the sheets is not hard to come by on a first date. But rather than the tangled convergence of ego and emotion that physical intimacy is, the sex in this series is actually a refuge from sex, which—no matter how hard one might try to keep it pure—pretty quickly gets tangled up with ego and emotion. Sex in this series is like a sandbox. Its presence here is as unreal as its absence was on network television forty years ago.

THE DOMINANT FICTION projected by commercial society is that you can gratify yourself at no cost except to your wallet or your pocketbook; and *Sex and the City* has taken that illusion for reality. The show sublimates actual sex into ideal sex-in-an-emotional-vacuum in the same way that sitcoms from the 1950s sublimated actual family relations into ideal family relations. *Sex and the City* is *Leave It to Beaver* after dark. An absolute disjunction exists between the way the show portrays the women's harrowing experiences and the way it depicts their blithely bawdy conversations. It is like watching two different programs. And when the four are not talking about sex, they speak about experience in a kind of sales rep's idiom: "Soul mates: reality or torture device?"

Now, a part of the reason for the show's portrayal of women seeking sex for sex's sake is that the series' two creators, Darren Star and Michael Patrick King, are gay. On this level, *Sex and the City* is part of a long imaginative streak in popular art, a trend that includes Cole Porter and Lorenz Hart and George Cukor and Rock Hudson and most of the writers of the 1970s series *Bewitched* and many other gay figures whose portrayals of heterosexual life brilliantly subverted heterosexual conventions even as they were providing models for (unwitting) straight boys and girls. But there is a quality to *Sex and the City*'s subversions that is more bitter than playful, an element that is almost vindictive.

Running through *Sex and the City* is a subtext that amounts to a manifesto for a certain kind of raw, rough, promiscuous, anonymous gay male sex. Star and King sounded the call to arms in one of the very first episodes, when they had Stanford Blatch, Carrie's loyal gay friend, declare that "the only place where you can find love is the gay community. It's straight love that's closeted." A few seasons later, the women sit around watching gay-male porn films. "That's the way to do it," says Samantha, "no 'I love you'—just good old-fashioned fucking." Nobody contradicts her. One half-hour-long episode had the women finding happiness for a full ten minutes in a gay men's dance club. Another sent Carrie and Samantha, both blonds, on a train across the country, joking all the way about *Some Like It Hot*. Some of the quartet's boyfriends in the show's first two seasons actually wore their sweaters tucked into their pants; and if the actors playing these straight guys weren't gay, I'm Montgomery Clift. *Sex and the City*'s ongoing impersonation is admirably resourceful and daring. But the show's misogyny is not admirable at all.

Commenting on Sarah Jessica Parker's pregnancy, Michael Patrick King said: "Sarah's our workhorse, our show pony. We put her in high heels and tell her to run thirty blocks. Now, all of a sudden, she has to be babied." In its caricature of women who talk about sex like men, and, like men, have orgasms every time they have sex, the show represents a kind of counterattack on women's biology. The expensive, mismatched, chic-ugly clothes that Carrie wears; Sarah Jessica Parker's confused interpretations of her character as a black girl one episode and a self-conscious suburban cutie the next; Samantha's robotic-erotic, studlike manner (and the atrocious acting of Kim Cattrall, who could not stand still and convince you that she is a person standing still); the women's starry-eyed gold digging; their countless humiliations: the picture of heterosexual life projected by *Sex and the City,* though it sometimes hits the nail right on the head, is the biggest hoax perpetrated on straight single women in the history of entertainment. The series' misogyny is matched by its homophobia: the only regular gay characters, Stanford and Anthony, are self-hating and flaming, respectively. Perhaps the exhilaration that the show provokes in some of its fans stems from the reactionary character of its assumptions about sexual identity.

YET *SEX AND THE CITY*'S assault on heterosexual romantic hope goes much deeper than its creators' psychosexual antics. More than an ingenious affirmation of a certain type of gay-male sexuality, the show is a surrender to a certain type of socioeconomic arrangement. For the series has skillfully turned what society still deems a deficiency of emotional strength—singleness—into what the economy considers an asset of calculated advantage—self-interest. Inviolable individuality is, after all, the hidden condition of Relationshipism.

By the fourth season, with the exception of Charlotte, who has been divorced, the four women were in their late thirties and still unmarried, and you began to realize that the show's premise of its protagonists searching in the city for love and happiness was meant from the beginning to culminate in disappointment—but disappointment funnily, sexily, even glamorously portrayed, until disappointment itself started to look like love and happiness, and the object of the search, someone to share your life with, acquired the aspect of a dystopian and dysfunctional fantasy. The men whom the four women meet are selfish, unfaithful, uncouth, hyperneurotic shits, which seems about right; yet the show brings no decent guys their way except for the handful of men whom the women themselves immediately or eventually alienate—like the virile, kind, cultivated, gorgeous police detective whose near perfection makes a nervous Miranda drink herself into a stupor on their first date, prompting him to flee her apartment after leaving behind the address of her local Alcoholics Anonymous chapter (a very funny episode); or Aidan, the virile, kind, and gorgeous furniture maker whom Carrie first sexually betrays and then, when a year later he forgives her and comes back, refuses to commit to, thus driving him away for good. Indeed, kindness in men arouses anxiety and suspicion in the women: Carrie sabotages a relationship with a smart, gentle magazine editor when he catches her rifling through his apartment, looking for the incriminating evidence that she is sure will prove that he's too good to be true. (She doesn't find it.)

The women, even the hapless, vulnerable, serious-minded Miranda, are magnetically drawn to callous, selfish men. It seems that the qualities that are sure to hurt them are also the qualities that they believe will protect them in *Sex and the City*'s money-

and status-obsessed New York, a dazzling Darwinian demesne in which to move ahead you have to move fast, and to move fast you have to move alone. And so the four heroines are attracted to hard-hearted, fleet-footed guys, who are almost always affluent, and who are guaranteed to leave the women hard-hearted and fleet-footedly alone—that is, to leave them alone as fluid, insatiable consumers, unobstructed by a limiting couplehood.

The really revolutionary thing—in sitcom terms—about *Sex and the City* is that the show does not satirize the lucre-inflated bowels of Manhattan; it celebrates them, and it prefers them to the city's unquantifiable heart. The show has a kind of cartoon ideology of Manhattan. Every episode begins with a generalization about the city's glamour, wealth, cool, and cultural uniqueness that is breathtakingly disconnected from the actual New York: "Most single people in Manhattan do not buy furniture or hang pictures until faced with the arrival of out-of-towners." Huh? The show's creators actually seem terrified of what they nervously perceive as Gotham's reality. What are meant to pass as jaded *aperçus* really just reflect yuppie anxiety: "If you own, and he rents, it's emasculating."

Sex and the City is so much the creature of its fantasy of New York that its characters do not resemble any actual person who lives in New York. The four women never, until a couple of spats in the later seasons, fight with each other; and never express jealousy of each other; and never—except for Miranda when she is pregnant—collapse from exhaustion or work late. It is not even clear how the four of them—a scattered socialite, a workaholic and ambitious corporate lawyer, a power-hungry nymphomaniac, a newspaper columnist so narcissistic that she is hooked up mainly with her own clothes—would ever have become friends.

The sitcom's traditional role has been to comfort the viewer who feels burdened by the unreality of American expectations.

Perhaps the greatest, and most innovative, feat of *Sex and the City* has been to unsettle viewers with the spectacle of people who have every material thing worth possessing—and night after night of great sex to boot—and to keep them masochistically coming back for more, as if to avoid the show's images of material and sexual perfection were to admit one's material and sexual imperfections. Like *New York* magazine, with its endless lists of "best" and "top," and *The New York Observer*—where "Sex and the City" first appeared as a column—with its slavish pursuit of the hip and the exclusive, *Sex and the City* has won a good part of its audience by instilling in its viewers massive amounts of anxiety, a mood that can be allayed only by turning on the show and belonging to it. Like Carrie's elusive, eternally uncommitted Mr. Big, *Sex and the City* is the remedy for the distress that it causes.

With *Sex and the City,* the folks at HBO have created just this kind of cold and remote object of desire; a commodity eternally alluring, like the show's conception of Manhattan itself. "I'm dating the city," reveals Carrie, with typical wide-eyed cynicism, in a recent episode in which, after (yet again) having been humiliated in the rain by a stranger she tried to pick up, she seems resigned to the fact that she is chronically single. But Carrie is played by an actress in a television series called *Sex and the City* who transparently is playing an actress acting the part of Carrie, who writes a column called "Sex and the City," which in the course of the series becomes a movie called *Sex and the City,* which is about a columnist named Carrie who writes a column called "Sex and the City," which becomes a movie, and on and on.

In other words, Carrie is really dating the idea of New York purveyed by *Sex and the City;* she is really dating her television. And it is beyond significant that this relationship—between a person and an appliance that projects the illusion of other people without exacting from the ego a price for being with other people—seems to be the only relationship in which this wildly popular series' creators, who fashioned the show in their own image, actually believe.

The Gay Science:
Queer Theory, Literature, and the
Sexualization of Everything

I.

I USED TO KNOW A WOMAN who was in thrall to a particular anecdote. She told the tale again and again. Many years before, when her son was just a few years old, she had taken him and a couple of his playmates to a friend's house, where there were some little girls about the same age as her charges. After spending the afternoon there, my friend put her crew in the car and started to drive off. As they moved away, the girls ran to the edge of the front yard, waving to the boys. "Good-bye, penises!" they cried. And the boys waved back and cried, "Good-bye, vaginas!" Whenever my friend related her anecdote, she seemed surprised by her own wonder at it, and mysteriously consoled.

In one fell swoop, the delightful story proclaims the elemental nature of sex and then demotes sex to a triviality. We all know that the pleasures of penises and vaginas are essential and significant and mysterious, but we also know that we amount to more than penises and vaginas. We also know that those pleasures are themselves more than the sum of our genitals, and also that our lives are more than the sum of our pleasures. We do know this. Don't we?

Maybe we don't. To judge by American culture, there is only sex. My friend's tale might easily have been told of two groups of adults—Hollywood adults maybe, since Hollywood's idea of intellectual seriousness is often to discover sexual desire beneath all forms of political power and social convention; or maybe two groups of poets and novelists, since it seems that every other novel or book of poetry now has the sizzling word "desire" in the title; or legislators applying themselves to conduct in the workplace, or newspaper editors, or independent prosecutors. Just about every figure in the arena of our public life, it sometimes seems, wants a kinder, more genitally obsessed nation. But nowhere has the sexualization of reality proceeded so intensely and so relentlessly as in the seminar room.

The contemporary academic obsession with sexuality and "the body" has nothing to do with the Freudian-inspired criticism of the 1940s and 1950s. On the contrary. For about the past fifteen years, some prominent and influential American academics, mostly literature professors, have applied ideas about language and literature to sexuality rather than the other way around. This development has its origin in the complicated rift between hermeneutics and poststructuralism, and you have to understand that rift to understand how academia, and how society through academia, has sexualized everything.

Hermeneutics is the practice of reflecting on the way in which we interpret and understand meaning. Its operations are about as old as Western civilization; but a revolution in hermeneutics, and its advent as a discipline in its own right, took place in Germany in the early nineteenth century. That was when Friedrich Schleiermacher partially broke with the traditional idea that the goal of interpretation was understanding. Instead, Schleiermacher made understanding synonymous with interpretation; and so understanding, though still achievable, became an essentially unfinished and unauthoritative attainment, a series of provisional satisfactions in the course of an endless labor.

Modern hermeneutics, from Schleiermacher through Hans-Georg Gadamer's *Truth and Method* (1960), has run in two currents. The first was the gradual conditioning of meaning and value on the shifting templates of psychology, history, and, most of all, language. In this outlook, the self was always on the verge of cognitive calamity. But the second current was founded on Gadamer's belief that mutual comprehension and shared values between people were possible. The so-called hermeneutic circle—to understand the whole, you have to grasp the parts, which changes your perception of the whole; to understand a part, you have to grasp the whole, which changes your perception of the part—was not a ceaseless flux. It was an affirmation that ultimate meaning exists as an elusive mystery, that it can be grasped in shards and echoes, and that the preservation of a secret itself communicates a cherishable meaning.

Gadamer borrowed many of his ideas from Heidegger, but Heidegger had sown the iron seeds of hermeneutical extremism. He lowered the boom on hermeneutics by raising the stakes: he made the hermeneutical enterprise synonymous with existence itself. For Heidegger, "Being" is the ultimate truth of existence: to go about the business of living in the deepest sense is to go about the business of interpreting truth and finally understanding it. Such "Being," however, is beyond rational articulation. So obscure, so mystifying, so all-encompassing is Heidegger's Being that, his vatic pretensions notwithstanding, it leaves nothing to interpret but other interpretations.

AND THIS WAS the loftily regressive situation from which the French poststructuralists embarked. Dismissing Heidegger's foundation of Being as a quaint metaphysical holdover, they retained his assault on reason. They made their happy escape from shared meaning.

Poststructuralists disdain traditional hermeneutics, despite all that hermeneutics has taught poststructuralism about the conditional nature of cognition and judgment. The poststructuralists cannot forgive hermeneutics for never attaching itself to the "critique of ideology." As they see it, partly under the influences of Nietzsche and the Frankfurt School, the idea that people are fundamentally the same in their profoundest values is not ethically descriptive or prescriptive. It is, rather, a mask for a system of power, in which universalism is easily disappointed into leveling, murderous coercions.

Thus the French poststructuralists came to celebrate any expression of "difference": madness, crime, perversion, transgression, unmeaning, absence, silence. Foucault, Derrida, and Althusser differed in many respects, but together they broke the hermeneutic circle into an endless number of parallel lines that never meet. And they did not consider this step a sufficient obliteration of the traditional quest for stable, common meaning. Poststructuralism was still bothered by traces of the original hermeneutical belief that shared meaning and shared mystery could exist together. Enter the penises and the vaginas.

Sex is both the most explicit thing we do and the most secret. It is the most conventional thing, and potentially the most "other," the most "transgressive," in the sense that society does not accept all of the manifestations of sexuality. Indeed, for the poststructuralists, the secrecy of sex is the most consequential concealment of the actuality of "difference." Find the sex, and you will have found the seat of social and political authority. But authority is repression, and must be unmasked. And so the poststructuralists set out to make sex as indeterminate, as "other," as depleted, as they had made language.

This was their endgame: liberate by sex, and then liberate from sex. The dissolution of reason into the human juices marked its final disappearance. Queer theory, though nearly a decade old, is the thriving culmination of the poststructuralists' sexual turn. It contains all of that development's various influences and tendencies. Its scripture, its watershed source, is the first volume of Michel Foucault's *History of Sexuality,* which appeared in Paris in 1976, and in English translation in this country two years later. Foucault is to queer theory, and to the larger culture, what Freud has been to psychoanalysis, and to the larger culture.

II.

Of course, there was also the influence of the American scene. The legislation closing gay bathhouses and sex clubs, implemented at the height of the AIDS epidemic during the late eighties and early nineties, had a lot to do with the birth of queer politics and queer theory. Though many gays welcomed the regulations as life-saving and tragically overdue, "queers" saw them as attempts to suppress gay sexuality. Out of this controversy there arose anew the old 1960s conflict between gay reformers and gay liberationists, with the queers building on the ambitions of the latter. Driven by the engines of multiculturalism, the queer enterprise took off from there: queers use radical doubts about identity to revolutionize the idea of the "personal," just as, two or three decades ago, many present-day gay liberals used the radical certitudes of the personal to revolutionize the idea of the "political." Thus the ascendancy of queer theory over queer politics.

As the threat of AIDs has diminished in the affluent sectors of the West, queer politics has subsided into what amounts to colorfully ineffective performance-groups, such as the one calling itself Sex Panic. But queer theory has gained in its sense of mission. Queer theoretical ideas have their roots in long-repressed aspirations for a universal sexual transformation; for a recognition of the ubiquity of homosexual desire; for an end to marriage and "sex roles"; for a unifying theory exposing connections between sexual oppression, economic inequality, and colonialist domination.

Like the liberationists of the 1960s, queer theorists have a totalizing framework; but they have no truck with 1960s notions of gay identity and gay pride. They wish to dissolve the categories of sexual identity and, with them, the way in which society has invested sexual identity with moral value, endorsing some sexual identities and stigmatizing others. Queers are engaged in a vast theoretical project of breaking up fixed sexual identities into the fluidity of sexual acts or practices. Instead of whom you have sex with, queer theory is interested in how you obtain sexual pleasure.

Queer denotes "genitality," masturbation, and "fisting"; cross-dressing, transvestitism, and sadomasochism; and especially the meaning-neutral and value-neutral "body." Queers regard this shift in emphasis as a shift in historical paradigm. As Donald Morton observes in "Birth of the Cyberqueer":

> Rather than as a local effect, the return of the queer has to be understood as the result, in the domain of sexuality, of the (post)modern encounter with—and rejection of—Enlightenment views concerning the role of the conceptual, rational, systematic, structural, normative, progressive, liberatory, revolutionary, and so forth, in social change.

Morton's casual identification of "normative" with "revolutionary," of "progressive" with "liberatory," is representative of some of the confusions and contradictions (and so forth) in queer theory.

For Eve Kosofsky Sedgwick, similarly,

> the now chronic modern crisis of homo/heterosexual definition has affected our culture through its ineffaceable marking particularly of the categories secrecy/disclosure, knowledge/ignorance, private/public, masculine/feminine, majority/minority, innocence/initiation, natural/artificial, new/old, discipline/terrorism, canonic/non-canonic, wholeness/decadence, urban/provincial, domestic/foreign, health/illness, same/different, active/passive, in/out, cognition/paranoia, art/kitsch, utopia/apocalypse, sincerity/sentimentality, and voluntarity/addiction.

And Michael Warner, in his introduction to a volume of essays called *Fear of Queer Planet,* writes that

> every person who comes to a queer self-understanding knows in one way or another that her stigmatization is connected with gender, the family, notions of individual freedom, the state, public speech, consumption and desire, nature and culture, maturation, reproductive politics, racial and national fantasy, class identity, truth and trust, censorship, intimate life and social display, terror and violence, health care, and deep cultural norms about the bearing of the body. . . . Queers do a kind of practical social reflection just in finding ways of being queer.

With such gargantuan ambitions, it is no wonder that the ideal of queerness sometimes seems indistinguishable from the hormonal and glandular processes that make up sex itself. Indeed, for Sedgwick, "what it takes—all it takes—to make the description 'queer' a true one is the impulsion [sic] to use it in the first person." Identity and "impulsion"—that is, desire—fuse into a single entity.

And if Eve Sedgwick has escaped the prison of contradiction, then David Halperin has escaped the prison of definition. In *Saint Foucault: Towards a Gay Hagiography,* Halperin goes Sedgwick one better and announces that queer is "an identity without an essence." Queerness is fluid, even as it dreams of fluids. Halperin, too, has a vision of global change: "Queer . . . envisions a variety of possibilities for reordering the relations among sexual behaviors, erotic identities, constructions of gender, forms of knowledge, regimes of enunciation, logics of representation, modes of self-constitution, and practices of community—for restructuring, that is, the relations among power, truth, and desire." Thus queerness, obsessed with transgression as the route to power, is finally a scatology in search of an eschatology. Michel Foucault, meet Norman O. Brown.

Naturally, the queer utopians reject the compromising liberal finitude of equal rights and equal protection under the law. They wish to "queer" society, to expose the essential "queerness" of everyone and everything. Queers do not want a place at the table. They want universal acknowledgment that the table has three legs. And yet, in queer writing, "queerness" always comes down to being gay. Worse, it often seems that calling oneself queer is a tactic for not acknowledging that one is merely gay, for not shouldering the burdens of coming out or the responsibilities that come with accepting the inevitable reality of a sexual identity and getting on with the rest of life.

Queers defiantly want to bring the closet out into public view while adamantly refusing to leave it. That is why queers take the premises of gay identity politics to an extreme and proclaim an unending "politics of difference." They adopt the ugly slur "queer" so as to keep the gap between gay people and straight people wide and yawning, especially when it is in danger of being bridged. Yet their project of "queering" society, politics, history, and literature is the expression of a terrible fear of difference.

III.

In *The History of Sexuality,* Volume I—again, the bible of queer theory—Foucault offered a chastening and disheartening diagnosis of the situation of sexuality in society. His American followers have turned his pessimism into a prescription for a better world.

For Foucault, modern society controls erotic life by broadcasting through various channels ever-evolving definitions of sexuality. Foucault called this complex network of domination the "deployment of sexuality." Such a process is part of the modern "discursive regime" that, like earlier discursive regimes throughout history, imposes what we take to be our identity through a web of social customs, moral and linguistic conventions, and official bodies of knowledge.

Yet the domination is not all on one side. It is everywhere. In constructing types of sexuality—one man's simple desire for another man, say, becomes stigmatized as "homosexuality"—modern society also gives people an outlet for expressing their erotic desires through these regulated constructions. And so the Freudian model of repression is a false one. There is no "natural" sex urge that requires only to be sprung from confinement. Modern society will go on constructing desire from all points. It will go on simultaneously legitimizing, stigmatizing, regulating, and making available an assortment of sexualities, which themselves will demand a greater freedom of expression, but always through constructed and regulated channels of desire.

With such a vision of life, Foucault obviously had no hope for a redeemed and perfected erotic world. He had a virtually pagan view of history as cyclical and nonprogressive. Of the discursive regimes cycling discontinuously through history there is no end. And there is no relief from the modern deployment of sexuality. That is why, toward the end of his life, Foucault found philosophical solace in the Stoic philosophers' ethic of self-cultivation through self-discipline. (Practically, he found it in sadomasochism's highly aestheticized rituals.)

Not surprisingly, Foucault held sexual liberationists in contempt. He ends *The History of Sexuality,* Volume I, by declaring that "the irony of this deployment [of sexuality] is in having us believe that our 'liberation' is in the balance." Elsewhere in the same volume, he writes that "we must not think that by saying yes to sex, one says no to power." He disdains the modern tendency to think "sex, the explanation for everything." He laments the "austere monarchy of sex," the way in which we have "become dedicated to the endless task of forcing [sex's] secret, of exacting the truest of confessions from a shadow." He regards it as pathetic that "we demand [of sex] that it tell us our truth." He believed (as did Christopher Lasch) that the most potent modern construction of sexuality was the endless Freudian-derived therapeutic obsession with sexuality.

Just as Heidegger wanted to return to a pre-Socratic purity of being, Foucault wanted to return to ancient pleasures, to a moment before the deafening modern invention and regulation of sexuality. He thought (bless him) that the time had come to stop thinking about sex. "The rallying point for the counterattack against the deployment of sexuality," this great pessimist wrote at the conclusion of *The History of Sexuality,* Volume I, with typical hyperbole, "ought not to be sex-desire, but bodies and pleasures." And the site for his "counterattack" was precisely the Stoic philosophers' faith in the private conditioning of private appetites.

Yet Foucault's followers, consecrated to absolute fluidity, prefer to ignore all this. "Foucault's 'self' . . . is not a personal substance," Halperin inanely insists in *Saint Foucault,* "or essence, but . . . a strategic possibility." And here is how Gayle Rubin uses Foucault in "Thinking Sex," one of the seminal essays behind queer theory, published in 1984: "The time has come to think about sex. . . . Contemporary conflicts over sexual values and erotic conduct . . . acquire immense symbolic weight. Consequently, sexuality should be treated with special respect in times of great social stress." You can hear the ghostly laughter wafting all the way down the Boulevard Saint-Germain.

This is where Eve Kosofsky Sedgwick, the mother of queer theory, and her chief disciple, Michael Moon, come in. Sedgwick's *Between Men: English Literature and Male Homosocial Desire* (1985) and *Epistemology of the Closet* (1990) are the keystones of queer thinking. In her books and her essays, she does not, like Gayle Rubin, make the semantic mistake of "thinking sex." Instead of saying yes to sex as a way of saying no to power, Sedgwick says yes to "bodies and pleasures" as a way of saying no to power. She makes "bodies and pleasures" the explanation for everything, dedicates herself to the endless task of forcing the secret of "bodies and pleasures" from a shadow, and demands that "bodies and pleasures" tell us our truth.

In other words, she ends up like Rubin anyway, deploying the very deployment of sexuality that Foucault decried as a noisy plague on the erotic life. It is a dead end spawned by Foucault himself, though he turned to Greece and Rome and left his contradictions behind. Yet Sedgwick is in total intellectual and unironic servitude to what she has made of Foucault. From three different works by Sedgwick, written over the course of seven years: "Foucault's demonstration, whose results I will take to be axiomatic . . . "; "A span of thought that arches at least from Plato to Foucault . . . "; "the gorgeous narrative work done by the Foucauldian paranoid, transforming the simultaneous chaoses of institutions into a consecutive, drop-dead-elegant diagram of spiralling escapes and recaptures . . . ."

A LOT HAS BEEN WRITTEN about the influence of Nietzsche and Heidegger on Foucault, but I don't believe anyone has pointed out the significant influences of French film and the *nouveau roman*. (Foucault's name probably first appeared in an American publication in 1963, in an essay that Susan Sontag published in *Partisan Review* on Nathalie Sarraute and the *nouveau roman*, where he pops up last in Sontag's list of French commentators on that new literary style.) Like Alain Robbe-Grillet, Sarraute strove for a zero-degree objectivity that would reveal a zero-degree subjectivity. Robbe-Grillet wished for "the possibility of presenting with all the appearance of incontestable objectivity what is . . . only imagination." He invited the reader to supply gaps in meaning with the reader's own meaning; he juxtaposed isolated objects or "shots"; he plausibly imposed a crazy illogic. And he found in film the most felicitous vehicle for such expression.

Shortly after Robbe-Grillet publicized his ideas, Foucault began to offer his own. He insisted on filling in history's silences with the meanings that he chose for them; and he explained an entire society and culture by isolating from its context a cultural practice or institution; and he rested his rationally presented judgments on his presumption of a universal irrationality. That is to say, Foucault became the first cinematic philosopher. He jump-cut around history.

This is exactly the intellectual style that Sedgwick has adopted in her weirdly mechanistic language. (You will find her matter-of-factly mentioning "adult/child object choice," for example, as just another option on the erotic menu.) She "presents with all the appearance of incontestable objectivity what is . . . only imagination." And this is fine, because, remember—"all it takes to make the description 'queer' a true one is the impulsion to use it in the first person." So all it takes to find a particular meaning in a literary work is the impulsion to wrench it from "silence"; to isolate it from anything else in the work; and then simply to say, in defiance of all common sense, that it is there.

Once you isolate this particular meaning from its organic connections to the rest of the work, you may connect it to everything in the universe outside the work. This is because all identity and meaning are socially constructed, and because the way in which these constructions are fashioned and imposed is the key to all private and public "realities" in modern life. After all, Foucault says so. And what results from this sort of criticism is the "queering" of literature.

IV.

Consider Sedgwick's reading of this passage from Henry James's *Notebooks,* written during a visit to California when he was sixty-two:

> I sit here, after long weeks, at any rate, in front of my arrears, with an inward accumulation of material of which I feel the wealth, and as to which I can only invoke my familiar demon of patience, who always comes, doesn't he?, when I call. He is here with me in front of this cool green Pacific—he sits close and I feel his soft breath, which cools and steadies and inspires, on my cheek. Everything sinks

in: nothing is lost; everything abides and fertilizes and re-
news its golden promise, making me think with closed
eyes of deep and grateful longing when, in the full summer days of L[amb] H[ouse], my long dusty adventure
over, I shall be able to [plunge] my hand, my arm, *in,* deep
and far, and up to the shoulder—into the heavy bag of re-
membrance—of suggestion—of imagination—of art—
and fish out every little figure and felicity, every little fact
and fancy that can be to my purpose. These things are all
packed away, now, thicker than I can penetrate, deeper
than I can fathom, and there let them rest for the present,
in their sacred cool darkness, till I shall let in upon them
the mild still light of dear old L[amb] H[ouse]—in which
they will begin to gleam and glitter and take form like the
gold and jewels of a mine.

For Sedgwick, this passage about the importance of reaching
down into memory for literary creation is not about the importance of reaching down into memory for literary creation. No,
the passage "shows how in James a greater self-knowledge and a
greater acceptance and *specificity* of homosexual desire transform
this half-conscious enforcing rhetoric of anality, numbness, and
silence into a much richer, pregnant address to James's male
muse, an invocation to fisting-as-écriture." Why, in heaven's
name, did James hang fire on this topic for so long? Similarly, in
Wings of the Dove, we find an older and wiser James "placing the
reader less in identification with the crammed rectum and more
in identification with the probing digit." Don't ask.

Sedgwick sees in history's silences an extraordinary amount of
shit. *(Wings of the Pigeon.)* And it is all there because Sedgwick
sees it there. And because she is "queer," marginal, "perverse,"
stigmatized, what she has seen has not been hitherto overlooked,

it has been hitherto silenced, just as the queer Henry James had to silence himself. So now the real James (never mind that identity is constructed) will be heard; and now you will listen to Sedgwick because she has truth and virtue (never mind that all meaning is constructed) on her side.

Sedgwick might go fancily on about how "queer" means so many different things, about how "genitality" is the antidote to the constrictions of "sexual identity," but her project always comes down to outing authors through their writing—to liberating them from their repressive historical moment. Needless to say, Henry James is the obsessive favorite for Sedgwick. His enigmatic sexuality makes him such a rich occasion for an analysis of the way in which "heterosexist" society buries same-sex desire under "compulsory" sexualities. And if no one knows for sure what James's sexuality was—alas, all we have are the novels, stories, essays, notebooks and so forth—all the better. A hoarding, secretive anal eroticism can become James's calling card.

The legion of Sedgwick's disciples have adopted the anal strategy as their own, too. In *Novel Gazing: Queer Readings in Fiction* (1997), a collection of essays edited by Sedgwick, Duke University graduate student John Vincent alerts us to the "face/butt metonymy" in Swinburne's poetry. Yet it is the rectum of the Master, brutally robbed of speech by history, in which one finds a veritable buried treasure of "recuperative" meanings. Here is the Duke University graduate student Renu Bora writing about James, also in *Novel Gazing:*

> I picture James's head hovering over a consummated toilet, a glossy, smooth turd lolling in the waters, pride summoning lost pleasures. Perhaps it "passed" (a favorite James term) too perfectly. Perhaps it was less than slippery, and he gripped it within his bowels like a mischievous

boy, playing peekaboo with the exit, hiding it upstairs, clinging to it as to a departing lover. Perhaps this dream only teased him.

The turd of independent minds.

THUS QUEER THEORY IS PARTLY about the more militant gay-liberationist goals of the 1960s "passing" into the tortured textual readings of the 1980s and the 1990s. Consider Sedgwick's theory of "homosocial desire." Propounded in 1985 in *Between Men*—it is more a feminist work than a queer one, with a faint but definite homophobic undercurrent—Sedgwick's theory rocked the groves of academe. It is not complicated. It holds that homosocialness derives from a sentence in Lévi-Strauss's *The Elementary Structures of Kinship,* quoted by Sedgwick in *Between Men:* "The total relationship of exchange which constitutes marriage is not established between a man and a woman, but between two groups of men, and the woman figures only as one of the objects in the exchange, not as one of the partners."

Of course, Foucault is not far behind in Sedgwick's use of Lévi-Strauss. This, again, is because Foucault stressed the importance of making history's silences speak: "There is not one but many silences, and they are an integral part of the strategies that underlie and permeate discourses." That, for queer theory, is the *carte blanche* that launched a thousand *bêtes noires.* What meaning is being suppressed in Lévi-Strauss's formulation? Well, what meaning would you like him to be suppressing?

For Sedgwick, the analytical prize is this: men really desire each other, but society's prohibitions against homosexuality force them to repress that desire. Instead they marry women and channel their homosexual impulses into keeping women subordinate through marriage, while using marriage as a means to bond with other men for social advantage. The homosocial element lies in this bonding, which also causes homosexual panic whenever the forbidden homosexual impulse rises to the surface. In such a way, the entire structure of Western capitalism (Sedgwick looks to English literature to prove her theory, but she makes it obvious that she thinks it applies to Western civilization in general) is supported by a frustration of homosexual desire.

Thus *Between Men* extracts its peculiar argument from one sentence in the work of a French structural anthropologist, who in fact never could prove the general truth of the proposition expressed in that sentence, and never returned to it. And even riskier is Sedgwick's combination of Lévi-Strauss and Foucault. For Foucault saw the absurdity of applying the former's notion of primitive kinship structures to modern society long before Sedgwick went ahead and applied it. As Gayle Rubin puts it in "Thinking Sex," in a passage paraphrasing Foucault, "kinbased systems of social organization . . . [are] surely not an adequate formulation for sexuality in Western industrial societies."

But—and this is where things really get confusing—Rubin herself had used Lévi-Strauss's theory in just such a way a decade before, in an essay called "The Traffic in Women." In *Between Men,* Sedgwick acknowledges Rubin's earlier use of Lévi-Strauss's idea, even though Rubin had already disowned that idea and exposed its illogic. Don't these people have e-mail? This is the kind of thing that Michael Warner has in mind when he celebrates queer theory's "focus on messy representation."

SEDGWICK CITES ALSO another important source for her theory of homosocial desire. It is Freud's essay on Dr. Schreber and "the mechanism of paranoia." Along with countless references to masturbation ("The Aesthetic in Kant is both substantively indistinguishable from, and at the same time definitionally opposed against, autoerotic pleasure") and to our friend the rectum, the subject of Freud's treatment of Schreber's paranoia appears throughout Sedgwick's work.

Freud notoriously claimed that all paranoia derived from an individual's repression of homosexual desire. Schreber's feeling that he was being persecuted by another man arose, for Freud, from Schreber's hidden desire for that man. Here is Freud's formulation of the paranoiac process: "The proposition 'I (a man) love him' is contradicted [repressed] by . . . 'I do not love him—I hate him.' . . . [T]he proposition 'I hate him' becomes transformed by projection into another one: 'He hates (persecutes) me,' which will justify me in hating him."

Such psychic slipperiness enables Sedgwick, in *Between Men,* to cite Freud on Schreber as justification for the way in which "this study discusses a continuum, a potential structural congruence, and a (shifting) relation of meaning between male homosexual relationships and the male patriarchal relations by which women are oppressed." In other words, Sedgwick can find homosocialness anywhere she wants to find it.

Of course, by adopting Freud's theory, Sedgwick gets herself tangled up again. For if men marry women—or simply have sex with women—both to suppress their desire for each other and to bond with each other for social advantage, they can hardly be expressing, at the same time, their hatred for each other. Not to mention the fact that if Schreber's case exemplified homosocialness, society would fall to pieces in a New York minute. And what about mere friendship between men who do not desire each other sexually? Or genuine love and passion between men and women? But no matter. So Sedgwick contradicts herself. Queer theory contains multitudes.

Interestingly, Sedgwick's use of Schreber reverses Whitman: "And what I assume you shall assume,/For every atom belonging to me as good belongs to you." Queer theorists adore Whitman, but they are democracy's dark side. For their flaunting of their "difference" is driven by their belief that everyone is, or must be, the same as them—a belief that they find continually frustrated. The queer theorist's conviction that everyone desires everyone else is the obverse of the queer theorist's mission to accuse everyone of desiring everyone else. Perhaps that is why queer theory is flourishing at a moment when, in our culture, sexual recrimination has become a more instantly gratifying form of sexual indulgence.

V.

Eve Kosofsky Sedgwick has complained about being "misspelled, misquoted, mis-paraphrased" by journalists who "wouldn't have been caught dead reading my work: the essay of mine that got the most free publicity, 'Jane Austen and the Masturbating Girl,' did so without having been read by a single one of the people who invoked it . . . the attacks on me personally were based on such scummy evidential procedures." I'm sure she's right. Sedgwick is one of the most influential academics at work today, and no one seems to read her closely, if at all. Still, if you do stay patiently and carefully with her writing, you find yourself in a twisting labyrinth of mad interpretations.

Or is it that she does not read well, and took up theory and concocted those deliberately outrageous essay-titles to disguise her deficiency? The first literary reading in *Between Men,* of Shakespeare's sonnets, is typical of the way that Sedgwick does literary criticism. Of the 154 sonnets, remember, the first 126 are addressed to a "fair youth," and all the rest but the last two spoken to the legendary "dark lady." The first part famously has a homoerotic undercurrent; but the poet also urges the fair youth to find a woman, marry, and have children.

As always, Sedgwick begins by laying down the theoretical framework. She adduces René Girard's notions of triangular desire. Marx appears. Lévi-Straussian binaries are posited and then deconstructed. There is an enveloping aroma of Foucault ("while genital sexuality is a good place to look for a concentration of language about power relationships . . . "). Connect, connect, connect. She freezes the camera on "Marilyn Monroe": "The speaker treats the youth, rhetorically, as a dumb blonde." Isolate, isolate, isolate. The line "Thou single wilt prove none" does not mean, as it usually is taken to mean, that without marriage the young man will be alone, or will have no heirs. Rather, it means "essentially the same thing as the brutal highschool-boy axiom, 'Use it or lose it.'" Masturbation, as usual, appears; even though it actually is absent. Sedgwick claims that the dark lady is masturbating, and then she compliments herself for saying so by giving Shakespeare a pat on the back: "To attribute masturbatory pleasure to the woman is unusual in these poems—unusually benign and empathetic, I would say."

And then we get the essay's premise, which is also the essay's foregone conclusion: with the dark lady sonnets, "we are in the presence of male heterosexual desire, in the form of a desire [i.e., homosexual desire] to consolidate partnership with authoritative males in and through the bodies of females." This, Sedgwick tells us, is the significance of the phrase "the bay where all men ride," which the poet employs in trying to seduce the dark lady. The poet does indeed mean that the thought of other men having been in the dark lady's "bay" arouses him. But not for Sedgwick. She explains that if the poet's certainty that the dark lady has been with other men excites him, it must be because he has homosexual impulses. Never mind that men might like promiscuous women for another reason.

Sedgwick's vaulting reductions do not only narrow the range of interpretive possibilities. They also narrow the range of erotic possibilities. And then there remains the biggest question that Sedgwick's elaborate cookie-cutter method of reading raises: Why would the poet want to use a common wench like the dark lady—she has, he tells us, a cumbersome gait, a bad complexion, and horrible breath—to bond with "authoritative males" when he has already "bonded" with the obviously powerful and high-born fair youth (who was also Shakespeare's patron)? And why would anyone want to write 154 sonnets about a business trans-action, anyway? All Sedgwick tells us is that "male homosexual bonds may have a subsumed and marginalized relation to male heterosexuality similar to the relation of femaleness to maleness, but different because carried out within an already dominated male-homosocial sphere." Foucault disseminated his generaliza-tions with a lot more flair; and he never dreamed of applying them to literature.

ONE OF SEDGWICK'S most influential essays treats "The Beast in the Jungle," Henry James's long story about a monstrously self-ish man who cannot see that his woman friend's unrequited love for him is slowly killing her. John Marcher binds May Bartram to him by sharing with her his terrifying fantasy of a "beast in the jungle" waiting in the future to pounce on him. It will be an event that could destroy him, he fears. And it is why he must in-definitely postpone his participation in life.

John Marcher consumes May Bartram with his asocial mus-ings; and she begins to waste away and dies. At the story's famous conclusion, he visits her grave in the cemetery, sees another mourner, a man, and envies him his impassioned grief. He real-izes that he has lived a life without passion or human meaning and that "the escape would have been to love" May Bartram, but that he had only thought of her "in the chill of his egotism and the light of her use." Hallucinating, he sees the beast about to leap on him, and flings himself face down on May Bartram's grave.

Sedgwick called her essay "The Beast in the Closet" and made it the centerpiece of *Epistemology of the Closet*. Her argument is that Marcher, compelled by society to pretend that he is heterosexual, has been emotionally and sexually paralyzed by homosexual panic. Such repressed desire is symbolized by the beast in the jungle, what the narrator also refers to as Marcher's "secret." And rather than being in love with Marcher, May Bartram spends the entire story trying to help him become gay so that he might find emotional and sexual happiness with another man. What a fine woman.

Sedgwick is bothered by the conventional interpretation of James's story. It is, she believes, patriarchal, misogynist, and homophobic. The critics who offer it have the audacity to "reunite" James and his protagonist "in the confident, shared, masculine knowledge of what she [May Bartram] Really Wanted and what she Really Needed. And what she Really Wanted and Really Needed show, of course, an uncanny closeness to what Marcher Really (should have) Wanted and Needed, himself." The critics, in other words, assume that May was in love with Marcher, and that ignoring her love spelled his spiritual doom.

In rebuttal, Sedgwick offers up the standard isolated moments. There are coyly knowing allusions to James's use of the word "queer." And there is personal testament: "To speak less equivocally from my own eros and experience, there is a particular relation to truth and authority that a mapping of male homosexual panic offers to a woman in the emotional vicinity." There is also the display of virtuous politics: the tale follows "a classic trajectory of male entitlement." And there is insider chitchat: the encounter in the cemetery with the other mourner reveals "a slightest potential of Whitmanian cruisiness."

And there is, as usual, a swaddling intellectual dependency. Sedgwick applies to literature every theoretical platitude that she has ever gathered. She is banal-retentive. For her, the cemetery encounter actually describes Marcher's sexual desire for the other mourner, which he represses and converts into paranoia and envy: "Marcher's closet-sharpened suspicions." (Freud on Schreber.) The other mourner's loss is "the castratory one of the phallus figured as mother." (Lacan.) And the story itself—"For John Marcher, let us hypothesize, the future secret. . . . I hypothesize that what May Bartram would have liked for Marcher, the narrative she wished to nurture for him," comes down to Marcher's liberation from "compulsory heterosexuality." (Adrienne Rich, "Compulsory Heterosexuality and Lesbian Existence.") You won't find these annotations in Sedgwick's essay.

The beast in James's jungle cannot possibly be Marcher's repressed homosexuality. I do not say so from my own eros and experience. I am not a silencing, homophobic maniac. I merely insist, as a consequence of what I see on the printed page, that James wants the beast to refer to the love that Marcher could have with May, and also to the despair that afflicts him when he proves indifferent to such a possibility. We learn that the beast is "the deepest thing within" Marcher; we also learn that Marcher first met May years before, at an excavation site in Pompeii. And in the story's very first sentence, May's speech "startles" Marcher, just as he expects to be shocked by the beast.

Consider also the remarkable way in which James associates variations on the words "spring" and "to spring" with both the springlike May and the beast. Her relationship with Marcher had "sprung into being with her first penetrating glance." Standing by May's grave, Marcher "rested without power to move, as if some spring in him . . . had been broken forever." And the name Marcher, of course, alludes to the month when spring holds out hope beyond winter. As for the beast:

> The Beast had lurked indeed, and the Beast, at its hour, had sprung; it had sprung in that twilight of the cold April when, pale, ill, wasted, but all beautiful, and perhaps even then recoverable, she [May] had risen from her chair to stand before him and let him imaginably guess [that she loves him]. It had sprung as he didn't guess; it had sprung as she hopelessly turned from him, and the mark, by the time he left her, had fallen where it was to fall.

From spring to fall: "The Beast in the Jungle" is, among other things, about a May-December romance that never was. In "recuperating" James's identity as a closeted homosexual (I have always assumed that he was one), Sedgwick erases his identity as an artist.

How does Sedgwick get away with this awful stuff? Her success is owed in part to her intermittent use of a reveal-all-hurts-and-wounds style of writing. After all, winning a reader's sympathy (as opposed to earning a reader's respect) is now a certified rhetorical stratagem; and the literary critic, too, has her uses for the confessionalism of the day. It enables her to write unsympathetically about subjects that have an elusive complexity. And anyone who cavils is vicious; an anti- or a-phobe.

> I can say generally that the vicarious investments most visible to me have had to do with my experiences as a woman; as a fat woman; as a nonprocreative adult; as someone who is, under several different discursive regimes, a sexual pervert; and, under some, a Jew.

> As a child, I hated and envied the frequent and apparently
> dégagé use my parents liked to make of the word *humiliat-*
> *ing*, a word that seemed so pivotal to my life that I could
> not believe it could *not* be to theirs.

Sedgwick's preternatural sense of alienness is perhaps why she
is so convinced that the "scummy evidential" reaction to "Jane
Austen and the Masturbating Girl" reflected a dangerous opposition to onanism. True, she gravely concedes that "today there is
no corpus of law or of medicine about masturbation; it sways no
electoral politics; institutional violence and street violence do not
surround it, nor does an epistemology of accusation." No, thank
God, there is no street violence surrounding masturbation today.
Still, trouble is brewing:

> Yet when so many confident jeremiads are spontaneously
> launched at her explicit invocation, it seems that the
> power of the masturbator to guarantee a Truth from which
> she herself is excluded has not lessened in two centuries.
> To have so powerful a form of sexuality run so fully
> athwart the precious and embattled sexual identities
> whose meaning and outlines we always insist on thinking
> we know, is only part of the revelatory power of the Muse
> of masturbation.

And yet, despite all the forces of darkness gathering out there,
I have to report that "Jane Austen and the Masturbating Girl"
does not live up to its promising title. And it is promising. For
why shouldn't a literary critic write about masturbation? Or, for
that matter, about rectums and excrement? Norman O. Brown's
chapter called "The Excremental Vision" in *Life Against Death*
analyzes with brilliance, wit, and style the role of the anus and

human feces in Swift's writing. For the analysis of masturbation, I envision an essay starting with Rousseau and the connection between his idea of a totalizing "general will" and his bouts of masturbation; and moving on to Rilke's aimless, unemployed hands in the *Notebooks of Malte Laurids Brigge;* and then to Kafka's *The Trial,* where the words "hand" or "hands" are repeated dozens of times in a sophisticated, ironic burlesque of sexual and romantic frustration; and finally to Gide's *The Counterfeiters,* in which a young boy named Little Boris, a compulsive masturbator, kills himself.

IT MAY BE SEDGWICK and her crowd are not comfortable with how great writers have consciously set out to portray one of the queers' favorite topics. Anyway, Sedgwick on Austen does not illuminate. I spent an entire, evidentially motivated day immersed in her fantasy about *Sense and Sensibility.* The essay's "point," if you can call it that, is that Marianne Dashwood's emotional and psychological distress is the result not of her rebuff by Willoughby, but of, yep, masturbation.

Sedgwick's argument consists of quoting a series of excerpts from a French medical text written about one hundred years after Austen wrote *Sense and Sensibility.* The author is one Demetrius Zambaco—a figure whom Sedgwick never discusses or even identifies—who describes what he believes are the effects of masturbation on two young girls. Some of these effects strikingly resemble Austen's dramatization of Marianne's malady. And therefore, Sedgwick reasons, Marianne must be masturbating.

Such an arcane analogy alone would be a shaky enough basis for an argument about literature and life. Worse, it appears that Sedgwick stumbled. Three years before Sedgwick delivered her paper on Austen to the MLA in 1989, Zambaco was exposed as a fraud by none other than Jeffrey Mousaieff Masson

in *A Dark Science: Women, Sexuality, and Psychiatry in the Nineteenth Century.* The volume is a collection of nineteenth-
century clinical writings that includes Zambaco's full text, and a
preface by Catharine MacKinnon. Yet Sedgwick went right
ahead and published her paper in 1991 without making the
slightest reference in her arguments to Masson's book, even to
rebut him. She didn't even revise her paper to identify Zambaco. She merely mentioned Masson's volume in passing, in a
brief footnote.

Sedgwick's evasiveness is understandable. For, according to
MacKinnon, Zambaco and the other writers in Masson's book
"trade in half-truths." Their "diagnoses are not true because their
etiology . . . is not true." Zambaco is a "sadomasochist." Masson
writes that "Zambaco's view about the sexuality of the two girls
is a fantasy"; and he considers Zambaco's text to be "shockingly
brutal, offensive, and pornographic." It's impossible to disagree:
Zambaco's treatment consisted of repeatedly applying a red-hot
iron to the clitoris of one of the girls, until the patients were removed from his care. But Sedgwick uses Zambaco's diagnosis of
the two girls' condition as a justification for her view that Austen
is describing a similar condition for Marianne. In other words,
Sedgwick believes that the sadistic, misogynistic doctor and the
exquisitely profound novelist share the same understanding of
women. This is the fumbled connection at the core of Sedgwick's
notorious essay.

Oh, she does try to connect Marianne's masturbation with a
lesbian relationship between Marianne and her sister Elinor,
though "connect" is, in this context, far too merry a word:

Is this, then, a hetero- or a homoerotic novel (or moment
in a novel)? No doubt it must be said to be both, if love is

vectored toward an object and Elinor's here flies toward Marianne, Marianne's in turn toward Willoughby. . . . Even before this, of course, the homo/hetero question is problematical for its anachronism . . . if we are to trust Foucault, the conceptual amalgam represented in the very term "sexual identity," the cementing of every issue of individuality, filiation, truth, and utterance to some representational metonymy of the genital. . . .

And if Sedgwick could demonstrate that Marianne Dashwood has been masturbating—say, by the miraculous discovery of a letter from Jane to her sister Cassandra ("Mr. Plumptre walked home with us yesterday & ate soup and talked of Chawton—this morning after breakfast destroyed entire chapter with wedding of Marianne and Digit—Henry dines tonight with Mr. Digwood")? It would be like demonstrating that at a certain point in the novel Marianne is sitting on a chair rather than on the sofa upon which generations of scholars have believed her to be sitting. The novel would still be longing for attention. And Marianne would still be in love with Willoughby, not with her finger.

Curiously, since Sedgwick published her essay on Jane Austen in 1991, she has more and more come to sound like the anti-Sedgwick. Consider her interest in Silvan Tomkins. (In 1995, she co-wrote the long introductory essay for *Shame and Its Sisters: A Silvan Tomkins Reader,* a volume that she also co-edited.) Tomkins was, essentially, an eccentric behavioral psychologist who, among other things, drew up personality evaluation tests for the Educational Testing Service. That is to say, he was just the sort of psychological expert that Foucault spent his life trying, fairly or unfairly, to expose. Yet Tomkins is also another kind of perfect guru for Sedgwick. For one thing, he describes sex in Sedgwick's mechanistic ("if love is vectored toward an object") and abstract terms. An excerpt from Tomkins:

> Many normal adults . . . utilize genital interpenetration as a way of heightening the oral incorporative wish or the earliest claustral wish. Sexual intercourse, as we shall see, lends itself as a vehicle to every variety of investment of social affect.

In other words, sex is an effect of affects. And the most primary "affect," for Tomkins, is shame. By using Tomkins, then, Sedgwick makes her publicly proclaimed feelings of "humiliation" theoretically more fundamental than the impossibly complicated matter of sex.

And this is what Sedgwick and the queer theorists seem to have wanted all along: to turn the "body" ("the two writing bodies of Marx and Engels," says Michael Warner) into an impersonal, quantifiable spaceship in which they can flee from the emotional and psychological tumult of sex. That is, from themselves. Perhaps such a self-disowning is why, in the introduction to her book on Tomkins, published in 1995, Sedgwick sardonically turns against even Foucault.

> Some consequences of such readings of Foucault: The most important question to ask about any cultural manifestation is, subversive or hegemonic? Intense moralism often characterizes such readings.

But this is precisely the earth-shaking question that Sedgwick had been asking for her entire career! From Shakespeare to Jane

Austen to Henry James: Sedgwick has subjected one literary work after another to an intensely moralizing interpretation.

Sedgwick may or may not be "straight," but she sure is full circle. For just as the homophobe strips the homosexual person of his human amplitude—the queer particularity of selfhood—and reduces him to his sexual practices, Sedgwick and her colleagues strip the homosexual person of his human amplitude and reduce him to his sexual practices. That is why the more you read the queers, the more their idea of "queer" sounds like a new kind of oppressive "normalcy."

VI.

Why am I being so hard, so mean? Because the result of Sedgwick's inestimable influence has been, among her followers—all of whom either are college teachers or will someday be college teachers—a deadness, not just to beauty and fineness of perception and fragile inner life, but also to human suffering. Michael Moon's new book, *A Small Boy and Others,* is interesting only as an illustration of this.

Of the seven chapters of Moon's book, three are concerned with Henry James. (*A Small Boy and Others,* in fact, is the title of one of James's autobiographies.) In James's wonderful story "The Pupil," the touching and fairly uncomplicated relationship between a tutor and a young boy named Morgan in his care reveals, in Moon's expert hands, each one's sexual desire for the other. The story is not about what James seems to have meant it to be about: two injured souls supporting each other amidst the shabbily genteel Moreens' cruel manipulations of both the tutor and their son. And it is the boy's mother, Moon has discovered, who has extended to the tutor the "invitation to desire Morgan." This, Moon tells us, is because the mother herself has probably been engaging in incest with her eleven-year-old boy.

Moon works up this last point by patiently and calmly explaining that the *"gants de Suède"* that Mrs. Moreen draws through her hands are made of a material that is described as "undressed kid" in "English-language guides to proper dress from midcentury forward." And "kid," Moon discloses, also means "child." (Impressive references to William Morris and the Earl of Shaftesbury drive home this point.) "Undressed kid," therefore, means "undressed child." Get it?

It follows from this that, in having Mrs. Moreen draw her gloves through her hands, James wants us to understand that she is unconsciously reenacting sex with her son. What role incest plays in this story, though, Moon never tells us. He merely "recuperates" it in this one isolated moment. And he never returns to it, which is not surprising, since a work of art can no more be split up into atomized particles than pleasure can be isolated from emotion, meaning, and value. As if to acknowledge this technical obstacle, Moon goes on to draw a helpful extraliterary conclusion from the story. With a kind of eerie remoteness, he writes:

> Like little Morgan and his tutor and the other "small boys" and young men that figure in these texts, we all often find ourselves possessing what seems to be both more knowledge than we can use and less than we need when we try to think about such difficult issues as our own relations to children and young people, including our students.

Comparing James's "The Pupil" to the film *Blue Velvet,* Moon describes Dennis Hopper's brutal beating of Kyle Maclachlan as representing "the two men's desire for each other that the

newly discovered sadomasochistic bond that unites them in-
duces them to feel." How the Master would have loved that
scene! *Midnight Cowboy,* moreover, is not about the shelter of
intimacy that the physically crippled Dustin Hoffman and the
psychically wounded Jon Voight find with each other away
from economic and sexual confusions; it is, says Moon, "a film
about how two men can have a meaningful S-M relationship
without admitting to being homosexuals." Moon has sadomasochism on the brain.

In *A Small Boy and Others,* the seventy-year-old James writes
about how, as a young boy visiting the Louvre, he "felt myself
most happily cross that bridge over to Style constituted by the
wondrous Galerie d'Apollon . . . a prodigious tube or tunnel
through which I inhaled little by little, that is again and again, a
general sense of glory." Professor Moon has an orals question
about this passage: "What's large enough for one to walk through
and small enough to take into one's mouth?" And so the young
James and his tutor are perhaps having sex. And the older James
goes to a Yiddish play on the Lower East Side perhaps because he
wants to have sex with the famous Yiddish actor Boris
Thomashefsky. And on, and on, and on, and on, and on.

Queer America, I am putting my straight shoulder to the
wheel, but I don't like what this is all about. For this cannot be
literary criticism, and this cannot be life, and this cannot be sex.
When we reduce our lives to "bodies and pleasures," we reduce
bodies and pleasures to an ongoing debate about the meaning of
our lives. And then we reduce love to work, and work, without
the promise and reward of love, to a senseless finality. And the
worst of it is that, as the effect of making a physical presence into
a cold abstraction, we will start to become indifferent to—or
perhaps connoisseurs of—physical pain in other people. Then we

will have broken the sympathetic bond between the heart and the flesh. And then the taste of our own lips will be all that we can rely on to summon our erotic past out of distant memory. And then we will all be traveling away from ourselves and each other along a very dark road indeed. Sexualizing all of life takes all of life out of sex. Good-bye, penises. Good-bye, vaginas.

Eyes Wide Shut:
What the Critics Failed to See
in Kubrick's Last Film

Eyes Wide Shut is one of the most moving, playful, and complex movies I have ever seen. I love the way Stanley Kubrick expresses the film's theme of social and psychological doubleness through a *double entendre* in the film's very title—"I's Wide Shut"—and through his choice, for the title song, of a waltz by Dmitri Shostakovich, a guileful composer famous for writing music whose subtle motifs seemed to celebrate Stalin but actually undermined him. I love the film's spare, almost allegorical portrait of the tension and complexity at the heart of a marriage. So imagine my alarm when, picking up one magazine and newspaper after another, I read reviews calling Kubrick's film a disaster and a titanic error, trite and self-important, one of the worst movies the critics had ever seen.

> I can state unequivocally that the late Stanley Kubrick, in his final film, "Eyes Wide Shut," has staged the most pompous orgy in the history of the movies. (David Denby in *The New Yorker*)

Ridiculously though intellectually overhyped for the very marginal entertainment, edification and titillation it provides over its somewhat turgid 159-minute running time.
(Andrew Sarris in the *New York Observer*)

This two hour and 39 minute gloss on Arthur Schnitzler's fantasmagoric novella feels like a rough draft at best.
(J. Hoberman in *The Village Voice*)

In *Eyes Wide Shut* nothing works.
(Louis Menand in *The New York Review of Books*)

An unfortunate misstep.
(Michiko Kakutani in the *New York Times*)

I soon began to discover something even more startling. Not a single critic, not even those few who claimed to like *Eyes Wide Shut,* made any attempt to understand the film on its own artistic terms. Instead, the critics denounced the film for not living up to the claims its publicists had made for it, reduced it to a question of its director's personality, measured it by how much information it conveyed about the familiar world around us. And I realized that something that had been stirring around in the depths of the culture had risen to the surface.

After years of vindictive, leveling memoirs of artistic figures; after countless novels, plays, films, paintings, and installations constructed to address one social issue or another; after dozens of books have been published proclaiming the importance of the "great books" and "humanist ideas" to such a point of inflation that the effect was to bury the specificity of great books and of original ideas—after the storm of all this self-indulgence had passed, a new cultural reality had taken shape. Our official arbiters of culture have lost the gift of being able to comprehend a work of art that does not reflect their immediate experience; they have become afraid of genuine art. Art-phobia is now the dominant sensibility of the official culture, and art-phobia annihilated Stanley Kubrick's autumnal work.

Much talk—some of it real, a lot of it fake—has been in the air over the last decade about empathy for the "other," for people different from us. But no one has dwelled on the essential otherness of a work of art. There is, after all, that hackneyed but profound notion of a willing suspension of disbelief. Genuine art makes you stake your credulity on the patently counterfeit. It takes you by surprise. And for art to take you by surprise, you have to put yourself in the power of another world—the work of art—and in the power of another person—the artist.

Yet everything in our society, so saturated with economic imperatives, tells us not to surrender our interests even for a moment, tells us that the only forms of cultural expression we can trust are those that give us instant gratification, useful information, or a reflected image of ourselves. So we are flooded with the kind of art that deprecates attentiveness, tells us about the issues of the day, and corresponds to our own personalities. And if a genuine work of art appears that has none of these qualities, critics impose them anyway, for they fear that if they surrender themselves to the work's strangeness, they will seem vulnerable and naive and intellectually unreliable.

EYES WIDE SHUT is the story of an affluent Manhattan doctor named Bill Harford (Tom Cruise) and his wife, Alice (Nicole Kidman). One night during Christmas season, Bill and Alice go to a lavish holiday ball thrown by one of Bill's patients, the shady and superwealthy Victor Ziegler. Alice dances with a dashing Hungarian stranger, who tries to seduce her, and Bill is almost lured from the party by a pair of stunning models. Arriving home, Bill and Alice make love. The next night Alice smokes a joint and tells Bill about the Hungarian's advances; he chuckles and shrugs it off. Annoyed by her husband's indifference to the power of her sexuality, Alice, in revenge, reveals that during the previous summer she found herself so attracted to a naval officer who was staying in their hotel that she would have given up Bill and their seven-year-old daughter, Helena, to be with him. Bill becomes obsessed with Alice's story, and he plays over and over in his mind the image—done in black-and-white tones by Kubrick—of Alice making furious love with the officer. The rest of the movie follows Bill as he moves through a world whose hidden erotic nature his obsession has uncovered: his adventures include encounters with a prostitute and with a nymphet in a costume shop and end with a masked orgy in a Long Island mansion at which Bill is discovered, exposed as an intruder, and nearly punished, until a mysterious woman offers herself up as a sacrifice in order to save his life. He escapes, and the film ends with Bill and Alice and Helena searching for Christmas presents in a toy store.

Now, it is perfectly possible not to like this film; I know more than a few sensitive and intelligent people who felt they could have lived without it. The film has its longueurs; it is full of puzzles, riddles, and games; it is highly orchestrated and stylized, like a cross between Krzysztof Kieslowski and Noh drama. It is perfectly possible not to like Kieslowski or Noh drama either; for that matter, it is possible to dislike Ezra Pound's *Cantos* or Henrik Ibsen's plays or Andrea del Sarto's paintings. But one cannot simply dismiss them. One must make one's negative judgment of them also a mode of understanding them.

There is pleasure as a form of diversion, and there is pleasure as a form of attention. *South Park* is in the former category; I can say that I dislike it, and no one is going to ask me for an interpretation that will support my dislike, for the simple reason that if I interpreted it, I would be ignoring the movie's simple, diverting nature. I would get laughed at. But I cannot just dismiss *Hedda Gabler* without interpreting it. If I did, I would be ignoring the play's purpose of laying claim to the attention. I would be in no position to judge its worthiness.

The critics were in no position to judge the worthiness of *Eyes Wide Shut;* they took the wrong tack. Since the film's producers had mounted such an immensely noisy publicity campaign—Kubrick's last film; one of the world's greatest directors tackles the subject of sex, sex, sex by staging the most erotic orgy scene ever filmed; see Nicole Kidman nude; see Tom Cruise nude; see the couple married in real life make love on the screen—the critics had to show that they were not going to allow bullying commerce to determine their experience of the film. So they decided not to respond to the film. They decided to respond to the hype. And the result was that the hype totally determined their experience of the film. They wrote about it as if it were a work of diversion and not a work of attention.

Consider this admission from Andrew Sarris, writing in *The New York Observer:* "Perhaps if *Eyes Wide Shut* just popped out of the blue without all the infernal hype and infomercials I might have appreciated it more for its uncommon virtues." This is a truly astounding thing to say, since no one was stopping Sarris from ignoring the hype and appreciating the virtues. Such weariness toward the commercial world was flaunted by most of the critics. J. Hoberman began his review by disclosing the information that Warner Bros. produced the film and that *Time*-Warner Bros.' "corporate sibling"—"shamelessly" promoted it. So what?

Pope Julius shamelessly promoted the ceiling of the Sistine Chapel. In *The New York Review of Books,* Louis Menand went farthest of all. Asserting that Kubrick hadn't finished the film, he concluded that even if he had, it wouldn't have mattered anyway, because the people who made the film "became inflated by their own hype." And what if the people who made the film actually did not become inflated by their own hype? How would Menand know either way? But the critics would not be restrained. They had to prove that they were not about to have the wool pulled over their eyes by commercial culture—even if they had to trample on a work of art to prove it.

IT JUST SO HAPPENS that right around the time *Eyes Wide Shut* opened in the theaters, a book came out about Kubrick and the film that gave the critics exactly what they were looking for. *Eyes Wide Open,* by Frederic Raphael, is a memoir of the director by a screenwriter who shares with Kubrick a writing credit on the film. The book is an act of revenge. Raphael is convinced that Kubrick stifled his talent and commandeered the script. As payback for Kubrick's indifference to his genius, Raphael paints a devastatingly corrosive picture of the director as an obsessive tyrant who squeezes the life out of scripts, scriptwriters, and actors. And since this portrait of Kubrick corresponded in fact, if not in tone, to some other recent accounts of him, the critics seized on Raphael's memoir as a guide to the film.

In truth, they had no choice, even if they knew that Raphael's memoir was "self-promoting," as Menand put it. Raphael's image of Kubrick as a tyrant went to the core of the general artist-phobia. And once this picture of Kubrick—the mean, controlling genius, the maniacal director who shot scenes forty or fifty times—was in the air, no one could write about the movie without taking this information into account. Those who did would look like they were out of the loop. They would give the embarrassing appearance of people who, in 1999, did not know how to assimilate information.

I have never before read reviews in which the issue was the working habits of the director rather than the qualities of the film itself. Menand, on one of Kidman's scenes: "She really gives it, in what was plainly the ninety-ninth take, an earnest effort." How could Menand possibly know that this was the ninety-ninth take? He is substituting information that he has gotten about how the director operates for what he, as a critic, should be doing, which is to make sense of how the scene works.

Andrew Sarris solemnly dwelled a bit on Andrew Sarris ("I am booking [*Full Metal Jacket*] this term for my Columbia genre class on the War Film"), and then he pronounced judgment on *Eyes Wide Shut* using Raphael's framework: "more control-freak unreality than visual genius." David Denby also responded to Raphael's picture of Kubrick as a figure of oppressive authority who instills fear: "Even, however, if you let your imagination run wild, the atmosphere—sombre, trancelike, unimpassioned—should hold you in check. The orgy is frozen in ritual, and devoted not to pleasure but to authority and fear." Yet this formidable and reliable critic never bothered to ask himself whether Kubrick deliberately made the orgy seem devoted to authority and fear.

According to Raphael, Kubrick insisted that he stick faithfully to Schnitzler's novel. Here, too, the critics swallowed Raphael whole:

MENAND: Schnitzler's story is set in turn-of-the-century Vienna and Kubrick's movie is set in contemporary New York City, but otherwise the adaptation is pretty faithful.

HOBERMAN: The script . . . is . . . surprisingly faithful to the 1926 Schnitzler original.

KAKUTANI: The movie was faithfully adapted from a 1926 novella called "Rhapsody: A Dream Novel" by the Viennese writer Arthur Schnitzler.

The fact is that the screenplay follows only the skeleton of the novel. (Was everybody able to get a copy of the Schnitzler in time to meet their deadlines? It's been out of print for years, and I spent days finding mine.) In the novel, the Bill character answers Alice's confession of an adulterous desire with his own tale of adulterous desire. In the movie, he doesn't. In the novel, the Bill character says he remembers having seen the man Alice desires. In the movie, Bill does not. In the novel, the Bill character leaves the prostitute because he is revolted by her. In the movie, Bill is interrupted by a call from his wife on his cell phone. In the novel, there is no Ziegler character. In the novel, the password Bill uses to gain entrance to the orgy is "Denmark." In the movie, it is "Fidelio." Remarkably, no critic I've quoted even brought up the password. This is a pretty bad lapse for reviews that called Kubrick's meditation on marriage an empty aesthetic exercise, since the opera *Fidelio* is Beethoven's hymn to conjugal love. Indeed, Kubrick structures his film with gorgeously subtle references to *Fidelio* and Christmas and Ovid and Homer, though none of the critics here interpreted any of these allusions either. Nothing of the sort exists in Schnitzler's tale.

The critics may have gotten the relationship between the film and its source material all wrong, but that didn't stop them from taking Raphael's cue and lambasting the movie for not getting the relationship between its setting and contemporary New York right. Although the movie wears its expressionistic and symbolic style on its sleeve right from the start—the Shostakovich waltz playing over the titles stops when Alice turns off her radio—the critics wrote as if Kubrick had aimed and failed to make a *Frontline* documentary about life in present-day New York. Denby even accused Schnitzler of anachronism. ("Writing in Vienna in the mid-twenties, Schnitzler may have sensed that his material, in terms of consciousness of sex, was already dated, so he set the book earlier, before the First World War.") Now, why would Schnitzler write a novel about themes that he thought were already dated? He was Arthur Schnitzler, friend of Freud and Klimt and Schoenberg, not some idiot. And it's not even clear that his novel takes place at the turn of the century. Raphael is the one who says that; the time period is never stated in the novel. The whole question is, of course, moot. Novelists and filmmakers set their work in the past when they want to avoid the distracting immediate particulars of their own time and place, when they want to strip their stories down to essences and ultimates. That's what Kubrick does in *Eyes Wide Shut,* but the critics did not consider that. That would have been unfamiliar and demanding and respectful of the viewer's desire to imaginatively inhabit other worlds. Calculating the proximity of Kubrick's New York City to life in the real New York City, on the other hand, assures viewers that they never have to venture away from their own experience.

Attacking a work of art on the grounds that it doesn't reflect contemporary appearances and conventions was bad enough, but the critics really outdid themselves on the subject of sex. The portrayal of an orgy, after all, had been the centerpiece of the film's publicity campaign. Therefore, the publicists had to be thoroughly debunked. Yet in debunking all the hype about the sex, the critics never got beyond the hype about the sex. They seemed intent on proving how sexy they were, and how sophisticated they were about sexiness, because when sexiness is marketed as vigorously as it is in America today, one had better appear to have mastered the market. Never mind that *Eyes Wide Shut* is not about sexiness but about sex. I've already quoted Denby on the "pompous" and "unimpassioned" nature of the orgy ("I found myself bored" with the film, he sighs near the end of his review).

MENAND: A ring of kneeling supermodels (identical proud firm breasts, straight hair, no hips) wearing only masks and black thongs and looking extremely chilly. . . . It is a very tacky orgy.

HOBERMAN (after alerting *Voice* readers that the orgy takes place "somewhere in the richest, most Republican districts of Long Island"): Hardly the sexual heart of darkness, this decorous gavotte is more studied than a fashion shoot and rather less explicit. The final shock: Two men dancing . . . together!

SARRIS: It can be revealed at last that there are acres and acres of female pubic hair on display, but no male members . . . [in] the otherwise boring free-for-all orgy sequence.

KAKUTANI: The masked orgy, much hyped in advance publicity for the movie, feels more ludicrous than provocative, more voyeuristic than scary. . . . It is curiously devoid of sexual energy. . . . The entire orgy sequence feels deliberate and contrived.

These are the terms, set by the film's promoters and determined by the enveloping dynamics of commercial culture, in which the critics judged Stanley Kubrick's last film.

EYES WIDE SHUT is a descendant of Bernardo Bertolucci's *Last Tango in Paris*. Both films examine the relationship of fucking to fraternity, of sex to society, and both reach the same conclusion: for the social order to survive, the instincts have to be recognized for what they are and then restored to their hiding place behind society's curtains. This is a sturdy old theme, but that is not the same thing as a dated theme. The trick is in inflecting the old theme with idiosyncracy and fresh insight, and in honestly refracting it through the colors of one's time, without miring it in mere documentary particulars.

In *Last Tango in Paris,* Marlon Brando plays the down-on-his-luck owner of a cheap hotel in Paris. Crushed by his wife's suicide, enraged by her infidelity, he begins an affair with a young woman from a bourgeois family. He insists on anonymity. Pure sex is all he wants, with an emphasis on anal sex, for anal eroticism represents a total reversal of conventional romantic love, and Brando is in a rage against what he now considers the fraudulence of romantic ideas. Although she is engaged to be married, the young woman, played by Maria Schneider, submerges herself in the affair. She accepts and enjoys Brando's sexual demands and starts making her own.

One day, Schneider arrives at the apartment they have rented to find it empty. She is distraught, and when Brando rushes up to her in the street, she tells him that she never wants to see him again. But Brando has fallen in love with her. He is the true romantic; only a romantic could rebel so extravagantly against the shattering of romantic illusions. He tells Schneider his name and describes his life to her. A proper bourgeois girl, she is appalled by his lowly status (Schneider's facial expressions are hilarious here), though she has pledged herself to him. She is the true sexual nihilist, who would betray her fiancé with Brando but will not marry a man whose social status is lower than hers, even if she loves him.

In the film's closing scene, Brando chases Schneider through the streets and follows her upstairs to her family's apartment. There he playfully puts on her late father's army cap—he was a colonel in French North Africa—and then, removing it, tells Schneider that he loves her. Horrified by his irreverence, cornered, afraid, Schneider shoots him dead with her father's army pistol. Thus society executes Brando for wanting to bring the instincts back into alignment with emotional life. It is the bourgeoisie, represented by Schneider, who pruriently wish to keep them apart.

Our tame middle-class critics so wanted Kubrick's orgy to be dark and dangerous and full of sexual energy, but Kubrick wanted to show that sex without emotion is ritualistic, contrived, and in thrall to authority and fear. He was too wild for them. Everyone droned on about how unerotic Kubrick's orgy is, but no one talked about how intensely erotic is Bill's fantasy of Alice making love with the naval officer. It is so erotic because Alice is the object not only of Bill's desire but also of his love.

No one tried to fathom the film's purposes. Just about every critic also mocked what they considered to be Cruise and Kidman's stilted performances. They seemed to be acting like actors, everyone complained. At one point in his review, Menand obliquely refers to rumors that the real-life Cruise and Kidman have a sham marriage and that Cruise is actually gay. "Who cares?" asks the impressively unimpressible Menand. "It doesn't matter, because they have no chemistry in the movie, either."

Well, Kubrick must have been pretty stupid to spend three years filming actors who couldn't act. But Kubrick wasn't stupid. In a film about life's essential doubleness, Kubrick presents Cruise and Kidman with double lives. They are actors in a film, and they are people we think we know something about. Their real marriage exists beneath the rumors of trouble, just as the troubles of their film-marriage exist beneath its apparent success. They act with dreamy formality because they exist between dream and reality. Kubrick wants us to watch Cruise and Kidman and think about what people appear to be and who they really are.

Kubrick's genius in *Eyes Wide Shut* is to make us look at the film the way the film looks at life. The title announces the film's perspective: we stare life in the face and miss what is truly going on right under our noses. Bill is a doctor; his job is to defy the corruptions of time and repair injured bodies. Thus he is willfully blind to the way the demands of bodies hasten the ravages of time. Physical desire ruins friendships, destroys marriages, discombobulates thoughts and feelings. Underneath Bill's sober medical optimism lies the hazardous dynamism of sexual fantasy and sexual desire. That is why Alice hides her pot in a Band-Aid tin. And because desire is an agent of metamorphosis, Ovid, the author of *Metamorphoses,* becomes one of the film's presiding presences.

The danger Bill and Alice face is that either domestic emotions will stifle sex or that unbridled sexual indulgence will kill off the individuality that nourishes emotional attachment. This is a dated theme? (That's like telling Hamlet to lighten up—everyone's father dies, for goodness' sake.) Such a dilemma is why the movie begins with a shot of Kidman's back and her unforgettable ass. We see her back when she dances with the Hungarian; Bill sees a man grabbing a woman's behind in a doorway as he wanders the streets; a partly obscured sign over a store reads "ass" through a window behind Bill and a gay desk clerk in a hotel as they talk; Ziegler delivers his stunning monologue about the banal inevitability of sexual desire to Bill's back; Helena picks up a giant teddy bear from behind in the film's final scene and asks if Santa will buy it for her.

The back, the ass, represent our animal side. They do not convey our individuality. Only our face does that. But the risk is that if we surrender ourselves absolutely to our anonymous animal side, we slide helplessly toward death, the absolute anonymity. For this reason, there are masks in Bill's patient's apartment and in the prostitute's place, too, and this is why Kubrick makes the orgy a masked affair. When Bill finds out that the mysterious woman at the orgy who may have saved his life has died, he goes to the morgue, steps over to her body, and almost kisses her face. Her face has become a death mask, and his urge to kiss it signifies that he has submitted too thoroughly to his obsession. And to Alice's machinations.

For just as every enchantress Odysseus meets on his voyage home is an echo of his thralldom to Penelope, every woman Bill meets is a version of Alice. (The numerous references in *Eyes Wide Shut* to *2001: A Space Odyssey;* the naval officer; and the large model of a ship in Ziegler's billiard room emphasize the film's allusions to Homer.) This is why the prostitute is beautiful and educated. And this is why Bill is constantly being interrupted just as he is about to satisfy his desires. He allowed an interruption to come between him and Alice, and now he must be punished in the very same terms over and over again. Just as the husband in *Fidelio* is in prison, so is Bill: twice we see him standing behind bars, outside the costume store and outside the gate of the Long Island mansion. With her tale, Alice has orchestrated his fate for him. At any moment she can betray him with her naval officer, just as at any moment Penelope can betray Odysseus with her suitors.

The movie does not resemble New York? How can it when it has such a large poetic and symbolic dimension? Kubrick paints vast pictures with minute strokes. As Bill is being tormented by his black-and-white fantasy, Alice sits at home watching television, helping Helena with her homework, and eating a black-and-white cookie. Consider, too, the movie she is watching. In the scene we see and hear, George Segal is sitting in a café in Rome, across from the Colosseum. A waiter brings him something, and Segal says, *"Grazie."* The waiter says "You're welcome." "If I were Italian," Segal mutters to himself, "he would have answered me in Italian." What a wonderful, whimsical way to improvise on the film's theme of the expectations and disappointments of desire. We live in the subjunctive: if only we could be someone else and get what we want. But when Bill gets what he wants and enters the orgy, he sees nothing but sterile coupling. There is the fantasy of absolute gratification, cynically projected from every corner of the culture, and there is the reality of the cookie and the child and the homework and the companion you have chosen, and for whom, despite everything, you sit at home waiting. Compared with the everyday reality of sex and emotion, our fantasies of gratification are, yes, pompous and solemn in the extreme. That is why the film's recurrent motif is of the Christmas tree. For desire is like Christmas: it always promises more than it delivers.

KUBRICK'S FILM IS HARDLY, as some critics have said, an instance of antierotic moralism. It is, instead, honest about the power and necessity and permanence of erotic life. It is about the simultaneity of irreconcilable desires. As the film proceeds, the dialogue increasingly takes the form of *double entendre*: "Would you like to come inside?" the prostitute asks Bill. The gay desk clerk refers to two tough-looking guys "you'd not like to fool around with" and giggles. Ziegler gestures to the pool table and says he has been "knocking a few balls around." The orgy itself runs parallel to the ball at the beginning, even as it parodies social life. The Hungarian with the long nose finds his mirror image in a man wearing a mask with the very same nose. Pairs proliferate throughout the film, reminders of our double natures. A sculpture in Ziegler's house, seen at the beginning of the film, is of two figures, a wingèd one bending over another without wings; people lift both their arms and raise both their hands; there are symmetrical doors and coffee cups; in Ziegler's billiard room, you see two pineapples, a perfect image of the banal duality of our desires.

I don't know how the critics could have missed the tenderness of Kubrick's themes, the way he has Cruise and Kidman look at each other out of each one's unfathomable depths—I's wide shut—the way he has Kidman stroke Cruise's head after she tells him her violent second fantasy, as if she is taking a maternal pity on the man whom she, as the furious lover, cannot help tormenting.

Indeed, the movie ends with a clement apprehension of a marriage's fragile world. When Bill finally returns home at the end of his adventures, he finds the mask he wore to the orgy, and which he thought he lost, on the bed next to the sleeping Alice. This is what they both have created, unwittingly, through their psychosexual *pas de deux*: the menace of an utterly lost individuality. Bill begins to sob, but he is sobbing for two opposite reasons, inextricably entwined: he is afraid that his marriage has been destroyed, and throughout his adventures he has failed to satisfy his desires. And so when Alice says to Bill in the movie's last line, "You know, there is something very important we need to do as soon as possible. . . . Fuck," she is reiterating the doubleness. Fucking is exactly what they have to do, but sexual desire is what got them into trouble in the first place. For there is no such thing as fucking in a vacuum.

In the end, nothing is resolved, but the fundamental irresolution at the heart of life is briefly illumined. Such is Stanley Kubrick's final film. You can understand the film and honorably still not like it, but you cannot proclaim your dislike of the film without basing it on your understanding. At a time when we are surrounded by movies about killing, and movies about murdering, and movies about slaughtering; by cheap caricatured reflections of human life; by dishonest and money-driven and career-driven drivel at every turn—at a time like this, you'd think someone would have given a genuine work of honest art its due. Oh, how I wish I were in Italy.

García Lorca and the
Flight from Desire

Poet, playwright, composer, pianist, guitarist, draftsman, actor, director, set and costume designer, Federico García Lorca made the ceaseless hunger of desire his obsessive theme. He called it *negra pena*, "black pain," and *perro en corazón*, "dog in the heart." Here is the final stanza from his "Sleepwalker's Ballad" (all translations are mine):

> Up over the face of the well
> the gypsy girl swayed and she swayed.
> Green her flesh and her hair so green
> and her eyes are full of cold silver.
> An icy piece of light from the moon
> Keeps her aloft on the water.
> The night grew close and intimate
> like the square of a small town.
> Drunken policemen pounded on the
>   door.
> Greenly how I want you so greenly.
> Green wind. Branches that are green.
> The ship aloft on the sea.
> And the horse on the mountain.

Lorca creates an atmosphere of impossible proportions, out of which nevertheless rises a dreamy congruity between the futility of desire and the intensity of desire. He is the celebrated master of such a mortal dissonance. And yet, for all the acknowledgement of his greatness, Lorca has always suffered a little at the hands of his admirers.

The most sober readers of Lorca's poetry and plays, it seems, cannot help having their idea of the poet distorted by the romantic image Lorca cultivated of the passionate Andalusian gypsy. And Lorca's death, at the age of thirty-eight, before a Fascist firing squad in the opening days of the Spanish Civil War, only intensified the dramatic aura around his life. One man boasted afterward that he had helped to kill Lorca, shooting "two bullets into his ass for being a queer"—an especially grotesque fate for a shrewd yet childlike man who was driven throughout his brief existence to resist imposed identities, whether political, sexual, or artistic.

Even William Carlos Williams, that lapidary anti-romantic, lost his footing when he considered Lorca. "His murder," Williams wrote, "is perhaps as he would have wished it to be: to die on the horns of the bull." It's a response that strangely resembles that of Salvador Dalí, Lorca's onetime friend and intimate: "The moment I learned of his death. . . I cried 'Olé!' I thought that for Federico Garcia Lorca it was the most beautiful way of dying: killed by the Civil War."

Lorca himself had trouble restraining the image of Lorca. "Don't pull that Lorca business on me!" he once shouted at an actor who was imitating his operatic style of recitation. (When Frank O'Hara wrote, "I'm getting rather Lorcaesque lately / and I don't like it," he was saying pretty much the same thing.) This is why Leslie Stainton's clear-eyed new biography, *Lorca: A Dream of Life*, the first in English in a decade, is so welcome, despite its limitations. Stainton's supercautious detachment can fade into remoteness, and her remoteness sometimes dissipates into appraisals of Lorca's writing so blandly general that they might apply to just about any poet at all. There isn't anything substantially new about Lorca's life here, either. Yet Stainton has told the story vividly and with real narrative drive, and has thus offered an occasion for the kind of reevaluation of the poet that she herself does not venture.

It's high time for a fresh consideration of Lorca, because his reputation thrives in two mythic-historical categories—one encompassing writers supposedly cursed by fate as the price of their genius (Keats, Chatterton, Rimbaud, Leopardi), and the other writers wounded and then done in by historical forces as punishment for their genius (Walter Benjamin, Osip Mandelstam, Isaac Babel, Bruno Schulz). We forgive these myths their obfuscations for different reasons: in the first case, we like to see a rough destiny redeemed by vindicating history; in the second, we like to see terrible history shamed by a vindicated destiny.

In fact, Lorca was both genuinely apolitical and sincerely enraged at the backwardness and inequality of Spanish society. The son of a wealthy landowning father and an educated, doting mother, he was emotionally connected to some prominent Socialists and was voluble about his unhappiness with Spanish social arrangements—that's why the Fascists came for him—but he refused to join a political party. His murderers, though, had an exaggerated sense of his ideological commitments and martyred him. And his admirers, in their rational impulse to vilify his killers, have obscured his true achievements by exaggerating his martyrdom.

As a dramatist, Lorca is known mainly for three plays, tragedies that appear to portray the consequences of a static society's repression of sexual instincts: *Blood Wedding*, *Yerma*, and *The House of Bernada Alba*. As a poet, his reputation rests on two volumes of verse: the *Gypsy Ballads*—which includes the "Sleepwalker's Ballad"—and *Poet in New York*. The latter he wrote during a brief stay in New York in the late twenties, when he enrolled as a student at Columbia University and lived in a Columbia dorm.

Lorca's previous biographers and now Stainton have made much of his supposed state of mind when he was in New York: lonely, depressed, alienated by the mammoth, modern city, tortured by his sexuality, and suffering in particular from a disastrous love affair with a roué who had toyed with his affections and left him for a woman. A corrosive personal anguish is certainly the dominant emotion in *Poet in New York*. But what needs to be explored is the connection between the emphatic dark note in his poetry and the fact that Lorca, in Stainton's words, "left the United States with renewed faith in his work. . . and a newfound enthusiasm for life." Stainton, as she often does, conveys this information in isolation, instead of embedding it in evidence from Lorca's life or in a convincing interpretation, and then, almost mechanically, moves on.

Lorca may have been depressed in New York, but much more significant is the mastery of his wrenching poems in *Poet in New York*. Such vertiginous introspection in art requires supreme inner poise. The paradoxical relationship between Lorca's psychic harmony and his increasingly nimble expression of anguish on the page does much to explain how he used his encounter with American blacks in his poetry. In New York, the Andalusian-born poet, who proudly claimed both Gypsy blood and Jewish blood, developed an almost fanatical, occasionally comic, and sometimes arrogantly condescending attraction to Harlem, and to the cause of black enfranchisement. Stainton writes, "Appalled by newspaper ads promoting powders to lighten black skin and pomades to flatten black hair, Lorca criticized those African Americans who would deny their race, and he rashly called for black violence to counter the cruelty of white America. One day, he wrote, black America will crush its oppressor, and blood 'will flow / on rooftops everywhere, / and burn the blond women's chlorophyll.'"

But Lorca wrote these lines, and other verses portraying American blacks as helpless and their situation as hopeless, during the Harlem Renaissance—a uniquely hopeful moment in black life in America. There is a case to be made for reading the vision of human misery in *Poet in New York* not as a projection of Lorca's inner state but, rather, as an ecstatic celebration of his new artistic strength. With his extreme depictions of the African American "other," and of the infernal American city, Lorca had, perhaps, contrived a way to normalize his own suffering.

LORCA'S GROUNDBREAKING biographer was the Irish scholar Ian Gibson, who set to work on Lorca's life just three years after Franco's death, and thus three years into Spain's rapidly emerging democracy. The political context obviously spurred Gibson to create something more than a biography, and he ended up producing a sprawling, dense, fascinating study of Spanish society and politics. Though Gibson's book remains the definitive work on Lorca, Stainton has done more to emphasize the man rather than his context. Unlike Gibson, however, she takes no interpretive chances.

Consider these lines from Lorca's magnificent elegy for his beloved friend Ignacio Sánchez Mejías, a famous bullfighter who, having just made a comeback after years of retirement (he needed the money), was mortally wounded in the ring:

I do not want to see it!

Tell that to the moon when it comes,
that I do not want to see the blood
of Ignacio all over the arena.

I do not want to see it!

The wide-open moon,
tranquil horse-clouds,
and the gray bullring a dream
with willows in its walls.

I do not want to see it!

This is Lorca's reply to the straight machismo that spurned his gay machismo, and it is all the more meaningful because Ignacio loved men as well as women. Gibson relates this fact about Ignacio's private life. Oddly, Stainton, who elsewhere writes of Lorca's homosexuality with sensitivity and insight, neglects to mention it. Yet to know how Lorca configured a destiny for himself in his art, you first have to see the pattern that his sexuality imposed on his life. "Ode to Walt Whitman," for instance, composed for *Poet in New York*, is a furious diatribe against the "*maricas*," the "faggots" of the world, "murderers of doves," who "give boys / drops of filthy death with bitter poison," counterposed by a paean to an idealized Whitman, possessed of "virile beauty," with "thighs as virgin-pure as Apollo's." Stainton takes the straightforward psychological approach and regards the ugly lines as embodying Lorca's anxiety about his effeminacy. But it seems just as plausible that they express the crude beginnings of Lorca's vision of an escape from desire itself.

Lorca is, indeed, a poet of desire, but he is, ultimately, the poet of an intense yearning to be free from desire. His tragedies, though conventionally read as attacks on sexual repression, are more truly protests against the condition of sexual longing. For Lorca was Spain's last great Catholic poet, though his Catholicism was soaked in Surrealism. He honors the poet who "gives up dreaming and gives up desiring. He no longer desires. He loves." The aspiration toward love beyond desire is Lorca's reply to the Surrealists' worship of desire, and the spiritual stillness that he sought approached a kind of oblivion.

In high modernist style, Lorca fashioned a theory as a pedestal for his art: death as the embarkation point of creation; an inner, self-obliterating frenzy as the source of poetic inspiration. He exalted "duende," which in Spanish folklore is a goblin energy demonically allied with death. Many people have been misled by his famous analogy between the artist's duende and the bullfighter's. Lorca was not celebrating the bullfight or adoring death; he was subtly undermining the toreador and asserting in his place the creative virility of a certain homosexual poet, who was occasionally vexed by his own effeminacy. "The duende wounds," Lorca wrote. "In the healing of that wound, which never closes, lie the strange, invented qualities of a man's work." It is the healing that has the highest value for Lorca, and not the destruction caused by the wound. The most viciously homophobic newspaper in Spain, which agitated for the arrest of *los ambiguous*, was in fact called *El Duende*. Death was its muse. With his idea of duende, Lorca turned the cruelty he hated in Spanish society and culture—and which lay nascent within himself—on its head.

One of the secrets of Lorca's poetry lies in his use of the word *cosa*, "thing." It is the way he colonizes the realm of extinction. Here are excerpts from three phases of his brief career:

Guitar begins
weeping. . .
Impossible to
silence.
It weeps for distant things.

("The Guitar")

Under the gypsy moon
things are looking at her
and she cannot see them.

("Sleepwalker's Ballad")

I want to cry because I have the urge
    to cry,
the way children in the last row cry,
because I am not a man, or a poet,
    or a leaf,
but a wounded pulse that patrols and
    serenades and hangs waiting for
the things of the other side.

("Double Poem of Lake Eden")

"Distant things," invisible things, "the things of the other side": into the arena of death Lorca imports this world's precious palpability. He confers eternity on finitude just as he humanizes infinity. This cunning transubstantiation, contrary to the vision cherished by the acolytes of his martyrdom, is the only kind of death Lorca ever desired.

PART FOUR

Life in the Palm of Art's Hand

Dante and the Subversive Ego

Long before it was the name of a magazine, "self" was at the heart of the greatest fiction and poetry. And there is seemingly no end of autobiography that rises to the level of literature: Augustine, St. Theresa, Montaigne, Goethe, Carlyle, Mill, and on and on. The historical list of what we exasperatedly call "memoir" is long, and the tides of self-immersion have now reached universal shores. Identity, what to do with our burden and bounty of inwardness, the connection between what goes on inside the mind and what happens outside of it—such questions have, in our culture, become the work of more and more people. Everybody is poking around in his or her interior.

Nowadays, the general question of the self almost exclusively takes the form of investigations into one's own experience. There are the old-style revival meetings known as talk shows, the personal websites on which a camera thrillingly follows the site-owner through his or her day at home, the "storytelling" monologists reciting their lives on stages throughout the country. Even Hollywood's lingering, screen-filling close-ups (film's version of the first person) now occur in almost every frame. But the written word, the most intimate form of self-expression, remains the most common form of self-exploration. Reporters have been placing themselves more and more emphatically at the center of the events they describe since the

New Journalism of the seventies. Memoirs and fictionalized autobiographies, usually about extreme afflictions endured and overcome, have been pouring out of publishing houses for the past twenty years. And the American novel hews closer and closer to the first person, even, somehow, when it's written in the third person: consider Jonathan Franzen's *The Corrections,* in which the author, the narrator, and the characters all speak in the same voice.

In this culture of almost occult self-centeredness, nothing riles cultural commentators as much as the slightest reference to the self. The reaction is both understandable and surprising, but it recently acquired the proportions of the perverse. Has there been another moment in history when a society's reaction to the murder of thousands of its citizens was a sigh of intellectual relief at the prospect of cultural liberation?

> Up until the moment the twin towers fell, America was deep in a cocoon of self-gratification and self-improvement. (Maureen Dowd)

> It seemed this week as if the World Trade Center disaster, like a plague of Egypt, had stripped off layers of the city's narcissism and venality. *(New York Times)*

> Is each generation entering its new phase of life with a new attitude? Are aging boomers overcoming narcissism? (op-ed in *USA Today,* on possible results of the September 11 attacks)

> Narcissism and cynicism are attitudes of the last century. (Stephen Novick, the vice chairman and chief creative officer of marketing giant Grey Global Group, on the culture after September 11, quoted in *Newsday* on October 11)

So is this the end of the culture of narcissism? "Yes, well, that would be nice, wouldn't it?" said Dr. Gail Saltz, a psychoanalyst with a practice on the Upper East Side. (in the *New York Observer*)

Return to Narcissism With Emmys. (headline in the *Baltimore Sun,* October 29)

Since Christopher Lasch coined the phrase "culture of narcissism" twenty-three years ago in his jeremiad against American self-obsession, the term "narcissism" has been used to encompass everything from self-gratification to the seemingly infinite modes of American self-expression. So when these reporters and commentators refer to narcissism, they tend to mean any cultural activity that revolves around the self. Insofar as they are taking exception to American solipsism and selfishness, their aversion, though not their timing, makes sense. But insofar as these writers are expressing glee at the possibility that foreign terrorists have finally rid us of talk shows ("self-improvement") and close-ups and reminiscing monologists and memoirs, then they are as wrong as they are callous and crude, for these glib excoriations of self-centeredness actually conceal the origins of their target, which lie deep in America's social and economic arrangement.

The dynamic is dizzying: A rugged, rough-and-tumble economy makes individuals radically vulnerable and thus radically vigilant about their every move. A business culture produces a condition of permanently stimulated appetite, in which any issue touching the consuming self holds the most interest and the highest value. So people—many people—turn inward to find that part of themselves that is connected to a larger life, that exists beyond their self-interest and their banal desires. And what happens then?

The captains of the culture deplore all the vigilant self-absorption and defensive self-scrutiny as narcissistic.

But our self-investigations are not the problem—they are essential. What we need is an improvement in the art of making them. Indeed, ceaseless self-examination offers our brightest cultural prospect. It's the only way to cut our own path through the prevailing image of a collective "self," composed of vanity and trivial appetites, projected onto us by a commercial society. If we master the art of making them, our good self-examinations will help fend off the bad narcissisms.

The truth is, though, few people want to read honest self-description. A full, unsparing account of one's self would be a full, unsparing, and perhaps unbearable exposure of social and political and cultural reality. It would include not just our stories and afflictions and memories but our ability to injure and to deceive, to hurt and to kill. It would portray not just that vague entity called "my self" but the particular, individual ego that drives it.

Fortunately, a style of self-description exists to which we might aspire. When Dante Alighieri began his *Divine Comedy* around the year 1308, it was the first time in the history of imaginative literature that an author had placed himself at the center of his tale, and the poem endures as not only the first but the most effective epic of the self. So the appearance in the past ten years of no fewer than six translations of the *Inferno* and a recent brief biography of the poet might present a hopeful sign, reflecting some readers' sense that, if we want to step forward into the next phase of self-description, we would do well to step back into the fourteenth century.

IN A LETTER TO HIS PATRON, Can Grande, the ruler of Verona, Dante famously described the inner motion of the *Divine Comedy*, or *La Divina Commedia,* a poem in three parts *(Inferno, Purga-*

torio, Paradiso), about Dante's spiritual journey from darkness to light, guided through hell and purgatory by Virgil, Dante's ideal poet, and led through paradise by Beatrice, his ideal love. In the letter, excerpted by R. W. B. Lewis in his solid and informative little biography, Dante explained that the poem did not possess one meaning but "might rather be called polysemous, that is, having several meanings." Dante goes on to designate the poem's levels as the literal, the moral, the allegorical, and the anagogical, the last signifying an ultimate truth about existence. For the benefit of Can Grande, Dante conjured up the impression of an almost unbelievably self-conscious set of intentions.

Scholars have typically taken Dante at his word, characterizing the *Commedia* in terms of dry intellectual purpose, as if the poet had set out to organize, like a monthly budget, his epic's personal and political meanings, its strands of Aristotelianism and Thomism and canonical Catholicism, its commentaries on history and love and the evolution of the soul. But it's hard to imagine Dante making a moral addition here, an anagogical subtraction there. More likely, in his letter to Can Grande, Dante is putting forth as a poetic method the by-then conventional approach to interpreting the Bible; in doing so, he is also puffing up his benefactor by confiding a poet's creative secret. The polymath author knew the value of a little intellectual intimidation, too.

Dante didn't create his poem "polysemously," if that is construed to mean an arid, almost mathematical approach to symbolic layering. He composed it with passionate complexity. He lived polysemously; experience cut his imagination into facets that glitter all at once in the lines of his masterpiece. Born into impoverished nobility, his father a moneylender, Dante served his native Florence as soldier and statesman. The city-state was divided at the time into Guelphs—the party of the pope—and Ghibellines—the party of the Holy Roman Emperor. The

Alighieris belonged to the former party, but in the late 1200s, after the Ghibellines had been driven out of Florence once and for all, the Guelphs split themselves up into Whites (led by the Cerchi family) and Blacks (the Donati), the Whites taking the antipapal position of the Ghibellines. Dante, eventually convinced that only the emperor could unify Italy, cast his lot with the Whites. When the Blacks seized power in Florence in 1302, they condemned him to death, forcing him to leave his wife, Gemma Donati, and their four children in his beloved native city and to wander in exile from one hospitable prince to another for the rest of his life.

By the time of his death sentence, Dante had proven himself a man of action, riding with the Guelph cavalry in their conclusive rout of the Ghibellines. He had served as councilman, elector, and then prior—public posts that enabled his enemies to accuse Dante of taking bribes, just as Dante's father's enemies had accused the elder Alighieri of usury.

Yet it was Dante's conduct, not simply his allegiances, that inflamed his adversaries. According to Boccaccio, Dante made himself such a central figure in Florentine politics that, in Lewis's words, "no action was taken by the city council, no law was passed or abrogated, no issue of war or peace was decided unless Dante had his say." Lewis presents Dante as a saintly figure whose every political judgment put the common good above his own private prejudice or personal interest. "[Dante's] position was steadfast: no yielding to pressure . . . , no involvement with external affairs. The welfare of the commune must come before everything."

Yet Dante, though he belonged to the Whites, was married to a Donati, a high-status member of the Blacks. This may be why, during Dante's tenure as an influential politician, a number of Whites were exiled along with several Blacks, including the

White Guido Cavalcanti, Dante's friend but also his chief poetic rival. In fact, Dante, emboldened by family connections and his own reputation as a poet and intellectual, seems just as biased and vindictive as his contemporaries. He refused compromise when it suited his purpose, rejecting Pope Boniface VIII's offer of sending Charles of Valois to calm the strife in Florence. Boniface had his own designs, and the Blacks wanted to use Charles as their tool. And Dante, whose support came from the Whites, had his own reasons for turning down Boniface's overtures.

As for the charge of taking bribes, it's as plausible as the possibility that the partisan charge was trumped up. Dante desperately needed cash. "There were money problems," as Lewis politely characterizes Dante's situation. It's hard to imagine that, in his cultural context, Dante didn't take a few florins here and there in exchange for political favors. The Italians, after all, invented machine politics; replace "Florence" with "Chicago" and such run-of-the-mill improprieties seem merely to add to the rich enigma of Dante's personality. Dante himself, in the *Inferno*'s first canto, allows the "she-wolf" of avarice the most devastating influence on him of the three allegorical beasts (the lion of pride and the leopard of lust being the other two) who block his way as he tries to ascend the hill of goodness.

Maybe Dante's sense of his own public importance really was the courage of lofty conviction, but it seems more like an enormous ego's fantasy of infallibility and invincibility. In his treatise on the superiority of Italian over Latin as a literary language, written between 1304 and 1307, Dante had celebrated himself as a genius responsible for inventing a new form of poetic expression. His boast was right, but his extravagant egotism was too much, even in rough, violent, wild, bawdy fourteenth-century Florence, famous for its bisexuality, for making black clothes fashionable, and for breeding comedians, renowned throughout

Europe, who would crash a formal banquet and announce, "If I was not invited, the fault is not mine."

These were Dante's boundary-blurring times. His character both magnified and transcended their effects. If no poet before Dante had written an epic in which the author was the main character, neither had any poet employed the elevated, ancient form of the epic to slander and punish his personal and political enemies. Most breathtaking of all, no Christian poet had ever composed a work of literature in which he impudently placed himself, after his own death, in heaven, among the angels and the saints.

When, in the *Inferno,* Dante indicts the ego as the driving force behind the world's folly and cruelty and misfortune, he knows whereof he speaks. At one point, he implores Virgil to shove a sinner—a hated contemporary—back into the sea of mud that he has been consigned to. The self—his self—is always with Dante; he tells the truth about its cruel capacities and about its onerous nature. He would have laughed at the way our commentators dismiss the ego's exertions as "narcissism"; he would have recoiled from the way some of our writers narcissistically present the ego as harmlessly afflicted or disengaged. Dante makes the problem of ego his theme early on. In Canto II, he is following Virgil, who has invited Dante to make the long, painful journey with him upward to the divine light of paradise. Suddenly, Dante loses his nerve. Notice here the repetition of *"io."* Because Italian often drops the first-person pronoun, Dante's re-iteration of it brims with purpose:

> *Ma io, perche venirvi? o chi 'l concede?*
> *Io non Enea, io non Paulo sono;*
> *me degno a cio ne io ne altri 'l crede.*
> *Per che, se del venire io m'abbandono,*
> *temo che la venuta non sia folle.*

But why should I go there? who allows
it?
I am not Aeneas, nor am I Paul.
Neither I nor any think me fit for this.
And so, if I commit myself to come,
I fear it may be madness.

(Robert and Jean Hollander)

Only this wearying, incessant, relentlessly intrusive first person stands between Dante and Beatrice, who waits for him in
paradise. *"Se del venire io m'abbandono"*—another way to render
that is, "If I lose myself and come along." How fitting that at the
end of the *Inferno,* Dante's *io* has dissolved into union with his
guide: *"E quindi uscimmo a riveder le stelle."* "And so we emerged
to see, once again, the stars." At the conclusion of the *Purgatorio,*
the "I" reappears, now cleansed and purged and ready for the final ascent to paradise and Beatrice: *"Io ritornai de la santissima
onda/rifatto . . . "* "I returned from the most holy waves/remade
. . . " In the final lines of the epic, at the close of the *Paradiso,*
Dante writes:

> *A l'alta fantasia qui manco possa;*
> *ma gia volgeva il mio disio e 'l velle,*
> *si come rota ch'igualmente e mossa,*
> *l'amor che move il sole e l'altre stelle.*

Here power failed the lofty phantasy; but already
my desire and my will were revolved, like a wheel
that is evenly moved, by the Love which moves
the sun and the other stars.

(Charles S. Singleton)

"Disio" means "desire," in this case the intellectual desire for God. *"Velle"* means the will to attain that desire. Dante has finally melded his appetite with his intellect and resolved himself into *dis-io*, the I that is also the not-I, the state in which the self's desire has become fused with the self's longing to be annulled.

IF THE *Divine Comedy* is the great poem of the self, the *Inferno* is the poem's most intense episode of self-exploration. It is where Dante's attempt to overcome his ego, so necessary to his attainment of grace in paradise, is most strenuous and transparent.

Dante pioneered this new phase in self-centered writing—the elevation and transmogrification of the naked self into a subject fit for poetic exploration—in 1293, about a decade before he began the *Divine Comedy*. The *Vita Nuova* is the account of his real-life love for Beatrice Portinari, literature's most famous girl-next-door. Told in poetry and prose, the prose providing the self-conscious and analytical autobiographical framework for the self-surrendering sonnets and canzones, the work is an extraordinary fusion of egotism and spiritual yearning. In it, Dante describes Beatrice's sudden death, ending on a note of sorrow, piety, and braggadoccio, declaring that he will soon return to his beloved girl and write about her "that which has never been written of any woman." The entire work is a struggle between an intellect seeking to know God through the sublimation of physical desire—seeking to enter a "new life"—and a will smitten by eros and in thrall to fame.

The spirit of self-opposition rules the *Vita Nuova,* and it dominates the *Commedia,* in which Dante fulfills his boast of writing a new kind of poem. The torsion of self-conflict drives the entire epic, just as the friction between autobiographical—and egotistical—prose and self-surrendering poetry propelled the *Vita Nuova.*

Whether Dante is turning against his sinners their own sins or inflicting on them the opposite effect of their sins—flatterers drown in excrement; gluttons are pelted with dirty rain; suicides, rejecting faith, are mired in subjectivity—he has them living out the truth of themselves by acting against themselves. At one point, he uses the word *"contrapasso,"* or "counterstep" (my translation) to describe the nature of infernal punishment. The poet might have had such a counterstep in mind in the *Inferno's* first canto, in which he finds himself spiritually lost. He tries to advance up a hill toward the sun, but he has planted behind him his *"piè fermo,"* his "firm foot"—traditionally understood as the left foot, symbolizing appetite, whereas the right foot stands for intellect—and this foot slows him down.

In this way, Dante lays bare the truth of himself by avowing his individuality and then consciously acting against it. From the beginning, he dramatizes his *"contrapasso"* and his *"passo,"* as it were, his moral weakness and his moral strength, at the same time. Driven into despair by avarice, lust, and pride, he exposes his vulnerability to each. Frankly exposing his faults, he demonstrates his moral and his poetic worth. To overcome his ego, Dante first has to display it in all its blindness and folly. And his egotism is the way he fortifies himself, so as to withstand this self-exposure.

THERE IS A MOMENT in Canto XXV of the *Inferno* when Dante passes through the circle of hypocrites and thieves. The poet stops to announce that Ovid himself could not have imagined the kind of metamorphosis he is about to pull off—and with astonishing inventiveness he makes a man and a serpent exchange forms. It's a conspicuous flash of ego, one that seems the hypocritical antithesis of Christian humility; it even seems, in this circle of thieves, like an attempt to steal another poet's laurels. In the previous canto, Dante has already staked his claim to imaginative mastery with a metamorphosis that serves as a kind of warm-up. Since these two cantos are the only examples in the *Inferno* of Dante explicitly taking on another poet and then displaying his artistic powers, the first metamorphosis begs to be read as an artistic credo. The transformation consists of the poet reducing a man to ashes and then instantly recomposing him. Dante describes this startling quick-change in a very peculiar way:

> No *o* or *i* could be made with strokes as fast
> As he took fire and burned and withered away,
> Sinking; and when his ashes came to rest
> Ruined on the ground, the dust spontaneously
> Resumed its former shape.

(Robert Pinsky)

By reversing the two letters, "i" and "o," Dante associates the poetic evocation of the destruction of an individual with the effacement of the self, and he associates the effacement of the self with the ability to put pen to paper and make art. With a few strokes of his own pen, he exposes his capacity for hypocrisy and even for a kind of violent theft, he egotistically shows off his creative powers, and he identifies creativity with the abolition of the ego. The passage echoes with the *Inferno*'s deep pendular motion: self-assertion and self-obliteration, reckless appetite and chastening intellect, *"contrapasso"* and *"passo,"* destruction and creation—all of which will dissolve at the end of the poem into *"disio,"* the I that is also a not-I.

He never so vividly evokes himself as when he is dissolving himself in another person. His *Commedia* is where Ovid meets Stanislavsky. Entering the seventh circle, Dante sees the suicides, who have been cast into the form of trees with gnarled, twisted branches. Having uprooted themselves from their bodies, they spend eternity inhabiting strange bodies with alien roots. Dante, who throughout the *Inferno* is as tender about human suffering as he is vindictive toward his Florentine persecutors, is profoundly moved. Trying to grasp what is passing through Virgil's mind, he writes:

> *Io sentia d'ogne parte trarre guai*
> *e non vedea persona che 'l facesse;*
> *per ch'io tutto smarrito m'arrestai.*
> *Cred'io ch'ei credette ch'io credesse . . .*

> I could hear wailing, deep and pitiful,
> but there was no one anywhere about,
> and I grew so perplexed that I stood still.
> I think that he was thinking that I thought . . .

(Michael Palma)

As Robert and Jean Hollander observe in the commentary on their translation, the *"smarrito"* in Dante's third line echoes the *"smarrita"* in the famous third line of Canto I, meaning "lost" or "bewildered." The poet wants us to know that he himself was in such despair that he considered the folly of suicide. He is so upset by the agony that confronts him that he twists his syntax in the fourth line, but in such a way as to both express his own state of mind and illuminate the suicides' inner condition.

Often translated as "think," which pleases the ear, the fourth line cries out for "believe." (*"Credere"* can mean either but is closer to "believe.") For the suicides shunned faith—i.e., belief—and surrendered to hopelessness. Dante surrenders himself to this state of mind by beginning in the indicative and ending in the subjunctive, by twisting, as the suicides' limbs are twisted, the verb *"credere,"* from certainty to uncertainty, from outer reality to inward self-enclosure.

THE VERY LANGUAGE Dante employs fuses with what it describes. By transporting himself into each sinful other's state of mind, he both asserts his weakness and makes that assertion his strength. With Paolo and Francesca, such complicated mimicry rises to virtuoso heights. Caught *in flagrante* and murdered by Francesca's husband, the pair cling to each other in a whirlwind through eternity. Encountering them, Dante can barely control himself. He immediately melts into another nature. Flirting with the flirtatious Francesca, he assimilates the sweet, silvery style of her speech. Since her manner of speaking happens to be in the style of Dante's early verse, in the *Vita Nuova,* he does Francesca to perfection. Swept up in the intensity of an amorous encounter, as well as in a moment of self-recognition, the poet cruelly ignores Paolo.

But Dante is not, of course, there with the lustful in hell—not permanently, at least. He has got to distance himself from Francesca even as he is performing her. And so he has the murdered woman undercut her own starry-eyed language by having her abruptly describe Paolo's fatal kiss with crudeness and disgust: *"questi . . . la bocca mi basciò"* ("this one smacked a kiss right on my mouth"). Despite her bitter coarseness, Dante is so moved by her story that, in the canto's final line, he passes out: *"E caddi come corpo morto cade."* "And I dropped like a dead body drops." Yet this line's hard alliteration runs against the mellifluous courtliness of the preceding lines. It is like Zero Mostel coming onstage at the end of *Rigoletto* and delivering a Bronx cheer. The *"oi"* becomes an *"io"* once again, but an *"io"* a little less burdened by ego.

Primed by his own experience of life, Dante turned himself into a poet of incredible plasticity. In the circle of the sodomites, he seems surprised to encounter Brunetto Latini, an older literary figure from Florence who wrote a long and, by all accounts, mediocre didactic poem entitled the *Tesoretto*. Deeply sympathetic to his former friend, Dante nevertheless presents Latini, even here in hell, as blind to his fate and numbingly didactic. He speaks to Dante in a stilted, antiquated manner, marred by banal aphorisms: "Keep the grass far from the goat" (Allen Mandelbaum); "for it is not fit that the sweet fig should abide/and bear its fruit where bitter sorb trees grow" (Michael Palma). Dante effortlessly adopts Latini's trite, aphoristic style: "Let Fortune turn/her wheel as she will, and the farmer turn his spade . . . " (Richard Howard). Yet he uses this rhetoric to expose Latini's fatal flaw. It is not his erstwhile friend's sexuality that Dante, the worldly Florentine, condemns—he expresses sadness and surprise at finding Latini in hell—it is Latini's inability to see clearly and to write honestly.

Dante uses the verbs for "to turn" again and again. On the surface, he associates Latini's turning his back to other men for sexual purposes with Latini's blindness to Fortune's turning wheel, which has in this case produced such an unhappy outcome. Latini's turning away is a travesty of the poem's redemptive turning-toward-the-light. Dante himself, he tells Latini, was about to "turn" his back on his journey when Virgil arrived to save him in the nick of time—but Dante, in the end, turned toward the truth. At the end of the canto, he says that he sees Latini running to catch up with his fellow sodomites, and seeming

> . . . one of those
> who at Verona race for the green
> cloth across the
> fields; and of those he seemed
> the one who wins, not the one who
> loses.
>
> (Robert M. Durling)

But since Latini has lingered to speak with Dante and has to run after the other doomed souls, who are far ahead of him, he looks like one who loses, not like one who wins. Once again, like Latini, Dante is not saying what he means. By adopting Latini's saccharine aphoristic style, Dante both implicates himself in the sin of literary excess and lampoons those who employ pretty language to "turn" their backs on the truth. As always, the poet is egotistically using satire and mimicry to expose and diminish his own ego.

DANTE LIVED in cruel times, before the bourgeoisie tamed the ego by neurotically segregrating private and public life. Modernism took up the task of unmasking, and sometimes celebrating, the brutal instinct behind the public facade, but the twentieth century's perfection of genocide defeated that enterprise.

The question is whether we can once again infuse our necessary self-explorations, in whatever kind of cultural expression, with cruel candor about our individuality. There isn't much of a market for it. Having created, thanks to the discreet bourgeoisie, a society that discreetly allows an individual to do enormous harm, we have created a society in which people feel that they must disavow their individuality if they wish to be trusted and esteemed. Much American self-presentation has, as a result, internalized contemporary America's fear and hatred of the individual ego.

Memoirists and monologists and novelists and poets present themselves as having been robbed of their individuality by circumstances, as being sick, depressed, addicted, abused, bereaved, or generally virtuous but ineffectual. Journalists use the first person to block out the circumstances they are supposed to be describing, as if to reassure the reader that their egos will have no effect on the outside world (including the reader). In all these cases, such writers present themselves as faithful innocents incapable of doing harm. Yet somewhere the blind, cruel, foolish ego, which Dante so openly disclosed in order to defeat, is doing its blind, cruel, foolish work.

> *Fede e innocenza son reperte solo ne' parvoletti . . .*

Faith and innocence are found only in small children . . .

Sundays with *The Sopranos*

I.

IN 1968, A YEAR BEFORE MARIO PUZO'S *The Godfather* appeared—a novel that inaugurated the final phase of the gangster as a figure of spine-tingling mass diversion—a book was published that, along with everything else that was happening, permanently changed America's perception of violence. The book came at a time when the American capacity for violence was so general that it seemed anybody could erupt at any moment: a middle-class white kid at an Ivy League school, a mild-mannered black kid just trying to get by in the inner city, some run-of-the-mill redneck with a high-powered rifle, cops who just minutes ago were serving and protecting and now were busting citizens' heads. In Vietnam, American boys who had been drafted from all over the country were coming home in body bags, and in American cities crime was soaring—so it seemed that anybody could be the victim of violence at any moment, too. And then, in 1968, the country famously exploded.

The book in question was about the banality of evil, but it was not about systematic mass killing. Genocide, no matter how plain the perpetrators seem, always eclipses the "banality" of its practitioners; but killing among a group of people not dedicated to killing, people who murdered only when necessary, and mostly on economic grounds or for reasons of practical power relations—killing as a way to put bread on the table and to keep status anxiety at bay: this kind of crime was small enough in scale to keep the true ordinariness of its perpetrators in full view. The book contained these passages, and others like them:

Around 1950 or so Mildred decided that nothing will do except that we had to own a house. One day she calls me and she says she has found a house in Yonkers, New York. She wanted me to see it. I told her if she liked it, that was good enough for me. . . . By this time the boy had finished his days in school. It was one of the best in New York City. . . . He boarded there and came home only on holidays, as we wanted to keep him off the streets of the Bronx. . . . He married young, and I built three rooms onto the house in Yonkers for him and his wife. . . . I painted the whole house inside and out, and I used the best paint. I was very handy at home, that is, when I was home, as I was always busy with this and that. . . . As far as the neighbors were concerned, I was always a gentleman. Naturally by the hours I kept they got around to asking Mildred what did I do for a living. Mildred told them that I had the Lido, so they figured I was just a guy who ran a restaurant. Some of the neighbors would come into it every now and then, and they all said they liked the food very much. I ran a clean place. Any girl could come in there alone—you know, without being escorted—and if some guy bothers her, he gets thrown right out on his ass. . . .

A little after four o'clock there is this knock on the door [of the Lido]. . . . I open it, and in comes Pat Pagano and Fiore. They got Steve Franse with them. "Hey, Joe," Pat says, "we want Steve to see your joint."

Well, I fix drinks, and we talk about how the Lido is doing, and we walk around the front, and then we go into the kitchen. That's when it happens. Steve is a little guy, and Pat is pretty big. Pat grabs him from behind—he has got him in an armlock—and the other guy, Fiore, raps him in the mouth and belly. He gives it to him good. It's what we call "buckwheats," meaning spite-work.

I'm standing guard by the kitchen door when Pat lets go and Steve drops to the floor. He is on his back, and he is out. They wrap this chain around his neck. He starts to move once, so Pat puts his foot on his neck to keep him there. It only took a few minutes. . . .

I'll say one thing thinking about them days. I am a happy man that I brought up my kid naïve, so he wouldn't be in the life I was.

The book was Peter Maas's *The Valachi Papers*, and the laconic reminiscences came from Joseph Valachi, the first "made" member of the Mafia ever to break the code of silence and describe the inner workings of that hitherto mysterious organization. Without Valachi—and sooner or later a Valachi was bound to appear—there would have been no *Mean Streets,* no *Goodfellas,* no *Prizzi's Honor,* no *Married to the Mob,* no *Analyze This,* and, finally, no *Sopranos*—that stream of gangster entertainments created from the bottom up, films that made the world of people just like you and me seem to resemble the world of the violent criminals on the screen.

It is hard to know whether Valachi's revelations horrified readers at the time, or comforted them by demystifying the Mafia, or reassured them with a kind of violent distraction from violent developments. Americans have never really gotten outraged over the Mafia, maybe because it was Italians who were killing mostly other Italians, and Italians have often been the white Negroes of American culture, unfairly portrayed as being either too physical and instinctual to be completely white—Sylvester Stallone in the *Rocky* movies—or too parochial and prosaic to be black—John Travolta in *Saturday Night Fever*. (Stallone was the first choice to play Eddie Murphy's role in *Beverly Hills Cop*.) One thing is certain, though. The world of the gangster portrayed by Valachi and Maas, and in movies and on television, exerts a powerful influence over how Americans think of themselves: as entrepreneurs, as clients and consumers, as beings driven by appetite and enticed by America's promise of absolute gratification on just about every front.

II.

One of the remarkable things about *The Sopranos* is that it is the first television series about gangsters, to my knowledge, to have gangsters as the (at least partially) sympathetic protagonists. *The Sopranos'* lineage derives from American films that go way back to the 1930s, though its parent, of course, is *The Godfather,* which the series' characters quote from, dream about, and feel empowered by, but which also makes them feel, as Tony puts it in the show's very first episode, that they have come too late. In *The Sopranos*, Coppola's films have died and come back as legends. The heroic characters of Coppola's masterpiece—the Corleones, the "lion hearts"—are far removed from this (again to quote Tony's weary self-description) "fat crook from New Jersey" and his equally pedestrian crew.

With his panic attacks and his depression, his destructive mother and his emotional dependence on her, Tony has nothing in common with Vito Corleone or Michael Corleone, whose mothers play no full human role. Imagine Brando's Don fainting from anxiety—James Gandolfini's falls during his blackouts, which deliberately evoke physical power by its very dissolution, are like parodies of Brando's slow, grasping, refusing-to-yield collapse when he falls onto his car and then into the gutter after being shot at the fruit stand, and then when he is fatally stricken by a heart attack in his vegetable garden. Gandolfini's Tony Soprano is more reminiscent of Cody Jarrett, Jimmy Cagney's gangster in *White Heat* (1949), who suffered from migraine headaches and a mother fixation that makes Tony's tortured relationship to his mother look like a *Madonna and Child* by Raphael. But then, in a family named the Sopranos, it makes sense that the men would be haunted by the unacknowledged feminine undertow of their machismo.

Despite the fact that he is a sociopath and a killer, Tony also seems like a good guy at moments, though anyone who thinks that he really is a decent fellow, capable of change, is going to be brutally, probably fatally, disappointed. He is intermittently sympathetic because we see his bruised, tattered, stormy inner life, mostly through the window of his sessions with his therapist. We learn about the assortment of traumas, wounds, insecurities, buried aggressions, and stifled affections that make up Tony's— and every other person's—inner life. And those scenes of him operating privately, domestically with his wife, Carmela, and his children, Meadow and Anthony Jr., and his Uncle Junior, and his sister, Janis, have the effect of sometimes blurring our awareness of his savage "public" activities. These disclosures of Tony's psychic life and private life make it more difficult to judge his outer deeds. One minute he is destroying Sandy the sports-store owner, his boyhood friend who made the mistake of borrowing money he couldn't repay; the next minute he is snapping at Janis for dissing a black doctor, or rushing to the side of one or another of his mistresses who needs his help; and the minute after that he is explaining to an astonished Sandy, in a breathtaking and almost redeeming moment of self-awareness, that he is destroying him because "that's my nature."

In art, when evil acquires interiority, the result is tragedy; but in life, the result is confusion and a paralysis of judgment. How do you judge a guy who is such a vulnerable yet self-aware mess? Whaddya gonna do, send Macbeth to the electric chair? Now that we live in a totally psychologized culture, where even pet birds have interiority—there is a new DVD meant to calm lonely, alienated parrots—moral confusion is everywhere. This makes it hard to create tragedy in art, because nowadays representing the interiority of bad people does not offer a cathartic revelation, it merely rehearses the general chaos.

Chaos, however, is the spirit of comedy. And so the way back to tragedy in art might be to tease the comic quality out of the riot of interiority, and out of the rampant disclosure of private things that are hampering art, and then to find, when we are laughing so hard that it hurts, that the tragedy is to be found in the comedy. There is something modestly funny about Valachi saying, "I was very handy at home, that is, when I was home, as I was always busy with this and that." And there is something remedially tragic about it, too, as that peaceful homemaking circumstance and that violent one grow larger, and then finally clash. Anyone who thinks that *The Sopranos* is principally a comedy—who thinks that, for example, Tony Blundetto's impulsive brutal beating of the Korean businessman who was going to help him go straight is funny, as one critic described her reaction—is striking a pose. Still, what makes *The Sopranos* original, uncanny, riveting, and also funny is that it paints a deadly accurate portrait of a culture exhausted by psychology. The show is a semicomic playing-out to the absurd and bitter end of the endless contemporary revelations of inner life and private life that neutralize our attempts to make sense of right and wrong.

The series was created in a time when we are surrounded, in our treatment of public figures and celebrities, and in our "reality" shows, by disclosures of private and psychic life that make us feel inferior to no one, and liberated from being judged as much as from having to judge. Americans are everywhere taught to believe that inner psychic life is larger than the peopled world and the natural world around them. *The Sopranos* is the tonic counter-tendency to this universe in which analysis really is what Freud hoped it would be: interminable. The show's constant juxtaposition of private and psychic life with brutal outer actions and events has the effect of showing that all our introspecting and secret-telling is nothing compared with the actuality of the world around us, outside us.

For all his therapy, Tony is still a monster. For all the characters' strong loves and hates, someone is dying of cancer in nearly every episode. For all the show's dream sequences, outer life and external events still work their havoc on the characters. When the FBI catches someone with the goods, as in the case of Big Pussy Bonpensiero, or tricks someone into thinking that they have been caught with the goods—as in the case of the amoral and weirdly innocent Adriana—and threatens them with imprisonment, that person undergoes a transformation. When someone needs to survive, he does whatever brutal thing he has to do to survive, despite his immediately previous gestures to everyday familiar feeling: Tony Soprano kills his beloved cousin because such a heinous act is the only acceptable alternative to the destruction that the rival sociopaths in New York would visit upon his family. So *The Sopranos* makes all our interiorizing funny and absurd. That is its comedy. And it owes its tragedy, too, to the same fatalistic sense of the power of externalities—of the outer world of action and consequence, where the bad guys, for all their extenuating and even endearing psychological qualities, are still bad. When the camera, almost surreally, shows us Tony both looming and isolated in his environment, it shows us a man at the mercy of his environment, his inwardness flapping uselessly in the wind.

III.

Commentators on *The Sopranos* sound one note over and over again: Tony and the people in his world are us. They are the dysfunctional American family. They are the dysfunctional suburban American family. They are the embodiments of the petty liars and crooks who currently run the country. They are the embodiments of our greedy age of Enron and WorldCom, cheaters and corner-cutters who think that they can have everything for nothing. They are depressed like us, and angry like us, and confused teenagers like us, and bewildered parents like us, and adults whose gigantic sense of entitlement is perpetually disappointed, just the way ours is.

The assumption behind these comparisons is that, like all gangster movies, this gangster series uses a story about criminals to make a cathartic, moral, even romantic point about the buried qualities of everyday life. Yet what many people see as *The Sopranos'* normalization of the gangster—defining deviance down, to borrow Daniel Patrick Moynihan's phrase—was right from the start an essential quality of the crime drama, which, like the cowboy movie, was never really about its subject. Its subject was always something else. The achievement of *The Sopranos* is that it stands this model on its head.

In the early 1930s, gangster movies were the prototypes of today's police shows. Like the solitary cop who is in his department but at odds with his department—a true American hero, he invents his own conformity—the gangster-protagonist was both part of his world and endangered by it. The first great gangster movies appealed to Depression-era audiences because Cagney and Edward G. Robinson and Paul Muni satisfied the audience's hunger for vicarious rebellion *and* for the catharsis of seeing a hungry little guy, driven more by feelings than greed, slapped down by greedy and more ruthless big guys. As Robinson's Rico says in *Little Caesar,* "Money's all right, but it ain't everything." Rico was an insecure bully with a soft heart who couldn't kill his best friend when he had to and so was done in by harder men. Cagney, as Tom Powers in *The Public Enemy,* was a poor kid shoved into crime by his environment, who had a soft heart for his mother and for maternal women, and who also got finished off by mugs tougher even than he (and he was tough). And Muni in *Scarface,* tormented by incestuous desires, kills his best friend for seducing his sister, not realizing that the two of them had just gotten married. At that moment, like Rico and Tom, he becomes a victim of his own strong feelings, and, like them, he is felled by stronger and more brutal men, who are not susceptible to their emotions. His unnaturally violent life, the film seems to say, was the only possible outlet for stifled, unnatural feeling. For all three characters, their soft side is a quality that respectable society, in the form of the police, will not accept and that criminal society will not assimilate. Their vulnerable side is a pathological excess in both contexts. In other words, it is romantic.

Hollywood has always had a liking for the gangster. Showbiz and the underworld, after all, are the two places in American life where people who do not fit into mainstream society can flourish in a parallel universe. (What made *Get Shorty* so delightful was its tale of a gangster who slips effortlessly into the role of Hollywood big shot.) In the mid-1930s, however, an interesting change occurred, which is often attributed to the moralistic Hays Code urged by the government on Hollywood studios, but which really had more to do with the deepening misery of the Depression. The Hays Code frowned upon any glamorous psychological extenuation of the gangster's violence, and this certainly led to more simplistic portrayals of bad guys. Gone, for the most part, were the doomed and semipoignant mama's boys who killed to suppress the feminized side of their natures. Yet an increasingly despairing American population was not exactly in need of stories about how psychic pain led to evil deeds. It wanted stories about how inner distress could create a tortured good; and so Cagney and Robinson now appeared as driven, obsessive G-men and cops who were just as brutal and amoral as the now one-dimensionally evil gangsters they chased in the pursuit of justice.

Like the earlier gangster movies, however, these flicks still used their morally ambiguous characters to point outward, away from the film itself, to latent human complexities and capacities. And so the film noir that followed these films represented a further evolution in the development of the gangster type as symbolic of regular people. The ethically mottled protagonists in noir were not gangsters, but they were not cops either. They were private citizens, "private eyes," which meant that they could just as well be you or me. (All you need is a cute secretary and a door with your name on it.) Even the cops in post–World War II crime dramas, such as Cornel Wilde in *The Big Combo,* and Glenn Ford in *The Big Heat,* and maybe Dana Andrews in *Laura,* were so screwed up that they didn't seem like cops at all. They were ordinary people with small guns and big neuroses. (Have gun, will twitch.)

By the time film noir played itself out in the early 1960s, the crime drama had almost entirely lost its specificity. It was now possible to portray bad guys with such a capacity for good, and good guys with such a capacity for bad, that *The Godfather* could put on the big screen gangsters who were every bit as noble and heroic as, say, Elliot Ness had been twenty years earlier. This is why Tony Soprano and his pals are obsessed with *The Godfather. The Godfather's* sanitizing of criminality—a kind of waste management—is a boost to their feeble consciences. There is no ethical difference between Gary Cooper's show-down with evil in *High Noon*—another movie that obsesses Tony—and Michael Corleone's showdown with the rival mob-ster and the corrupt cop in that Bronx restaurant.

Culturally speaking, the premiere of Coppola's *Godfather* in 1972 was a watershed moment. It was at a time when the middle class was embracing the values of the counterculture—when, as Michael Harrington wrote that same year, "businessmen started hanging nonobjective art in the boardroom [and] Bohemia was deprived of the stifling atmosphere without which it could not breathe." Puzo's and Coppola's Mafia was just as subversive of law and order and conventional values as the SDS or even the Weath-ermen had been; but the Corleones combined antisocial behav-ior with the exceedingly conventional activity of making money. They were, you might say, highly unregulated capitalists. And Brando, the rebel without a cause before *Rebel Without a Cause*, T-shirted, tight-jeaned, crotch-swelled Brando, who was Elvis's favorite actor and the spirit of rock and roll before there was rock and roll—this actor was the perfect fusion of countercultural sen-timents with, in the form of the intensely traditional Don Cor-leone, middle-class sentiments.

In one stroke, then, Italian family-feeling met Italian American white-Negro sensuality, and countercultural rebellion met com-mercial instinct. In 1972, when the postwar boom blew itself out, the gangster movie came full circle from the gangster movies of the Depression. The gangster was once again romantic, but this time not in the tradition of "sick" romanticism, not as someone whose inner energies society had transformed into outer demons. After film noir's dissolution of moral categories, and its complex universalization of the gangster, and after *The Godfather*'s identifi-cation of the gangster with the most positive, energetic elements of American life, the gangster was finally ready to become Every-man. That is to say, the gangster became ripe for satire.

From *Prizzi's Honor* in 1985, and (the semisatirical) *Miller's Crossing* in 1990 (in which Gabriel Byrne was the first movie gangster to throw up from fear), and Brando's send-up of Don Corleone in *The Freshman* the same year, up to De Niro's send-up of his Don Corleone in *Analyze This* in 1999 (both Brando and De Niro were throwbacks in this regard to George Raft, who satirized his own gangster image in *Some Like It Hot*), the gangster film became more and more of a metaphor, an ironic comment on hidden social dynamics, on the gangsterish spirit behind American get-up-and-go. As the Mafia was being steadily curtailed by the forces of law enforcement, the mafioso was be-coming a comic, if lethal, figure.

Meanwhile, Quentin Tarantino was caricaturing violence it-self as a comic event. You began to get a spate of funny movies in which hit men were lovable and capable of love: *Grosse Pointe Blank, The Whole Nine Yards,* for example. All through the growth of the money culture in the 1980s and 1990s, a smiling avarice and entrepreneurial hardness in politics and society coincided with what one might call the comedification of murder and greed on the big screen. And it was hard to tell whether these films were satires on the ethos or expressions of the ethos, be-cause the comic gift bespeaks intellectual capacity and ironic self-knowledge, and a thug with those qualities becomes a pretty formidable human being. So does a funny, ironic businessman with thuggish qualities.

Until then, comedy had always been on the side of the vul-nerable outsider. But when the funny and deadly gangster be-came a figure of fun, he gradually displaced the funny and decidedly undeadly nebbish. Why laugh at weakness when you can laugh at strength? Which is to say, why laugh anymore at

Woody Allen and Albert Brooks? When De Niro vanquished Ben Stiller in *Meet the Parents,* the nebbish became extinct. (Adam Sandler, Jim Carrey, and Larry David are nuisances with an edge of menace, not nebbishes.) The gangster who spoke in stiff, formal, educated cadences, with a thick, ethnic accent, using clumsy syntax and hilarious malapropisms (Tony Soprano is the contemporary master of the form: "You're like an albacore around my neck," "Revenge is like cold cuts," and so on) and expressing homicidal sentiments, became a stock comic figure.

But it was a figure that was continuing to lose specificity as it was gaining symbolism. The injured, pathetic gangsters of the 1930s, and the morally ambiguous cops or private eyes of the 1940s and 1950s, and Coppola's larger-than-life heroic bad guys, and Scorsese's smaller-than-life regular-seeming bad guys: they were all allegories for The Evil in Our Hearts or The Way We Live Now. Like them, the funny-deadly gangster referred to something outside himself; but with this figure's arch and knowing send-up of himself, which incorporated or alluded to all the earlier forms of the gangster, the funny-deadly gangster seemed to signify curtains for the American mobster on the silver screen. The melting, through the medium of comedy, of the gangster into an ordinary American type (and vice versa) seemed to leave movie mobsters with no place to go but toward deeper identification with the Darwinian routines of American materialism, etc. Thanks to the satire, the regular American guy began to fill the role of the gangster, who had always beckoned toward the regular American guy anyway. Enter Tony Soprano.

IV.

From *The Sopranos'* opening episode, when Tony suffered his first panic attack, which made him immediately sympathetic, and then chased down and beat a man who owed him money, which made him immediately repellent, *The Sopranos* was a problem. Some people, intimidated by all the violence and confused by the "mixed signals," put up a front of being cool and unaffected by the most disturbing drama ever put on television. But the fact that you did not know how to respond to the show, and could not look to any cultural precedents for the correct interpretation, is the essence of *The Sopranos*' originality. After the culture's metaphorizing, and commodifying, and comedifying, of violence and degradation—as if, in the end, violence and degradation were cultural phenomena and not actual experiences—*The Sopranos* returned brutality and brutal sentiments to real life.

The vexing thing about the American gangster movie was always that, for all its implicit or explicit analogies between gangsterism and the hidden underside of the American way, it was always distracting you from the true nature of violence and brutality. But *The Sopranos* is remorseless in its de-idealization of its people. Its wit is never its last word about its subject. The show never lets you forget that you are enjoying an emotional and physical horror.

Tony and his gang are *not* us. You and I don't drive around town with a bruised and bloody corpse in our trunk, do we? And we wouldn't, right? They are not Kenneth Lay, and they are not the Bush administration. And the connection between Tony's real family and his crime "family" is not symbolic, or even ironic. How could even the most "dysfunctional" American family be like a crime family unless it was, actually, a crime family? Our whole culture is bedeviled by the simile, by the relentlessly mediating and protective preposition "like." Things are constantly—and democratically—sliding into other things; a movie, a book, a trial, a scandal become social and political palimpsests to be unpacked, analyzed, interpreted, so that by the end of all the commentary, life's real facts and events have been reduced to nice, cushy abstractions, with easy, comfortable morals and conclusions. Nothing is allowed, like, to just be, to follow its own nature. But a person is a particularity without end; a person cannot be appended to "like." Novelists know this better than anybody, and the quality of *The Sopranos* may accurately be described as novelistic. (Which is why, incidentally, it can be properly reviewed only when each season is over. Would a literary critic review only the first chapters of a novel?)

The Sopranos is a fugue of incomparable, ungraspable personalities. They don't fit into other categories. All their shifting takes place inside themselves. An example: Tony Soprano's soft, suffering psychic underside leads him to Dr. Jennifer Melfi, who is attracted to Tony's machismo because the men in her world—like the boyfriend who gets beaten up in front of her by Tony's detective friend—are soft and ambivalent, but she is also repelled by Tony's brutality, just as she was repelled by the attack on her boyfriend. She feels that she can help Tony, but she knows that she can't, though she doesn't really want to, except that she does, and Tony frightens her, but he attracts her, because she needs his elemental power in her life the way she needs a man in her life, though Tony is the last thing she needs, since she is strong and independent and humane (the only such character in this gallery of damaged and damaging people), despite the fact that Tony's influence makes her, at different times, weak, depressed, reliant on alcohol, dependent on her own shrink and her ex-husband, and coarse and unfeeling, though she remains a decent person and a caring mother. And yet after her rape and the release of the rapist on a technicality, she has the impulse to ask Tony to injure or to kill the rapist, but when Tony, knowing that something very bad has happened to her, asks her to tell him if there's anything that he can do to help, and she knows that here is her chance to empower herself by having her revenge on the man who assaulted her, she looks at Tony with precisely Tony's ferocity, and says, "No!" as if she had sublimated her urge to have the rapist killed into aggression against the man whose feral quality had inspired that urge, thus in one stroke obliterating Tony and her attraction to Tony, while unwittingly, or maybe semiconsciously, keeping the latter alive through the intensity of her response. All this, on American television!

Another example: Carmela Soprano has profited from Tony's thuggery, but tries to hide from herself the true nature of how she is living by, say, taking ritual trips with daughter Meadow to the Plaza Hotel, where Carmela wears long white gloves that make her stick out clumsily even from this not exactly refined crowd, as if the ugly reality of her life were sticking out behind her, which is her inescapable fate, this inescapable tawdriness. Carmela doesn't love Tony, she needs Tony, she hates Tony; the material things in her life that she escapes to in order to forget Tony have their origin and sustenance in Tony, so in their big bed, in their big bedroom, in front of their big television, at night, she can put her arms around her big Tony and fool herself into thinking that the husband she despises is actually the material things that she cherishes, and that her happiness is at one with her marriage. And yet she still looks to Furio, Tony's Italian henchman, for an escape from Tony; and to her son Anthony's guidance counselor Mr. Wegler, to whom she was drawn because he gave a break to her feckless son, and onto whom she displaces a father's function: she keeps trying to convince him to help her son, because she loves him the more he seems devoted to her family. And so she commits adultery for the first time in twenty years of marriage, but Wegler thinks that she is using him to help her son, and she thinks she loves him and so is unafraid to ask for a favor for her son, and she really does love him in her fantasy-escape world, so Wegler is wrong, but she really is using him, so

Wegler is right, and when he tells her that he wants to break it off, she threatens him with a sudden vicious glint in her eye, just as Tony would have done, because if she ever could live apart from Tony, she would have to act like him to make up for the fact that he wasn't there, and she can't do that for long, so she goes back to him after their separation, where she will suffer from him, and try to live apart from him, but in safety.

And there is Tony himself. He is at first the occasional victim of the show's unrewarding efforts to make him a Representative Man for contemporary times—Melfi is incited by Tony to speak with him about "the climate of rage in American society." Tony longs for the days of strong men and submissive women, he longs for a time when people followed the rules, when everything had its place in the social hierarchy: he longs, as he tells his son in anger, for 1954. This Tony resembles the movie gangster of yore in the way that he points to something outside himself, in this case to that quintessentially American figure, the rapacious innocent, the destructive creative, a veritable gangster who speaks of the rules even as he breaks them, who extols hierarchies even as he undermines them, who smiles his way through the hell he condones and helps to create. And on and on it goes. What better example of the willfully, cunningly, smilingly deluded American person than this middle-aged gangster who still holds in his mind the figure of Gary Cooper as a model of manliness and virtue, and who was told when he was a little boy that his imprisoned father was in Montana being a cowboy?

But by the middle of the first season, the character of Tony had obviously escaped his creators' rational purposes and begun to unfold, uncontrollably, in their imaginations. Tony started out as a "borderline personality"—the technical name for a clinical narcissist. He perfectly embodies the features of this very "now" condition: emptiness, fragmentedness, overwhelming shame, rage, manipulative charm alternating with spasms of self-loathing, and the capacity for "splitting," which is the tendency to idealize someone and then furiously to demonize them when they reject or disappoint: thus, when Melfi resists a tender and seemingly loving Tony's attempts to seduce her, he flies at her with rage, curses her, and almost kills her. Borderline personalities almost always have parents who suffer from the same syndrome, and in Tony's mother, Livia, a figure of almost Greek malevolence who actually plots to assassinate her son, clinical narcissism reaches the peak of its devastating imperfection. One of Tony's favorite imprecations, which he applies to all the other murderous nut-cases in his world, is "motherless fuck," which in the context of clinical narcissism acquires poetic power.

Yet in that inaugural season as the character of Tony became more particularized, the borderline personality blurred into the very concrete Tony Soprano, and the character acquired the particularity-without-end that is the condition of every great fictional creation. Tony is moved by animals, terrified by a bear, refuses to harm his treacherous Uncle Junior out of family feeling, detests the FBI yet allows them to play him a tape that tips him off to his mother and his uncle's plot against him, comes to his sister Janis's aid when she needs him but humiliates her in front of her new beau Bobby when he resents her happiness, has the cop who gave him a ticket reassigned, feels bad, tries to get the cop his job back, then shrugs the moral impulse off with "Fuck it, he got what he deserved."

The fugue of shifting meaning inside each character goes on and on. But all the meaning is ultimately meaningless. No wonder Tony in one episode keeps flushing the toilet to keep the FBI from electronically eavesdropping on a conversation; no wonder he spends an entire episode defecating and vomiting; no wonder Adriana throws up when the FBI terrorizes her. All this interiority, like all the psychological introspection with Melfi, has no place to go. You cannot interpret people like these. You have to judge them. In the end, *The Sopranos* is a long study of the specificity of human existence, of the finality of human temperament. Like Tony's inner life, the moral filth in this sublimely disabused show is simply there. The destiny of these people is, as some guys in certain neighborhoods of South Jersey—not to mention Sophocles—might say, what it is. What a blessing to have popular art that does not impair the sense of reality, but sharpens it.

A Writer Who Is Good for You

My wife is an admirer of Jane Austen but not, like me, a devotee. She recently informed me over breakfast that since I started going back to Austen's novels, I have become more polite but less sincere.

Her concern was the kind of thing Lionel Trilling must have had in mind when he wrote that the responses to Austen's work were nearly as interesting and important as the work itself. He went on to say that the reader trying to decide for or against Austen was "required to make no mere literary judgment but a decision about his own character and personality, and about his relation to society and all of life." Not liking Jane Austen's darkly streaked social comedies, Trilling believed, put a person under suspicion "let us face it—of a want of breeding."

Though Trilling found such an attitude "absurd and distasteful," he was the one who so extravagantly defined it. When he started admiring the "cool elegance" of Austen's surname, you felt almost embarrassed by the self-exposure. Yet it's hard to disagree with his assessment of Austen. No other author goes with such casual intimacy as she, for all her delicate soundings of formal social relations, into the vulnerable spot where society touches the root of self. And few authors are at the same time so quietly fearsome and so intensely consoling.

Who's afraid of Jane Austen—that uncanny panoptic minia-
turist who captures all the degrees of vanity, snobbery, and self-
deception, that piercing dramatizer of encounters between
emotion and convention, private hopes and public constraints?
The very thought of finding herself alone with Austen intimidated, of all people, Virginia Woolf. Describing what it might be
like to be in a room with her, Woolf imagined

> a sense of meaning withheld, a smile at something unseen,
> an atmosphere of perfect control and courtesy mixed with
> something finely satirical, which, were it not directed
> against things in general rather than against individuals,
> would, so I feel, make it alarming to find her at home.

Henry James, in whose fiction manners are often nonblunt
instruments of destruction, could be condescending about one of
his strongest influences, though he acknowledged her genius.
Austen's heroines had "small and second-rate minds and were
perfect little she-Philistines," he thought. "But I think that is
partly what makes them interesting today." And Austen irritated
Emerson: he found her novels "vulgar in tone, sterile in artistic
invention, imprisoned in the wretched conventions of English
society." All that her characters cared about was "marriageable-
ness." "Suicide," the great Transcendentalist proposed, "is more
respectable."

No one, it seems, has ever been neutral or aloof about Jane
Austen. From the time of her death, at the age of forty-one, in
1817, possibly from either Addison's or Hodgkin's disease, she has
been a contested figure. Her beloved sister Cassandra destroyed
many of her letters and made excisions in others, prompting biographers to suspect that she was trying to suppress evidence either of some deep depression or of unseemly malice or spleen.

Brief memoirs of Austen written by her descendants amount to hagiographies. Her great-nephew edited and bowdlerized the first edition of her letters in 1884, claiming that "no malice lurked beneath" Austen's wit, which is like saying that no alcohol lurks in claret.

By 1896 the word "Janeite" had come into the language as a term signifying literary fervor and adoration. To read some Janeite expressions of enthusiasm, one would think that Mansfield Park was the name of a local soccer team. Anti-Janeites accused their opponents of a lack of virility. (They especially disliked what they thought were Austen's portrayals of men as gossips without vocation.) Later, in the 1940s and 1950s, some critics tried to save Austen from her Janeite admirers, claiming that Austen's sense of decorum, of the forms of politeness and tact, were what the Janeites most prized but what Austen, with lethal irony, most wanted to subvert. She composed with a "regulated hatred," as one of these writers put it—a steady, subtle corrosiveness toward smothering conventionality. She was not, as Henry James had once mocked the Janeites' benign conception of her, "our dear, everybody's dear, Jane."

A hundred years after "Janeite" entered the language, Jane Austen is everywhere. It's a good bet that the highly entertaining, often intelligent and moving, and always inadequate film versions of her novels are more popular than the novels themselves. But there's no doubt that more people are reading her since the craze began.

Of course, contemporary women are likely to identify with smart, vital, and strong-willed heroines like Elizabeth Bennet and Emma Woodhouse. And there must be no lack of female empathy for the hemmed-in Fanny Price, for the heartstrong Marianne Dashwood and her self-suppressed sister Elinor, for the wise, sad, unfulfilled Anne Elliot. But some people must cherish Austen now simply because she trained her attention on a patch of living that, for the most part, has been abandoned in American imaginative writing. We are surrounded by consequential social circumstances, but we have few writers who can make sense of society without reducing it to an explanation. In his aversion to Austen, Emerson was true to his own inclinations. Too much Emerson—too much grandiose withdrawal, too much self-indulgence masquerading as self-creation—is probably the deepest cause of the Austen revival in this country.

Because she wrote at a time of rapid social flux, Austen offers an unexpected illumination of our situation. In late-eighteenth-century England the beginnings of industrial democracy were dismantling the old organic forms of community and throwing identity into question. An aristocracy of birth was giving way to an aristocracy of wealth. Modern commerce, with global ambitions, was creating a fluid, contingent, modern sense of self. Roles were changing, roots were tearing, the definition of the individual was evolving. It was then that Austen wrote great English novels. Now they are great American novels.

That's not to say that Austen approached the changing arrangements in her society and culture directly. She famously—or infamously—didn't. She has even been faulted for barely referring to the dramatic historical events she lived through: the French Revolution, the Napoleonic Wars, the expansion of colonialism. The literary scholar Edward Said accused her of giving approval in *Mansfield Park* to slavery; according to Said, Austen makes the restoration of order at the Bertrams' plantation in Antigua the foundation for their eventual moral renovation at home. Yet Mansfield was where, in 1772, a court passed down a decision prohibiting the holding of black slaves in England. Austen decided to set an estate called Mansfield in a novel that makes the quiet, ungrasping decency of Fanny Price, its humbly born heroine, a reproach to the upper classes' rapacious masculine activity. Austen's ultrasensitive social and moral antennae could, among other things, obliquely register, and pass stern judgment on, history's distant rumbling.

As an unmarried and almost penniless woman, Austen seized on laughter to live. Her outer life was entirely uneventful as far as we know. Her biographers therefore have had to lean heavily on her letters—in which the humor of battered pride and obstructed genius ranges from satiric to redemptive to cruel—and to resort to filling in space with descriptions of her family and accounts of her surroundings.

These two new biographies follow that tack. They're both solid, readable accounts, sticking close to Austen's life and milieu. Claire Tomalin's is more fun, and better written, though it sometimes seems hastily thrown together and desperately digressive. Tomalin is not herself a writer of fiction, but she has a novelist's imagination and playful insight. When she does comment—sparingly—on Austen's work, or lightly speculate on the formative weight of her social and cultural influences, she's usually absorbing and acute.

David Nokes's book is more tightly composed. Focusing exclusively on Austen's life and the lives of her relatives, Nokes never engages the fiction and barely refers to the social and cultural context. Strangely, he believes that he is doing iconoclastic work: "I have had the temerity not only to write about Jane Austen, but to do so in a manner which challenges the familiar image of her as a literary maiden aunt . . . to present her . . . as rebellious, satirical and wild." In fact critics and biographers have been presenting Austen as rebellious, satirical, and wild, and also as cold, anal, and malicious, for half a century. The former qualities can be found subtly insinuated in a biography by Jane Aiken Hodge, and the latter in one by John

Halperin, neither of whom Nokes mentions or cites. Nokes loves triumphantly to repeat this line from one of Austen's letters: "If I *am* a wild beast, I cannot help it. It is not my own fault." But he leaves out the sentence before it: "I am rather frightened by hearing that she wishes to be introduced to *me*." Austen was responding to someone's wish to meet the rumored author of *Sense and Sensibility* and *Pride and Prejudice;* with her usual combination of unwild insecurity and confident self-deprecation, she was envisioning herself as an animal on display in a cage.

Nokes's life is often perceptive, and it has a rich narrative density, but his details tend to pile up into a blearing mélange. A British don, he has a high Oxbridge tone, which together with a quaint eighteenth-century literary affect can be wearying: "She did not greatly repine at the absence of titled acquaintances." (And I do wish that starry-eyed, or distracted, American publishers would make their increasing ranks of British authors explain, to those of us who did not attend Harrow, the meaning of being someone's "fag" and similar heartwarming public-school expressions.)

Both biographies include abundant excerpts from the letters, with all their mundane descriptions couched in revelatory style, and also their flashes of embitterment.

> Pictures of perfection as you know, make me sick & wicked.

> They called, they came and they sat and they went. [on a visit from some local gentry]

> Her hair is done up with an elegance to do credit to any Education.

> I do not want people to be very agreable, as it saves me the trouble of liking them a great deal.

Mrs. Hall of Sherbourn was brought to bed yesterday of a dead child, some weeks before she expected, owing to a fright—I suppose she happened unawares to look at her husband.

Such intimate snippets of perception bring us as close to the living, breathing woman as it is possible to get—maybe, in the last quotation, closer than we'd like to get. But in Austen's day dying infants were a tragically common occurrence. Then, too, women were often exhausted to death, and families impoverished, by continual childbearing. Behind Austen's apparent cruelty was a hardness, and behind that perhaps a genuine outrage.

The person is in both biographies, but anyone curious about Austen the writer will have to go elsewhere. That's a shame. Austen's style is one of English literature's marvels. Her repartee is sometimes as dazzling as anything in Sheridan, and is one reason that her perpetual hope of seeing exciting theater was disappointed whenever she went. Here's an exchange from *Pride and Prejudice* between Elizabeth and Darcy, starting with Darcy:

"There is, I believe, in every disposition a tendency to some particular evil, a natural defect, which not even the best education can overcome."

"And *your* defect is a propensity to hate everybody."

"And yours," he replied with a smile, "is wilfully to misunderstand them."

And there are the superfine irony and the balletic insight, as in these two passages from *Emma*:

Human nature is so well-disposed towards those who are in interesting situations, that a young person, who either marries or dies, is sure of being kindly spoken of.

She did not repent what she had done; she still thought herself a better judge of such a point of female right and refinement than he could be; but yet she had a sort of habitual respect for his judgment in general, which made her dislike having it so loudly against her; and to have him sitting just opposite to her in angry state, was very disagreeable.

As Virginia Woolf once declared, it's hard to catch Jane Austen in the act of greatness. But Woolf was too much the aesthete, too much the gifted borderline solipsist, to do so. For Austen captured the way the mind works by following it out into the world. Her expository prose is on the verge of dissolving into dialogue, and her dialogue about to condense into expository prose. Consider these two passages, the first from *Mansfield Park* and the second from *Sense and Sensibility:*

"It often grieves me to the heart—to think of the contrast between them—to think that where nature has made so little difference, circumstances should have made so much. . . ."

Two ladies were waiting for their carriage, and one of them was giving the other an account of the intended match, in a voice so little attempting concealment, that it was impossible for him not to hear all.

Actually, the first passage is exposition and the second dialogue; I changed a pronoun and the tense in the former and a pronoun in the latter. I hope I've persuaded you. Even in the most elaborate expository passage the cadences seem almost spoken. Austen's sentences operate inwardly and outwardly at once—they go into a quiet corner of the mind and out into the busy world.

And just as Austen's characters are completed by their relations with other people, her sentences cannot function alone. Like her self-deceived heroines, they are usually a little blind. They bear hints of their own impending amplification, qualification, contradiction. That semantic instability drives us from one uneventful-seeming statement to the next; we feel propelled by a coming displacement of meaning ("She was quite concerned and ashamed, and resolved to do such things no more"). Austen's whole style is an evanescence laid solidly and matter-of-factly on the page like plates on a table.

That's especially plain when her sentences burst with male-style certainty—"It is a truth universally acknowledged, that a single man in possession of a good fortune, must be in want of a wife" (the celebrated first sentence of *Pride and Prejudice*). Austen ironized such propositions into insubstantiality—"However little known the feelings or views of such a man may be on his first entering a neighbourhood . . . " (the less celebrated second sentence). She set the blaring horns of social and psychological certainty against the piccolo of minute observation; and we hear the music in her meaning rather than in the physical sound of her words.

AUSTEN WAS A SATIRIST above all, with tragic and romantic moods. She had a flawless ear for moral counterpoint, for the hidden chords of how things ought to be and really were. She pitched her delicately endangered sentences, her psychology, her dialogue and drama, to some invisible key way at the back of her language, just as Mozart pitched his compositions to a frequency beyond human range, way at the back of his music. That's why even her clumsiest turns of plot, or her characters' foggiest motivations, are accommodated like straggling notes by a larger harmony.

Jane had six brothers: they included a clergyman, a failed banker who entered the clergy, and two naval officers. Two other brothers had radically different fates. One was adopted by distant relations, taken from the Austen home and eventually made the heir to a large fortune and estate; the other, born retarded, was sent when very young to a nearby village, where a family was paid to take care of him. Such opposing circumstances, arbitrary and disruptive, must have clinched the satirist's vocation, along with her beautifully contingent style. They might also help to explain why, for Austen, preserving social forms was as necessary as unmasking them.

That simultaneous tearing down of conventions and institutions and keeping them intact is finally what is so healing (a good word, badly misused) about Austen. It runs parallel to her exquisite balance of inner and social lives. After all, her novels, mostly filled with bad marriages, end with marriages that are perfect—so perfect that they seem like ideal rebukes to the reality of marriage in her fiction. A whole world is put into question, remains stable and whole, but is left dangling. After the First World War, shell-shocked veterans were advised to read Austen's novels for therapy, perhaps to restore their faith in a world that had been blown apart while at the same time respecting their sense of the world's fragility. Americans who are intelligent and skeptical, but who are frazzled by pundit-unmaskers, by academic see-throughers, by Hollywood exploders of social forms, may be drawn to Jane Austen for a similar reason.

Or, as Kipling has a character put it in "The Janeites," a story about a group of soldiers in the First World War who keep hold of their sanity by organizing a secret Austen cult and cherishing the way Austen carefully molds life's replenishing smaller motions: "There's no one to touch Jane when you're in a tight place."

Bernard Malamud and the
Comprehending Heart

BERNARD MALAMUD HAS NOT FARED well in posterity. The publication, in 1997, of his *Collected Stories* seemed to enshrine this master storyteller as little more than a caricature of an American Jewish writer. For Walter Goodman, writing in *The New York Times Book Review,* "Bernard Malamud's magic barrel overflows with schnorrers and schleppers," and Malamud exhibited his "joy in Second Avenue vaudeville shticks." Perhaps the oddest review appeared in *The New York Review of Books,* where Alfred Kazin compared Malamud's fictional world to Primo Levi's description of Auschwitz, and digressed into Malamud's class insecurities and nineteenth-century Russian anti-Semitism.

But the most damning contemporary impression of Malamud is that he was a writer whose "sense of virtue is too narrow" for current readers. That is how he is obviously alluded to in Philip Roth's *American Pastoral,* and a brief survey of some very intelligent literary friends and acquaintances mostly confirms such a judgment. The dismissal (or damning faint praise) seems to rest on a certain view of Malamud's early stories, set in struggling grocery stores and tailor shops and shoe-repair businesses; it seems especially to depend on a certain way of reading his novel

The Assistant. In those works, these critics say, suffering is equated with goodness, and goodness is constrictedly equated with duty and obligation.

It's unfair criticism, based on a fatal misreading. Look carefully at the early stories, and you will get a sense of Malamud, the son of an impoverished merchant, industriously chiseling his escape from a formative predicament by chiseling it into artistic perfection. This melancholy apprenticeship might account for the energy with which, in later fiction, Malamud applies himself to the idea of receiving spiritual rewards in exchange for suffering. It is like his personal triumph over the practice of receiving goods and services in exchange for money. Perhaps that's why Malamud, steeped in Russian literature, keeps returning in his short tales with an awestruck, occasionally comic, yet shy sympathy to the figure of the female prostitute. She is expert in the knowledge of human life under the pressure of relative worth.

Spanning forty-five years, these stories—collected here for the first time—display the wilder and wilder exfoliation of Malamud's obsessions, away from the threadbare confinement of the moving early tales. So well did Malamud fine-tune his soundings of morality that, in stories like "The Maid's Shoes," "The Elevator," and "A Choice of Profession," he anatomized narrow virtue as the harmful instrument of a timid egotism. And he did this ruefully, tenderly—he was no modernist scourge. With figures like Salzman in "The Magic Barrel," Susskind in "The Last Mohican," Rabbi Jonas Lifschitz in "The Silver Crown," and, less fantastically, Feliks Levitansky in "Man in the Drawer," Malamud created adversary-teachers who shatter their dully practical and reluctant pupils into self-knowledge. Among other wondrous things, these stories are like beautiful transmutations—and overcomings—of the psychoanalytic relationship into modernized wisdom tales. (Similar duos appear in Saul Bellow's *The Victim* and *Seize the Day,* while Philip Roth expediently split a single character, Nathan Zuckerman, into two different psychic entities.) And in "Angel Levine" and the wryly despairing "Black Is My Favorite Color," Malamud set modes of suffering at loggerheads in his portrayal of the relationship between blacks and Jews. The latter story in particular is a rehearsal for the racial apocalypse Malamud laceratingly portrayed in his 1971 novel, *The Tenants.*

Malamud's virtuous complexity is worth exploring. Consider *The Assistant,* widely alleged to be the *locus classicus* of Malamud's narrow sense of virtue. At the end of that novel, a rabbi eulogizes Morris Bober, the owner of a grocery store and one of the novel's central characters. The rabbi recalls that Bober once ran through the snow, without coat or hat or galoshes, to give a poor customer a nickel that she had mistakenly left on the counter. According to his daughter, Helen, Bober had many friends who admired him for such selflessness, the rabbi says. He goes on, "He was also a very hard worker, a man that never stopped working. How many mornings he got up in the dark and dressed himself in the cold, I can't count. . . . Fifteen, sixteen hours a day he was in the store, seven days a week, to make a living for his family. . . . This went on for twenty-two years. . . . And for this reason that he worked so hard and bitter, in his house, on his table, was always something to eat. So besides honest he was a good provider."

So far, one might say, so good. But after the rabbi finishes, Malamud describes the thoughts of Helen, the novel's heroine and moral center:

> Yes, he ran after this poor woman to give her back a nickel but he also trusted cheaters who took away what belonged

to him. . . . He gave away, in a sense, more than he owned. He was no saint; he was in a way weak, his only true strength in his sweet nature and his understanding. He knew, at least, what was good. And I didn't say he had many friends who admired him. That's the rabbi's invention. People liked him, but who can admire a man passing his life in such a store? He buried himself in it; he didn't have the imagination to know what was missing. He made himself a victim. He could, with a little more courage, have been more than he was.

The Assistant appeared in 1957. It must have been a tremendous unburdening, since Malamud never again wrote about merchants or stores. Instead he began, in 1958, to publish his series of stories about Arthur Fidelman, a hapless, finally unsuccessful painter. Fidelman has come to Italy to slough off his past and start anew, the possibility for a new life and the impossibility of a total escape from the past comprising a favorite Malamudian obsession. To simplify a remarkable set of stories, Fidelman zigzags toward failure through a tangled comedy of desublimation. He aspires to immortality through art; he settles for a momentary lay, so to speak, against confusion. What Fidelman lacks is Morris Bober's discipline at fulfilling his obligations and making a living. What Bober lacks is Fidelman's imaginative and courageous attempt to make a life.

Malamud prized courageous imagining: he was a moralist, not a moralizer. The spectacle of good people suffering provoked him. But the incommensurability between suffering and goodness fascinated him. Neglecting that, his admirers are partly responsible for the arguments of his detractors. They often describe this author as celebrating "the human"—you imagine him standing on a tenement roof singing, "If I were a poor grocer." But

Malamud knew that the quality of being human is often fatal to humanity, that selfishness, envy, and hatred are just as human as kindness, compassion, and love. In Malamud, being human is an ultimate consolation, yet it is also a primal sorrow.

Malamud turned the classical tragic situation of right against right on its side. He created little tragedies, or little tragicomedies, of hurt against hurt. A typical, though flawed, story is "The Loan," where a gentle, broken man named Kobotsky calls after many years on his old friend Lieb, hoping for money to buy a headstone for his wife's grave. Lieb has become a baker and prospered. His secret, he informs Kobotsky, is that he bakes his tears into his bread. (Wry bread, if you will.) The needy Kobotsky tells Lieb his tale: the death of his wife; his operation; his loss of employment; crippling arthritis; a widowed sister who lost her only son and whom Kobotsky had to help support; his boils, which made him ashamed to go outside. Moved, Lieb decides to lend Kobotsky the money.

But Bessie, Lieb's second wife, says no, falsely claiming that she and the baker have no money. She tells *her* tale: father slain by Bolsheviks; first husband dead of typhus; beloved brother and his wife murdered in Hitler's incinerators; twelve years of working her fingers to the bone in the bakery. "The baker, who had often heard this tale, munched, as he listened, chunks of bread." At story's end, a crestfallen Kobotsky goes away empty-handed, and Bessie rushes into the rear of the store just in time to pull some burnt loaves—"charred corpses"—from the ovens. There are no spiritual rewards for pain here. Suffering has made Kobotsky abject, and it has twisted Bessie's heart. The gruesome image of the blackened bread signifies a depressing chain of causation: suffering causes callousness, which destroys the humble redemption—the delicious tear-soaked bread—bestowed by suffering.

Malamud makes passing moral judgment on these characters a form of ignorance. He also leaves no doubt about where, from moment to moment, their moral culpability lies.

"ALL MEN ARE JEWS." Malamud's remark, implying that history has made Jews aware of the nature of morality in a way that is usually hidden from other people, is still routinely quoted whenever the subject of his work comes up. As a moral proposition, it's sentimentally silly. But I think Malamud meant it as an aesthetic premise, one that might lead to moral results within the realm of art.

Malamud seized on the Jewish gift for strong feeling and turned it into metaphysical proof of the existence of the one who is doing the feeling. He made emotions his territory the way Thomas Hardy—whom the young Malamud wrote a master's thesis on—claimed his heath for the dramatization of emotion. For that reason, the angel Malamud struggled with was the blubbery angel of sentimentality. And he hobbled it with the short story, for the most part (a few of these tales dive off the page like Tosca plunging to her death). If, to modify one famous definition of it, sentimentality is an author's emotional response in excess of his characters' emotions—early Malamud is always in danger of himself giving his characters the *"bissel rachmones"* ("the bit of mercy") they long for—then the short story is better than the novel at instilling formal discipline. That's why, with the exception of *The Fixer,* Malamud's novels rarely attain the astringent intellectual and affective control arrived at in the landscape of most of these tales.

A reader knows he is out in that Malamudian landscape when he hears sobbing. Of the fifty-five stories here, forty-four of them have characters who at one point break down and cry. You would have to go back to the *Aeneid*'s grand motif of *"lacrimae rerum"* to find a writer who put tears in the service of such a complex artistic discipline. You can measure Malamud's mastery of his characters' emotions—and, like some Jewish Aeneas, his own—by following the flow of saltwater through these tales.

Malamud's friend and longtime editor, Robert Giroux, mentions in his introduction to the stories that Malamud had an uncle named Charles Fidelman who worked as a promoter at the Yiddish theater on Second Avenue. (Fidelman was the maiden name of Malamud's mother, and the name must have been the source for the Arthur Fidelman of Malamud's stories.) It makes you wonder whether the young Malamud saw *King Lear,* a staple of the Yiddish theater's repertory, and whether it gave him a special purchase on, as it were, Shakespeare's version. In "Suppose a Wedding," a small, one-act play included in this collection, Malamud has its main character—Maurice Feuer, a Yiddish actor—quote lengthily from *Kaynig Lear und sein Tochter.*

I bring it up because *King Lear's* themes have a kinship with Malamud's own. Seeing is the play's central motif: on the one hand, seeing in order to appraise, count, and possess the hard material things of the world; and on the other, seeing inward and recognizing a common fragile humanity beyond the rational world of appearances—seeing as touching. When Gloucester, his eyes torn out of their sockets, says near the end of his life, "I see feelingly," he has learned—too late—to temper the rational will with the comprehending heart.

Tears are Malamud's characters' impulsive action against the hard laws of material circumstance, of economics, of ego; against the hard merciless logic of their own past acts and consequences. The eye fills up, momentarily blinded; the visible world blurs and vision turns inward. But what these characters see is not usually a common humanity. The utter weirdness that lies under the countable, controllable, possessable, and dispossessing world starts to thrive. What these Malamudian people end up seeing is the absolute strangeness of fate coupling with their character.

In the amateurish early short fiction, tears are mostly just tears. They hint at another dimension but don't quite find a formal place for it. Later, when Malamud gets his rhythmic stride, they provide transitions that hit the beat right where the story's inner and outer movements converge. "The Prison," a masterpiece, has Tommy Castelli hating his job in the candy store his father-in-law has bought for him. He regrets his past mistakes, particularly his robbery of a liquor shop, an incident that is at the root of his present miserable confinement. One day he sees a young girl stealing candy from the store. Before long, he notices that she comes in to steal once a week. He resolves to grab her the next time he sees her pilfering. Then he starts to cry.

That's when the weird way of the heart takes over. Fooling himself into thinking he's going to save the girl from turning out like him, Tommy waits for the right moment to take her aside and talk compassionately to her. But he keeps putting the moment off, and his inaction, fueled by hatred of his lot in the store, makes him her accomplice. When his stingy and suspicious wife finally catches the girl, Tommy, the reformed holdup man, defiantly declares that he has been in league with her. He thus turns out . . . just like him.

In Malamud, weeping is almost always genuine. His tears signal that a soul is sweating its strangeness. With "The Magic Barrel," Malamud's most celebrated story, the act of crying finds its most artful deployment. The story is a simple one: a very sober and very rational rabbinical student named Leo Finkle decides that "he might find it easier to win himself a congregation if he were married." He retains a matchmaker named Salzman ("salt man"—he knows his way around tears) and goes out on an arranged date. Sickened by the process, Leo has a crisis of faith, realizing "that I came to God not because I loved Him but because I did not." His rational, practical bent easing into self-pity, he covers his face and cries.

Yet he persists, and one day, when he finds himself alone in Salzman's office, Leo sees on Salzman's desk some photographs of eligible women. One picture catches Leo's attention. The woman's eyes are "hauntingly familiar yet absolutely strange"; they reveal that she "had somehow deeply suffered." Leo falls unaccountably in love with her, summons Salzman, and demands to meet her. Salzman at first seems horrified, then, "bursting into tears," histrionically proclaims the truth to Leo, which is that the photograph is of his daughter, and that his daughter is a prostitute. Leo goes to meet her anyway, though suspecting that Salzman had planned just such an outcome all along. As Leo approaches Salzman's daughter, Salzman leans against a wall around the corner saying kaddish, the prayer for the dead.

The tears occur at the story's two turning points: during Leo's crisis of faith, not long before he sees the photograph of Salzman's daughter; and at the moment of Salzman's revelation of his daughter's nature. They are portals to the story's layers of transformation. In a remarkable evocation, Malamud first describes Salzman like this: "He smelled frankly of fish." Now how can someone smell *frankly* of fish? I can tell you, frankly, that you smell of fish, but you yourself cannot smell of fish frankly—you either smell of fish or you don't.

Salzman is frank about his fish odor because it resembles a sexual odor, and the satisfaction of his clients' physical needs is one of the services he plainly offers. Salzman is a matchmaker, but he is also a pimp, who is also a father, who out of desperation manipulates a man's lonely flesh to save his daughter's soul. So Leo runs to the girl at the end with "flowers outthrust"—that is to say, with his member erect, with his rationality distended to the point of bursting. Simultaneously, he is rushing toward the satisfaction of his desire, toward the fulfillment of his heart, toward the possibility of earning God's grace. These themes make up one seamless intensity, an intensity that is indeed strange. A dry eye cannot discern it. A wet eye cannot control it.

I DWELL ON Malamud's strangeness to stress the wisdom and idiosyncrasy, the spicy capaciousness of his vision. And I suspect that the Christianity of Malamud's wife, and the apparently tender and supportive role she played for him, added to his idiosyncratic exploration of suffering's ethical permutations. When Malamud's characters ask for mercy, they are asserting its necessity in life, as though they were Christians encouraged by a certainty. Yet by the very act of pleading for it, they cast light on its absence, like Jews tutored by history.

The word "mercy," in fact, dangles from the page in Malamud like his recurrent motif of the unshaded lightbulb. The bulb's "yellow darkness" illuminates its own naked vulnerability the way the plea for mercy confirms a heart worth succoring. Never mind that help is rarely about to ring the doorbell—if there is a doorbell. (In the 1970s, the painter Philip Guston repeatedly used the image of the unshaded lightbulb with the same corrosive ironic pathos.) The Malamudian image takes various forms. A face that is suffering can be "lit with sadness," or eyes that have suffered can be "light in dark." This quality is one of the more profoundly ambiguous rewards Malamud's people get for having suffered. You think of hell's darkly burning fires in *Paradise Lost*. And his characters sometimes movingly study each other's interiority searching for signs of such knowledge born of suffering. Sorrow hangs from them like a diploma. Malamud's men and women often appeal to each other on the basis of that recognition—they recall the woman

in Kafka's *The Trial,* who found "nearly all accused [read "suffering"] men attractive."

However, the moral volatility of suffering in Bernard Malamud's work being what it is, when Malamud's weary men and
women finally get together, they are not all that kind to each
other. Suffering may not, in the narrowly virtuous sense, subside
into redemptive goodness in Malamud. But, as George Herbert
once wrote, imagining God talking about his unpredictable creation: "If goodness lead him not, yet weariness may toss him to
my breast." These short stories become essential at the point
where mortal ligaments begin to strain.

The Second Coming of
Richard Yates

THE CULTURE OF RETRIEVAL is inescapable today. There are the ubiquitous memoirists retrieving their early lives, and the songs barely a decade old being remixed, and the children of famous writers and directors and entertainers taking up their parents' occupations (and drawing on their parents' professional connections). We have had *Jane Eyre* the musical, recently on Broadway, a stage version of *The Producers,* also on Broadway, and a revival of *Hair* (can you imagine?) Off-Broadway. There's *The Golden Bowl* on film, a rewrite (if it successfully makes its way through litigation) of *Gone with the Wind*, and at least three small publishers bravely dedicated to reprinting forgotten works by forgotten authors. Americans disrespect the past? Yes and no. We adore the past so intensely that we refuse to let it die, but in fact our indiscriminate homage to it can be a form of disrespect. We are caught in a cycle more inane than vicious. Weakly stimulated by the present, we compulsively return to the past, which has the effect of eclipsing the present, which makes us return to the past.

The inescapability of the past was a thematic obsession of the novelist and short-story writer Richard Yates, and so the publication of his collected short stories—along with the republication of *Revolutionary Road* and *The Easter Parade*—fits nicely into all this relentless retrospection. It was Yates, in fact, who introduced into American fiction the theme of inertia as catalyst. Portraying characters arrested by their personal histories, mired in memory and thus destined for the most irrationally self-defeating action, he shifted fiction from the Hemingway track back to the Frank Norris track, from realism back to naturalism. That is to say, he brought American fiction from the drama of free will back to the crisis of determining circumstances. In Yates's fiction, childhood and adult memories of what parents wrought exert the same power over the characters' destinies that economic forces did in Norris's *McTeague* or Theodore Dreiser's *Sister Carrie.*

Strangely, you won't ever hear Yates mentioned in connection with the American naturalists. He has most often been compared with Hemingway, the great American realist. And he is an acknowledged influence on the style and sensibility of an entire line of writers—from Raymond Carver through Ann Beattie, Andre Dubus, Tobias Wolff, Richard Russo, Richard Ford, and Jayne Anne Phillips—who consider themselves to have been fathered by Hemingway and, as it were, brought up by Yates. These writers have long and eloquently regretted the latter's lapsed reputation and the unavailability (until now) of his work, pointing to his plain, unobtrusive prose and to his bleak take on life (traits that can be traced, in their view, to Hemingway's lapidary sentences and to his Lost Generation pessimism). The present decision—on the part of three separate publishers—to bring Yates back into print can probably be traced to the noble efforts of these writers on his behalf. In 1999, in *Boston Review,* the Yates champion Stewart O'Nan predicted that:

> Eventually the books will make it back in print, just as Faulkner's and Fitzgerald's did, and Yates will take his place in the American canon. How this will come about

it's impossible to say. Writers and editors are keenly aware of his situation, so perhaps his Malcolm Cowley is just moving up through the ranks at Norton or Doubleday.

Happily, Yates's books are indeed passing back into print. Inevitably, the response will be less a reconsideration than an uncritical celebration, since everybody loves a comeback, and since it is hard to resist an opportunity to redeem a writer whose work was often neglected during his lifetime. But if Yates was a writer of enormous talent, he had no less enormous limitations. By sentimentally ignoring those limitations, we miss the chance to see which of them occur as the necessary outgrowth of his gifts and which occur when his gifts falter.

First, there is Yates's style. His prose is so easy and natural and transparent that it suggests a profound humility before life's inscrutable sadness. Almost ego-less, it recalls Kafka's remark that writing is a form of prayer. And Yates's language bestows upon his men and women, tortured and silenced by life as they are, what might be called a clemency of accurate observation. At times he writes less like an artist than like a witness. His cool humble chronicling of his characters' slow doom (and his characters are almost uniformly doomed) can read like a redemptive freedom in an afterlife of art, as in the following passage from *The Easter Parade,* a novel that follows the long, unhappy lives of two sisters, Emily and Sarah Grimes:

> It took only a couple of days for Howard to move his belongings out of the apartment. He was very apologetic about everything. Only once, when he flicked the heavy silken rope of his neckties out of the closet, was there any kind of scene, and that turned into such a dreadful, squalid

scene—it ended with her falling on her knees to embrace his legs and begging him, begging him to stay—that Emily did the best she could to put it out of her mind.

The casually cruel flicking of the heavy silken ties is wonderful: Howard is leaving Emily for a younger woman, one who better satisfies his vanity. The repetition of "begging him," representing an abandonment of stylistic neutrality, is the only slightly false aesthetic note in the passage. Here, Yates's art—the art of the unaverted eye—briefly stumbles on his compassion. This is one of those fascinating moments when literary style becomes a moral, even a philosophical dilemma, no less than the question of whether a photojournalist should intervene on behalf of an innocent subject.

Such a style can be emotionally consoling in the way that it calmly reflects back to us an image of familiar pain, relieving our suffering with the sense that we do not suffer alone, but it is not always spiritually satisfying. Yates's style is very closely tied to the feelings it evokes. Hemingway's, by contrast, evokes an emotion of which he simultaneously makes intellectual sense. His style is no less unobtrusive to the eye, but it is a poeticized plainness, which rubs his characters against the reader's mind until the shape of each individual approaches the originality of a new idea. The reason we remember Hemingway's characters is that we've never seen them before; the reason we are moved so powerfully by Yates's characters, who then pass from our minds so quickly, is that we know them so well. Of course, Hemingway was a stoic, and stoicism is an idea that rules the emotions. Yates was a pessimist, and pessimism is a feeling that fends off thought.

In "The B.A.R. Man," now reprinted in *The Collected Stories,* Yates imagines with exquisite pacing and nuance the slow deterioration of an embittered and frustrated ex-soldier, John Fallon. But Fallon's eventual detonation flows from his predictable personality, and it conforms to the feeling that this near stereotype arouses in us. Fallon's fate is, typically, pronounced a certainty from the very first sentence: "Until he got his name on the police blotter, and in the papers, nobody had ever thought much of John Fallon."

The Collected Stories contains seven heretofore unpublished pieces, along with two that appeared in *Ploughshares* in the seventies, but the bulk, and heart, of the book consists of Yates's two story collections, *Eleven Kinds of Loneliness* (arguably his best-known work) and *Liars in Love.* The short form, with its special intensity, throws Yates's virtues and his deficiencies into stark relief. His truly magical storytelling whisks the attention from sentence to sentence, and not a word is wasted. Yet the stories often depend for their unfettered momentum on characterization that verges on stereotype. (Ralph and Gracie in "The Best of Everything" at times seem to be walking and talking on the set of *The Honeymooners:* "Whaddya—crazy?")

Yates's admirable sympathy for the plight of "ordinary people"—secretaries, cabdrivers, office clerks—is often dampened by a narrow emphasis on their ordinariness. The defensively arrogant young writer who narrates "Builders," from *Eleven Kinds of Loneliness*, might take himself to task for regarding Bernie—the cabdriver who has entangled him in his literary fantasies—as a vulgar, obnoxious, intellectually limited "Philistine," imprisoned "in the pathetic delusions of a taxicab driver." But at the end of the story, Bernie is still a pathetic Philistine while the narrator has become a minor hero simply by virtue of his realization that he has been a minor shit. There is something mildly vindictive about Yates's vindications of ordinary people, a streak of schadenfreude running through his horror at their ordeal. Even Yates's famous unflinching depiction of life's cruelty has its flawed underside. His honesty can be less like an artist's truthfulness than like a psychiatrist's candor. Each tale in *Eleven Kinds of Loneliness* is like a deeply affecting icon expressing a variation on a brute existential fact of life. Yet it is as if the loneliness had been gouged raw and bleeding from the body of life, and then processed into art by Yates's systematic pessimism. We are left with the powerful reiteration of an experience rather than its transformation. We are left, like beginning analysands, alone with the harsh illumination of isolated facts.

Call Yates's outlook, and that of his epigones, neo-naturalism. For him, it was the family, rather than the mine, or the factory, or the stockyards, that pulled destiny's strings. Pascal said that people could avoid all the trouble in their lives if they simply stayed in their own rooms. In Yates's world, people can't leave their childhood rooms, no matter how widely they travel the world as adults. This is not their trouble; rather, their trouble is a *fait accompli*, which it is their fictional duty to live out.

The short story "A Glutton for Punishment" is representative in this regard. It tells the tale of a man who as a boy so loved to feign death when playing cops and robbers with other children that he courts and welcomes failure all his life. The internal process driving Yates's characters is frequently so simple that it recalls that old desk gadget with the row of metal balls hanging on strings; by lifting the ball on one end and sending it swinging, the ball at the far end is propelled into the air without moving the ones in between. Yates's fictional circumstances are just like those motionless, intermediary balls. They have no weight, no meaning in themselves, except to serve as the kinetic conduit between cause and effect, between past and present, or future events. Between the first sentence and the last.

The Easter Parade carries this forced march to an extreme. The novel's first sentence is, "Neither of the Grimes sisters would have a happy life, and looking back it always seemed that the trouble began with their parents' divorce." One reads the novel waiting for this judgment—seemingly so cynical as to be naive—to be surprised by some kind of irony or extenuation, but what one encounters instead is a straightforward fictional syllogism that inexorably bears out its premise. Two girls are born to a transient alcoholic mother who is unable to maintain a relationship after the end of her marriage. Sarah Grimes marries an abusive husband and dies an alcoholic; Emily Grimes moves from apartment to apartment, and from job to job, unable to maintain an emotional relationship. *The Easter Parade* boasts what must be the only first sentence in the history of the novel that is also a sentencing.

SUCH A STRANGLEHOLD of the personal past is a romanticism in retreat, and Yates stands out among postwar American writers for the breadth of his disappointed romanticism and the distance of his retreat. Bellow, Ellison, Updike, Salinger, Cheever, Malamud, Mailer, Roth, et al., all searched everyday life for a different form of heroism, for a quotidian stoicism, for grace under new kinds of pressure. Yates gave up on everyday life.

When did disappointment become a dominant theme in literature? We cannot say that Dante is disappointed with his life as he wanders through that dark wood. It would be absurd to call Don Quixote disappointed by his futile search for Dulcinea, or Faust disappointed in his quest for absolute happiness and power. Defining events happen in those fictional worlds, and disappointment becomes a describable issue in a world where nothing defining happens. Disappointment attracted literature's attention when the modern world became ordered beyond the individual's comprehension, and when inner life—middle-class, bourgeois life—began to compensate for the lack of outer efficacy. As a response without recourse, an aborted action converted into a mood, disappointment has no outlet, only a terminus. That's why the first and greatest novel of disappointment, *Madame Bovary,* ends with the heroine's suicide.

Since disappointment is a purely mental state, it is one of the more unexpected developments in literature that disappointment should also be one of the great themes of realist fiction. Unmoored as it is from the external world, the mood of disappointment required a new technique. Flaubert invented one. First, he set *Madame Bovary* in the suburbs (back then, they called them "the provinces"), thus providing a reality more easily correlated to a static interior mood than the city could be. Then, in *Madame Bovary's* celebrated Agricultural Fair scene, he introduced the essentially theatrical device of the ironic contrast into the novel. By juxtaposing the high-flown romantic sentiments that Rodolphe, the adulterous Emma's lover, declares to her, against a local provincial official's pompous speech, and putting alongside this the smell of cow manure, Flaubert incorporated outer reality into the mood of disappointment. He invented a dynamic environment in which to portray the arrest of personal motion.

Yates called *Madame Bovary* one of his two favorite novels (*The Great Gatsby* was the other), and *Revolutionary Road* is a distinct echo of it. Published in 1961, at the height of the postwar exodus from the cities, *Revolutionary Road* was part of a flood of fictions chronicling life in the suburbs that were quickly expanding around New York City. Like Flaubert's work, most of these novels and short stories identified the suburbs with the extinction of human vitality. I can't think of any novel, though, that presents life in the suburbs with as black a monotone as *Revolutionary Road,* the story of Frank and April, a young couple whose dreams founder on their illusions. Of course, novelists instinctively disdain the suburbs for the simple reason that the novel was born in the modern city and the suburbs offer a far more limited field of operations. If it's true, as Irving Howe once wrote, that the troubles of life are the convenience of literature, then the convenience of the suburbs puts a definite crimp in subject matter.

Then, too, in postwar America, the suburbs held out the very same *promesse de bonheur* that romantic novels once dangled before Emma Bovary. If art's job is to puncture deceit with illusion, any writer who takes on the suburbs as an end in itself rather than as a fictional means to incalculable ends will turn out one hostile Ironic Contrast after another. In fact, writers like Updike and Cheever used the suburbs the way Hemingway used the battle-field: not simply as a place but as a place of unfolding. Even Roth's *Goodbye, Columbus,* corrosive satire that it is, allows its characters to do what they would—or what they could—with their environment. Yates portrays the suburbs as an enveloping condition:

> The Revolutionary Hill Estates had not been designed to accommodate a tragedy. Even at night, as if on purpose, the development held no looming shadows and no gaunt silhouettes. It was invincibly cheerful, a toyland of white and pastel houses whose bright, uncurtained windows winked blandly through a dappling of green and yellow leaves. Proud floodlights were trained on some of the lawns, on some of the neat front doors and on the hips of some of the berthed, ice-cream colored automobiles.
>
> A man running down these streets in desperate grief was indecently out of place.

In other words, if their histories don't get Yates's characters, their environment will. Frank, like his father, dies spiritually in a soulless job; April, like her father, dies by her own hand; and all this happens in their house on *Revolutionary Road,* where

America's revolutionary promise withers and dies in the coarse, materialistic suburbs.

Such an unyielding machinery of pessimism eventually shades into caricature, in much the way that Yates's characters themselves often shade into stereotype. Sometimes it seems that all it would take to bring a liberating light into Yates's world is the sudden appearance of a therapist, or a landscape architect.

YATES IS A VIRTUOSO CRAFTSMAN, and his mature style is enviable. We are fortunate to have him back in print. But the quality of his moral outlook will determine his place in American letters. The best place to begin puzzling out the ethic of Yates's aesthetic is *The Easter Parade,* in which Yates suppresses the bloated poeticizing of *Revolutionary Road,* allowing his themes to arise effortlessly from the final pages of the novel.

After a life of unrelieved disappointment, Emily Grimes arrives at the New England home of her nephew, Peter. A newly ordained minister who has recently married and fathered a daughter, Peter is the only person in the Grimes family who seems to have come through. He has escaped his own abusive father and alcoholic mother and made a separate life for himself in a small college town. Sensing that his "Aunt Emmy" has reached the end of her rope, he invites her to stay with his family for an indefinite period of time.

The great naturalist heroines, Zola's Thérèse Raquin, Stephen Crane's Maggie, Dreiser's Carrie, went down swinging. Desire leads Thérèse to murder, and the passionate decay of desire into hatred leads her to suicide; Maggie desperately turns to crime and prostitution to survive; Carrie is borne up by the destruction of the men who seduce her. Even ill-fated Emma Bovary, whom "Aunt Emmy" is meant to put us in mind of, took a willful solace in her illusions—then, too, she summons her own destruction by plunging headlong into her chosen escape. Emily Grimes, on the other hand, has to be the most passive heroine in the history of literature. She does not, in the course of the entire novel, express a single desire of her own, except, pathetically, the desire not to be hurt or disappointed.

Emily is a saint in a world without a God, and so her saintliness has no dignity and her suffering holds no meaning. You wonder whether Yates is pulling the rug out from under the religious impulse itself. The novel, after all, takes its title from the idea of resurrection. Yates, however, offers us a parody of resurrection: a beautiful, hopeful photograph of Emily's sister, Sarah, and her future husband, Tony, taken on Easter Day at the time of their courtship, reappears toward the end of the novel, after the revelation of Tony's wife-beating and Sarah's inherited masochism and alcoholism. It's as if Yates had replaced the idea of resurrection with the concept of the return of the repressed.

The fate of Emily seems, on the surface, more ambiguous. On the brink of a nervous collapse, she tries to turn back from Peter's house and hospitality at the last minute. Peter comes down his driveway after her, and Emily hears "a jingle of pocketed coins or keys." An instant later, when Peter suddenly realizes the extent of her distress, he asks her if she's tired and then stands "looking at her in a detached, speculative way now, more like an alert young psychiatrist than a priest."

"Yes, I'm tired," she said. "And do you know a funny thing? I'm almost fifty years old and I've never understood anything in my whole life."

"All right," he said quietly. "All right, Aunt Emmy. Now. Would you like to come in and meet the family?"

Considering that the Grimes sisters' "trouble began with their parents' divorce," Peter's invitation to enter yet another family romance could be read—indeed, almost demands to be read—as the bitterest of ironies. But since he seems happily married, with his family intact, perhaps Emily does stand, if unsteadily, at the threshold of redemption. Yet is it the redemption of religious grace or the promise of "alert" psychoanalytic "understanding" that offers no love or sympathy? Are those the jingling keys to heaven's gate (as Peter's name suggests), or are they the coins of selfishness and greed? It hardly seems to matter. The expectation of grace in a world without God and mere psychiatric understanding in a world without grace are like two sides of an obscene joke. That is Yates's zero-degree ethos.

Such unsparing sobriety makes up the solidity of Yates's achievement. Yates knew how to rivet the reader's attention on the quiet desperation of unacknowledged lives. His unpardonable failure (and perhaps his secret satisfaction) was never to give his implausibly ordinary men and women the freedom to respond.

Chekhov's "Cheap White Bone"

To return to Chekhov in this cultural moment makes you feel as if you were experiencing spring in Russia. His meticulously crafted fiction and plays seem absolutely free of artifice, as if telling stories were a natural function of his physical being, like a birdsong, and not a highly disciplined and self-conscious creative-intellectual activity. Yet so much writing about fiction now consists of tiresome debates over realism versus modernism, the nature of consciousness in the novel, character versus caricature, poetic language versus plain language—it is all a kind of analytical birdcage.

During the past forty years, the university has offered refuge to scores of artists and intellectuals and, for some time, an academic style has been flowing back into mainstream literary culture. It boggles the mind that Harold Bloom's impossibly dense and jargony *Zagat*-like guides to the best of the canon, to the greatest geniuses and to the wisest wisdom get defined as great "popular" criticism. Reading Bloom's abstractifying impositions, you start feeling anxious, as though you just realized that the exam was tomorrow and you hadn't begun studying for it. (The influence of anxiety!) The idea of literature as, in Kenneth Burke's phrase, "equipment for living," has just about gone the way of the typewriter.

And suddenly Chekhov's universe appears anew in this beautiful, if sometimes maladroitly translated—by Richard Pevear and Larissa Volokhonsky—new collection of his five short novels: Chekhov's acheful, unsparing eye; his unforgiving yet gentle irony; his characters' dignified pathos and their pathetic attempts to dignify themselves with big theories of how to live in this world; and the writer's uncanny evocation of their self-delusion as simultaneously ludicrous and heartbreaking. About Chekhov, Maxim Gorky wrote, "In the presence of Anton Pavlovich, everyone felt an unconscious desire to be simpler, more truthful, more himself." Reflecting on Chekhov, you find yourself using words like "sadness," and "longing," and "disappointment," and "love," and "kindness," and "hate"—you feel, inexorably, a sudden desire to talk not about literature, not about the conventions and strategies of fiction, but about life itself, as if Chekhov had not so much invented his stories as discovered them in a field, or inside a broken bottle.

"Zhizn zhizn" goes a Russian saying: Life is life. Experience ultimately defeats the most elevated attempts to make sense of it. Art, science, ideas (not to mention debates over realism versus modernism), all go down before the onslaught of time and sensation. An unmediated clarity—the illusion of actual experience unfolding through actual time—characterizes Chekhov's fiction, and also his plays, which revolutionized the theater in the way they stripped the stage of theatricality. Indeed, when the people in Chekhov's plays dream of transforming themselves through devotion to a plan for the betterment of humankind, or through love or travel, they are yearning for the type of dramatic twist that you find in a well-constructed plot. In Chekhov's plays, the promise and salvation of the theater are always waiting, unattainably, just offstage. The honest core of Chekhov's art is the acknowledgment that even art is helpless in the face of life.

Chekhov wrote *The Steppe,* appropriately the first tale in this volume, when he was twenty-eight, and it is a kind of manifesto of Chekhovian lifelikeness. A fatherless nine-year-old boy named Egorushka is taken by his uncle, a wealthy merchant, and a rich priest on a long journey far from Egorushka's mother and home, the purpose of which is to enroll the boy in school and thus give him a good start in life. At one point, realizing that they have to make a side trip, his guardians arrange to meet Egorushka later and leave him with a group of peasants who are part of a caravan bringing merchandise to market.

Throughout the trip, Egorushka animates the stark landscape with his own emotions: Trees, grass, sky, wildlife are "transfixed with anguish," and then bursting with a "passionate thirst for life," and then "lonely," and "anguished, hopeless" once again. His perceptions of the people he encounters also change as his moods shift, and as the people themselves shed appearances. Fearful, obsequious Jews are, a minute later, defiant, mocking Jews. A countess is worldly-seeming and enchanting one minute, and the naive dupe of a rogue the next—and so forth. The qualities of life that Egorushka witnesses on his journey are equally unstable. They run the gamut from callousness and cruelty to kindness and sorrow, with contrasting qualities often converging in the same incident or person. By the end of his odyssey, Egorushka has nearly died from pneumonia, as senseless an experience as death, or a brush with death, always is. When he is momentarily reunited with his uncle and the friendly priest, the latter takes him aside:

Well, how was the journey *puer bone* [my good boy]? . . . Sick of it, I suppose. . . . You go on and on, Lord forgive me, you look ahead, and the steppe still stretches out as continuously as before: there's no end of it to be seen! That's not traveling, it's sheer punishment.

After Egorushka is left alone by his guardians with a kind friend of the family, whom Egorushka has never met before, he wonders about this new embarkation into the future: "What sort of life would it be?" That is the story's final line, and it is the gentle war cry of Chekhovian irony. The shifting meanings, the uncertainty and instability, the dependence of his perception on his state of mind, the incalculable ratio of appearance to reality, the senselessness of affliction—Egorushka's journey has in fact been life itself: "You go on and on . . . you look ahead, and the steppe still stretches out as continuously as before: there's no end of it to be seen!" His own, private, untransmittable experience of life is, and will always be, the only truthful description of life that he will ever know. Somehow, Chekhov's art manages to transmit the untransmittable.

Such lifelikeness makes it difficult to talk about Chekhov in a critical way. What makes his stories poetic is precisely their freedom from the "literary." One of the many gifts of this collection is that the novellas reveal more about Chekhov's art than do his fleeting short stories. Strictly speaking, they are not novellas at all, but short tales that go on for longer than usual. They are expanding compressions; they deepen rather than progress. And therein lie their little windows onto Chekhov's art. The highly wrought details in the short stories that occur too briefly to be rationally apprehended unwind more lengthily in the short novels. Yet these aren't lapses in storytelling. They're tangible wonders.

What would be a detachable symbol or leitmotif in another writer remains, in Chekhov, embedded in his characters' lives as a concrete part of their experience. Consider the parasol in *Three Years,* one of the lesser known of Chekhov's works. Laptev, member of a rich merchant family and a colorless, anxious, passive, yet kind and decent man, falls wildly in love with a doctor's daughter, Yulia Sergeevna. Yulia's father is treating Nina, Laptev's dying sister, and Yulia often comes to visit Nina, who is also Yulia's friend. One day she leaves her parasol behind.

> At home, [Laptev] saw Yulia Sergeevna's forgotten parasol on a chair, seized it, and greedily kissed it. The parasol was of silk, no longer new, held by an elastic band; the handle was of simple, cheap white bone. Laptev opened it and held it over him, and it seemed to him that there was even a smell of happiness around him.

Laptev opens his souvenir and sits giddily under it. The next day, clutching the parasol, he rushes to Yulia's house, begs her to let him keep it, and then with innocent, crude impulsiveness asks her to marry him. Astounded and confused, she turns him down. Laptev is devastated. Yulia begins to think about his offer, however, and concludes that there was no reason "to refuse a decent, kind, loving man only because she did not like him." (Chekhov's irony always resolves itself into a poignancy. A negative becomes a positive in mid-laugh: You suddenly see what Yulia means.) She was getting old, no other opportunities presented themselves and Laptev could change her life for the better. She decides to marry him, even though "to marry him would mean saying good-bye forever to her dreams, her notions of happiness and married life."

There is much discussion in *Three Years* of happiness and love. Embittered by their union, Laptev and Yulia each come to believe that both are impossible. The pair drifts through the months and the years into despair. And then they find that they cannot live without each other. They discover that time has woven invisible threads of affinity—not merely habit—between them. They find that they miss each other when they're not together. They want to protect each other. They seem to enjoy each other sexually. They depend on each other's kindness, and—of utmost importance in

Chekhov—both of them are bored when the other isn't around. Laptev and Yulia come to realize that "love" does not exist; rather, it consists of the sometimes-present, sometimes-absent experiences—of the other person's kindness, or intelligence, or honesty, or reassuring presence, or wit, or physical chemistry, etc.—that keep two people together, at least until tomorrow. The conventional idea of love that so oppressed Laptev and Yulia is about as real as Laptev's idealizing of Yulia's parasol into a perfect love.

What is real is the parasol's "simple, cheap white bone," "held by an elastic band." In other words, the only reality is fragile human life: meaningless except for the meanings we deluded and deluding people keep projecting onto it. Toward the end of the story, Laptev brings the parasol to Yulia and tells her that he's abandoned the idea of ever being happy, but that he was happy one time in his life, when he sat all night under her umbrella. This is ironic in at least two ways: He is in fact still striving for happiness with Yulia by attempting to move her with memories of the parasol; and he is unwittingly telling her that on the one occasion in his life when his spirit soared, the source of joy was not Yulia but his fantasy of Yulia. He is still trying to impose meaning on life, still horrified by the blank, neutral slate life is, still trying to delude Yulia and comically deluding himself. The parasol becomes the perfect symbolic center of the story. And yet it never stops being a parasol; it never becomes "literary." It carries meaning for the reader only because it has accrued the very same meaning for the characters. Unlike, say, D. H. Lawrence's famous rocking horse, the parasol is not a privileged communiqué over the characters' heads between the reader and the writer. It belongs to the characters.

For all of his attempts to win happiness for himself, Laptev comes to the same realization as Yulia, aptly summarized by the protagonist of the masterpiece *My Life:* "How sad it is to live in the world." In the same way as Chekhov's art achieves the illusion of capturing experience unmediated by art, Chekhov's heroes and heroines learn to live without the mediations of big plans, great loves, large ideas. It is not, Chekhov means to say, that life is consistently sad. It is that every life, no matter how abundant its joys, is ultimately sad.

My Life, a sort of shlemiel story, has its protagonist, Misail, reaching his rueful conclusion after trying to live as authentically as he can. He spurns his rich, brutal father, rejects his high social class, marries for what he thinks is love, cares for his emotionally wounded sister. He shears the mediations off life and pares existence down to its simple white bone. At the end, he is outcast and bereft. We last see him alone, his now-deceased sister's young daughter his only companion. Orphans or near-orphans abound in Chekhov. The hero of the bizarre *Story of an Unknown Man,* a political spy named Vladimir Ivanych, who falls in love with his quarry's abandoned mistress, ends up taking care of her little girl after the mother dies in childbirth. It's as if these parentless children came into life already prepared for the fact that, as Laptev puts it, "there were no firm, lasting attachments." Their future lies in their beginning; they are presaddened. And yet these orphans are luckier than nearly all the heroes of the novellas, who have been physically abused, like Chekhov himself, by their fathers. If orphanhood is a presadness, for Chekhov it is also a state of grace.

But although Chekhov's world exists on the tide of persistent, gentle melancholy, it is far from a bleak place. "Life is given only once," says Vladimir Ivanych, speaking for all of Chekhov's protagonists, "and one would like to live it cheerfully, meaningfully, beautifully." The best of Chekhov's people surrender their illusions and try to endure life's inherent limitations and disappointments. And for this sober honesty they are rewarded with a substitute for the cushioning mediations that they've given up. They learn to forgive themselves and to forgive other people; they learn to be kind. "Kindness" is a word that occurs over and over again in Chekhov. It is a mode of being rather than a big idea about how to live, a quality of experience rather than a mediation of experience. It is cheer, meaning, and beauty self-created from within.

Kindness and irony blend indistinguishably at the end of the magnificent novella *The Duel*. Superficially, the duel of the title is between the ideas of a ruthless Darwinist named von Koren and an ineffectual humanist named Laevsky, an intellectual combat that ends in an actual duel with pistols. But the real struggle is between Laevsky and his lover, Nadezhda; and even more than that, between each one's perception of the other and the actual other. Laevsky has grown tired of Nadezhda. Stifled, bored, constantly irritated, he makes plans to leave her, but feelings of guilt and pity keep him stewing in misery by her side. What he doesn't know is that Nadezhda, vain and coquettish, has been slowly drifting away from him and impulsively, even innocently, conducting affairs with two other men. She also is mired in pity and guilt.

Like Laptev and Yulia, however, Laevsky suddenly realizes, in a beautifully modulated moment, that Nadezhda is his life. Nadezhda herself discovers that her vanity has brought her further than she wanted to go and placed her in the hands of a brute. When Laevsky catches Nadezhda with the man, the irony of both their positions propels them into a new situation. Shorn of their delusions, they marry and dwell in life's simple white bone, in a gray mist between happiness and unhappiness, borne up by their clemency toward each other, which itself is the product of their understanding of life's tragic limitations.

At the end of the novella, Laevsky and the other characters, all of whom have clashed with each other to some degree, stand at the edge of the sea. They are watching von Koren being rowed out to a ship that is waiting to take him on a zoological expedition. The water is very rough, and soon von Koren's little boat becomes harder and harder to see as it gets tossed about on the waves, yet another irony, since this cold-hearted eugenicist, who seeks to master nature, is now at nature's mercy. Straining to see von Koren, Laevsky thinks:

> The boat is thrown back . . . it makes two steps forward and one step back, but the oarsmen are stubborn, they work the oars tirelessly and do not fear the high waves. . . . So it is in life. . . . In search of the truth, people make two steps forward and one step back. Sufferings, mistakes, and the tedium of life throws them back, but the thirst for truth and a stubborn will drive them on and on. And who knows? Maybe they'll row their way to the real truth . . .

And Laevsky entertains these thoughts while watching and worrying over the safety of von Koren, who would gladly have killed Laevsky in their duel if he hadn't been suddenly distracted. Yet such irony doesn't undermine Laevsky's reflections; it amplifies them into kind comprehension. The entire novella opens out into Chekhov's trademark blend of irony and poignancy. Rather than issue a thunderous Tolstoyan judgment or proclamation or conclusion, which perhaps reminded him of a cruel father's tyranny, Chekhov finishes his tale with the stubborn facticity of the parasol. Its last sentence is: "It began to drizzle." What makes Chekhov so inestimably precious is that he is a writer who lets life have the last word. Which it does anyway. *Zhizn zhizn.*

ACKNOWLEDGMENTS

The brilliant and courageous Elizabeth Maguire passed her wand over me and created this book. I'm sorry that she died before she could see it, and before I could properly thank her. Joann Miller kept a wise, steadying hand on the author and his project, while Chris Greenberg guided the book through the labyrinth of publication with expertise and care. Laura Stine, who oversaw production of the book, is a meticulous wonder.

Gloria Loomis is the Platonic Form of the literary agent: wizard, Fury, and friend.

I wish to express my gratitude to all the editors who welcomed these essays into their pages, and to three in particular: Lewis Lapham, Ellen Rosenbush, and Steve Wasserman. And thank you, dear Rachel Shteir.

Without Leon Wieseltier, I would not have a life as a writer. I owe him more than I can say. I am indebted also to Martin Peretz for his support, and to Frank Foer.

Christina Gillham is the heart and soul of my existence. I am grateful that she found me.

CREDITS

"Harry Potter and the Fear of Not Flying." *The New Republic,* November 22, 1999. (As "Fear of Not Flying: Harry Potter and the Spirit of the Age").

"A Book of Virtues for the Righ-thinking Left." *The Atlantic Monthly,* January 1996. (As "How to Raise a Good Liberal: A Book of Virtues for the Right-thinking Left").

"Seize the Day Job: Sacrificing Saul Bellow on the Altar of One's Career." *Harper's,* March, 2001.

"Persecution and the Art of Painting." *The New Republic,* August 31, 1998.

"Prophets of Profit: How Artists Slyly Critique Their Wealthy Patrons." *Slate,* August 8, 2001.

"From Stalin to SoHo." *The New Republic,* February 16, 1998. (As "From Stalin to SoHo: Komar and Melamid and the Irony Racket").

"Barbara Kingsolver's Icy Virtue." *The New Republic,* March 22, 1999. (As "Sweet and Low: Barbara Kingsolver's Icy Virtue").

"Television and the Pope." *The New Republic,* May 2, 2005. (As "The Rapture").

"Updike's Bech." *The Los Angeles Times Book Review,* July 1, 2001. (As "You Don't Have to Be Jewish").

"The New King of Irony." *Talk,* April 2000.

"D. H. Lawrence and the Romantic Option." Introduction to D. H. Lawrence, *The Lost Girl.* New York: The Modern Library, 2003.

"Who Is Carrie Bradshaw Really Dating?" *The New Republic,* November 18, 2002. (As "Relationshipism: Who Is Carrie Bradshaw Really Dating?").

"The Gay Science: Queer Theory, Literature, and the Sexualization of Everything." *The New Republic,* November 9, 1998.

"*Eyes Wide Shut:* What the Critics Failed to See in Kubrick's Last Film." *Harper's,* October 1999.

"García Lorca and the Flight from Desire." *The New Yorker,* September 13, 1999. (As "Spanish Prisoner: the Perils of Idolatry").

"Dante and the Subversive Ego." *Harper's,* May 2002. (As "Out of the Dark Wood: Dante and the Subversive Ego").

"Sundays with *The Sopranos.*" *The New Republic,* December 13, 2004. (As "The Attraction of Repulsion").

"A Writer Who Is Good For You." *The Atlantic Monthly,* January 1998.

"Bernard Malamud and the Comprehending Heart." *Double Take,* Spring 1999. (As "The Comprehending Heart: Bernard Malamud Revisited").

"The Second Coming of Richard Yates." *Harper's,* July 2002.

"Chekhov's 'Cheap White Bone.'" *The Nation,* December 13, 2004. (As "Imitation of Life").

INDEX